S0-ADT-709

What Women Should Know About Men

Copyright © 2003 Herb Goldberg, Ph.D.
All rights reserved.

Electronic and soft-cover print versions published by
the Wellness Institute,Inc.
1007 Whitney Avenue, Gretna, LA 70056

Cover design by the Wellness Institute, Inc.

SelfHelpBooks.com is a division of the
Wellness Institute, Inc.
Gretna, LA 70056

ISBN 1587411156

What Women Should Know About Men

Herb Goldberg, Ph.D.

Table Of Contents

Can men love? Yes! In their way, they love as much as women do. But if women want to enjoy that love, they must first understand what men are about and how women's actions affect them. This book challenges women to learn what makes men tick and offers the reward of discovering that men's potential for love is ready and waiting.

Why This Book Was Written

What Women Should Know About Men is really about the power women potentially have in their relationships with men, and the way to use that power to bring out the best in men's relationship behaviors, while creating for women the kind of love experience they grew up to believe was possible.

The way women have traditionally been socialized to relate to men actually brings out many of men's worst personal features, and causes women to feel unloved at best, and abused at worst. Women's sense of being loveable is tied into childhood conditioning to be accomodating, reactive, agreeable, and 'Nice.' This way of relating builds into them a sense of powerlessness, low self-esteem and repressed anger. Overall, it generates feelings of being abused and victimized. This occurs no matter how they are actually treated. Ironically, 'nice' is poison in the male-female relationship for both the man who is on the receiving end of something that seems to be desirable but only generates guilt and a sense of unreality, and for the woman who believes that she is being loving and deliberately deprived of love by the selfish male. In spite of the consequences, the illusion that 'nice' is a virtue that produces love and is something that a woman should strive to be with a man continues. The end result is a woman who becomes increasingly bitter toward men who can't figure out what they are doing wrong.

The alternative to 'nice' is not mean or bitchy. Rather, the opposite to 'nice' in a relationship is to be authentic. To be authentic is to see the man as he is and to be able to draw and maintain boundaries, to acknowledge and confront conflict, to recognize one's anger and express it in a non-blaming way, to maintain a sense of separate self while getting close, to make clear choices rather than deferring to the man and to behave in a way that expresses self esteem and preserves a woman's sense of control and power.

What Women Should Know About Men will describe the psychological reality that, even though men may initially balk, they respond best to women who maintain their power and strength, who respect themselves and who do not automatically accomodate or try to please in order to be loved. The abuse that "nice' women experience can be viewed as an unconscious 'wake-up' call or a disguised message, prodding the woman to become her best and strongest self.

Herb Goldberg, Ph.D.
Los Angeles, CA

February, 2003

Chapter One

WOMEN'S POWER OVER MEN

We've heard it so many times that we figure it must be true: Men are afraid of commitment and don't give a hoot about the needs of the women who love them. While many men do have trouble relating to others, the truth is, they actually YEARN for a close, caring relationship - if only they knew how to have one! Without a close love relationship, most men lead painfully empty, unhappy lives. Really.

Women don't realize how much power over men this desperate need for love gives them. It also gives women something else - the confidence that, if only they will learn what men are really about, they can have a terrific relationship.

Many women think that the key to catching a man is to make themselves beautiful. Now I'm not going to tell you that great looks don't attract a man's attention. But what HOLDS and BINDS him is knowing that his partner really likes and wants him. He needs a woman whose interest -and desire - are based on knowing who he really is.

Deep down, a man knows (even when he doesn't KNOW he knows) when a woman really cares for him. When she has a bad attitude, he senses that it's just a matter of time before she'll start to nag him about his faults, try to change him and blame him for all the problems in the relationship.

Love is very frustrating, if not impossible, for the woman who comes to a relationship with a negative attitude about men. The woman who can't see her man for who he really is can't understand how her beliefs about men can affect the relationship. The woman who refuses to share responsibility for the couple's problems is doomed to fail. Why? Because the way she treats him will actually MAKE him let her down!

HOW DO YOU CATCH A MAN?
WOMEN ATTRACT A MAN'S INTEREST
IN TWO MAIN WAYS:

1) Using old-fashioned feminine ploys and sexual allure. Sad to say, this is still the most common approach to hooking a mate. True, you have a good chance of winning a man this way, but don't count on the thrill lasting. What started out as romantic and exciting soon becomes distant and even hurtful. The reason: Your man, who at first was intrigued, ends up angry once he realizes you don't accept and love him for himself but are simply using him.

2)   Getting to know and accept a man's strengths and weaknesses.

If you can recognize the good, the bad and the ugly, and still care for a man, combined with a woman's awareness of how she plays into and triggers the reactions she abhors, your budding relationship has a strong foundation and a good chance for success.

This book is a road map for developing this second, healthy type of relationship. I've tried hard not to take sides. I don't mean to romanticize men as people in need of special understanding. And I certainly don't believe that the burden of making a relationship work should be placed on the woman.

What I HAVE done is explain how a man's mind works. Women readers will learn what makes men tick and how to love them . . . and men will learn why it's been such a struggle for them to love and be loved.

Chapter Two

MEN IN LOVE

The quantity of love that an ordinary person can stand without serious damage is about 10 minutes in 50 years.

George Bernard Shaw

The personal lives of many men are like time bombs ticking away, ready to explode at any minute - but they don't even see it coming. As their relationships begin to fall apart, they have no idea of what they should do to improve things – or why they should bother. Let me show you what I mean.

Chris has a high-paying, responsible job in the boat building industry. Every day, he and his team face - and solve - complicated design and mechanical problems for major companies.

Chris' special talent is his ability to feel what's wrong - whether he's working on a car, computer or household appliance. It's as if he can get into the minds of the machines.

In sad contrast to his uncanny ability to understand machines is Chris' tremendous INABILITY to get into the heads of the people close to him: his two children by two different wives, the ex-wives themselves and the women he has dated since his second marriage broke up. All of them have been hurt by the way Chris ignores their feelings, trying to handle every problem with his cold, hard logic.

Chris thinks women are crazy. He can't figure out any other explanation. His affairs all start off full of openness, excitement and passion, women falling head over heels for him - till they end up hating him, that is. Each time he's dumped, Chris is shocked.

"I don't understand it and I don't think I'll ever get used to it," he says. "I'm honest from the beginning. The more I try to get them to know me as I am, so that we can have a friendship, the more I seem to fail.

"I give up on trying to be friends with a woman. And I don't believe they're sincere about really wanting to know me or to get really close."

Like many men, Chris is a raging success in the world of business - and a failure at love. His many breakups make it hard for him to open up to anyone new. He tries plunging himself deeper into his work, but more and more he finds that work just isn't enough. He's disappointed and frustrated: Nothing in his personal life works out, even though he believes that he is doing everything right.

Chris isn't alone. There are plenty of men out there who think they're doing all the right things but still somehow can't make love work.

WHAT MOST SELF-HELP BOOKS MISS

The best-seller lists are overflowing with self-help books targeted at women readers about men who "can't love" and "hate women"; about men who are either selfish sexists; misguided, pathetic wimps; workaholics and selfish lovers, or abusive addicts.

Not surprisingly, few men identify with these books. That's because they don't see themselves the way women see them. Now if there weren't some truth to these books, they wouldn't be so popular. But they all miss an important point: an accurate explanation of what makes men tick, what opens them up and what shuts them down - so that the woman who wants a healthy, happy relationship with a man can succeed.

In my practice as a therapist, I've seen many women who feel so frustrated, hurt and angry with their men that they refuse to make the effort to understand why he has behaved as he has, and what women's personal problem areas and process contribute to the pain they are experiencing, and in the end, can't appreciate any of the loving things he does.

Many of these women believe that the only way their relationship can survive is for their men (but not for THEM) to change. They feel that they have given until they can't give any more, while the man has taken without giving anything in return. But this attitude dooms the relationship, because both partners have to be willing to change for a a relationship to heal.

MEN AND WOMEN ARE VERY DIFFERENT

As we've seen with Chris, romance sweeps most people along in the beginning of their relationships. Starry-eyed, the man believes everything will work out and that he is really understood and loved. But then reality starts to kick in and the going gets rough, and what does the man do? He quits talking, convinced that trying to be heard and understood won't do any good. He becomes one of the "silent, closed-off" males that drive their women crazy.

The way men love and what they need in a relationship are very different from what women need. In fact, often they're the exact OPPOSITE. Unlike women, men have been taught to deny any weaknesses and personal needs, to stay in control and not get too close. It used to be that men were considered lovable and manly for these qualities. If nothing else, they help men succeed in the working world. But these qualities can really hurt a man in his personal life.

Take 55-year-old Patrick, who decided to retire when he had a near-fatal heart attack. Sitting alone in his beautiful, antique-filled home, he couldn't bring himself to ask anybody to help him, either to run errands or to stay with him while he recovered.

"I'm uncomfortable asking anyone to do things for me," he said. "Maybe it's too much of a commitment to let someone know I need them. The women might get the wrong idea and think it's an invitation to get too close, and I'm not ready for that. If I ask my men friends, they might say no, and then I'll get angry or hurt. I don't want to risk that."

So here was Patrick, who had always considered himself a lovable person, sitting alone hoping someone would call and the problem would solve itself. Wealthy, good-looking Patrick is a victim of this culture's lessons to men. He learned that to make money and impress others, he had to keep his distance. Like many men, he had learned to "stand tall and alone," to do for others, but to always keep an emotional distance.

And he got so good at this that he didn't even realize he was doing it.

WHEN SUCCESS EQUALS FAILURE

As the previous examples of Chris and Patrick show, the "ideal man" in our society doesn't have much hope of becoming the close, loving and intimate mate most women are looking for. Ironically, it's the very same traits that make him successful in business that lead to his downfall in his personal life!

Chris and Patrick did all the "right things" a man is told he's supposed to do to make himself lovable, but failed anyway. When Chris tried to deal with his women's feelings with "logical solutions," he drove them away. Patrick succeeded in work, but lived a lonely life by keeping emotionally distant. Over time, both became more accustomed to hiding their feelings, more frustrated and more incapable of having a good relationship.

Over the years, I have worked with many intelligent, sensitive and successful men who did very well at their jobs, but failed miserably at their relationships. The cold, logical approach that worked so well for them at work was exactly what destroyed their relationships. Then, instead of seeing how hard these men were actually trying to love them, the women in their lives saw only their flaws.

WHY MEN DON'T OPEN UP

Do they plan to make their partners unhappy? Of course not

As one man put it, "Even my sincerest efforts at being 'nice' seemed to get misunderstood, and I'd find myself being accused of being hostile or acting in patronizing, dishonest or manipulative ways. When I would joke or be playful to lighten things up, I was often told I was making fun of her or being sarcastic and hurtful. When I'd try to talk things out rationally or explain myself, it only made things worse, because I was told I was intellectualizing and being cold and distant.

"Nothing short of agreeing with her way of thinking and asking forgiveness seemed enough. Even then I was in a double bind, because apologizing would make me seem weak and intimidated. Going silent and being cold and withdrawn seemed the only solution. She'd be upset at how closed I was, but at least our differences had a bottom line. She could only guess at what I was feeling or thinking."

Was this man to blame for the breakdown of his relationships? Or was he the victim? Or was he part of a system that just doesn't work?

Few men purposely set out to be isolated, withdrawn and unloving. As a matter of fact, most men want exactly the opposite: a trusting, caring relationship.

That doesn't mean men aren't partly responsible for the death of their relationships or for the pain that many women feel. Deep down, men must know how tough it is to get close to them. After all, most of them can't even make close MEN friends.

Marty is a high-powered San Diego attorney in his mid40s whose personal life leaves, shall we say, a lot to be desired. He was on the brink of death from lung cancer, barely on speaking terms with the children of his broken marriage, and very bitter toward women after an expensive, painful divorce battle and an affair with a woman who left him when his business was bad.

Marty went on to meet and marry a woman he called his "soul mate," someone who he said he could fully trust and be vulnerable with for the first time in his life. To his dismay, he started having sexual problems.

When a doctor assured him that his "equipment" was working fine, he consulted a therapist to discuss his feelings, particularly about the woman he said he loved deeply.

Although Marty was sincerely worried about the problem, he quickly decided to give up therapy and work things out on his own. Well, not only was he unable to change his personality on his own, but he also couldn't talk about his problems to his new wife. Less than a year after they were married, the love of his life gave up in frustration and left him.

For most men, it's so unnatural to open up to a woman that they end up blowing the relationship. It all comes down to this: Men simply don't believe that they can expose their weaknesses and be treated with loving compassion.

PROBLEM? WHAT PROBLEM?

As we've discussed, most men are so focused on outside concerns like their jobs that they can't tune in to what others are feeling. Often they deny there's a problem at all until it's too late.

What's more, there's a big difference between the way women and men approach problems. Women are more able to ask for help and more willing to look within themselves for solutions. Men, on the other hand, see problems as the result of mistakes rather than of something that might have to do with their personality. They look for the same logical answers and mechanical solutions that work in the outside world, but can't find them.

Because of this, men operate "blindly" in relationships. Not only can't they change, they often don't even know what they NEED to change! Meanwhile, the people around them become enraged with them, and the men don't even realize what's happening. As far as they're concerned, they're still loved and lovable. They just go on building emotional walls, convinced that they need them for self-protection, not realizing they are hurting others in the process.

A well-known psychologist with a national radio talk show had a string of very public extramarital affairs. He believed that sexual freedom was healthy and that he was actually doing a favor for his wife and children, who would grow from his experience and love him all the more. What he couldn't see was the pain, anger and humiliation that his family members felt but were afraid to express.

While he preached openness and authenticity in relationships over the airwaves, this psychologist's family hated him for what he did, but they never told him. When his wife divorced him and ill health forced him to retire, he finally found out how little his loved ones thought of him. Instead of realizing how he had brought this situation upon himself, however, he blamed his family for being ungrateful.

WOMEN'S RAGE

While it's true that men have their problems in relationships, women don't help matters any with their furious reactions. Women, after all, have their own expectations, needs and romantic fantasies about closeness. Unfortunately, men don't fulfill them, not because they don't want to, but because they can't. And when men fail, despite their best efforts at loving, women get bitter.

Milton was a self-made, very successful businessman in his 50s whose wife had committed suicide and whose children despised him. They saw him as abrasive, arrogant and to-tally self-centered - the result of all his years of hustling to give his family what he never had.

If men were aware of the effect they have on others, would they choose to alienate and enrage those close to them and hurt themselves in the process? If women were aware of what was going on inside men, would they resent them as much?

Being fully aware of our role in a relationship isn't easy. It's one thing to point out the unpleasant things being done to us, quite another to see what we're doing to someone else. Women may feel misunderstood, victimized and exploited - but so do men. They feel as oppressed as women and as eager to achieve a successful love relationship.

Take the case of Miriam and her husband. Miriam, married for 12 years, was angry because her husband would fall asleep at family dinners with her parents and because he was "cruel" to their sons. He told her that the weekly dinner ritual with her parents depressed him and was bad for his health because he felt he had to eat the rich food and had to listen to her father's critical comments about how he conducted his busi-ness. What's more, during conversations with their children, he said, she would encourage them to "stand up to" their fa-ther and always sided with her parents.

But Miriam didn't listen. Enraged, she interpreted her husband's behavior as self-centered and insensitive. Only when they started therapy did she finally hear what he had to say.

FROM ENEMIES TO FRIENDS

The way a woman relates to a man can affect his ability to care and the way he responds to her. Women need to pay attention to what men are saying if they're ever going to quit being opponents and start to be loving friends.

There are so many differences between men and women: men"s isolation, woman's need to be close; men's cold' logic, woman's hot emotions. These opposites can make male/female relationships exciting. But when a man makes a joke that a woman takes in the wrong way, or a woman thinks she's being loving but is seen as pressuring, the defenses go up. Remember, both are victims. Both are caught up in the misunderstanding and pain.

When passionate romance—which is the way most relationships begin—turns into distance and dislike, we are all victims. When a seemingly compatible couple can't stop hurting each other, it is time to stop, take a few steps back and clear the air.

WOMEN'S LIBERATION; GOOD FOR MEN, TOO

We've come a long way in the past 30 years. Women no longer tolerate men making all the decisions. As women take their place in the business world, their relationships with men in the "outside" world will flourish.

Men, meanwhile, no longer accept that they're responsible for all the problems in a personal relationship. More and more, they are trying to get a handle on their own experience and are making an effort to understand others, too.

To love and be loved means to know and be known as we really are. Good relationships stem from a realistic understanding and acceptance of each other and ourselves.

Confronting our partners about their "crimes" seems easier than dealing with our own problems. It's not easy to look at ourselves, but it's worth it. In a society where we are free to choose a mate, our relationships have a lot to teach us. The person we attract and are attracted to is a reflection of who we are.

CHAPTER THREE

THE 12 BLIND SPOTS OF MEN

The way men look at the world creates huge blind spots when it comes to personal relationships. That's why they can't "see" what they're doing when they select the wrong partner, mishandle problems and misjudge the quality of their relationships.

HERE ARE SOME OF MEN'S MOST COMMON BLIND SPOTS AND THE CONFLICTS THEY CAUSE:

1   "I will be automatically loved for my achievements."

The football hero scoring a goal, the young man paying for an expensive night out, the husband working two jobs, the businessman giving his family "the best" - each of these men believes that these are sufficient proof of love and will earn him loving rewards in return. When people don't respond that way, he feels betrayed.

2   The more successful I am, the happier my partner will be." The man who believes this fails to see that the very same qualities that make him a success in the outside world - aggressiveness, distance, etc. - may actually turn off and even hurt those closest to him.

3   "My ideas about life are absolute truth, and everyone around me better agree." The men who think this way - and there are many of them - don't realize that their thoughts are just one man's opinion.

Eventually such a man discovers that those who are close to him don't think the way he thinks or act the way he thinks they should act. When he pushes to get them to do things his way, they end up resenting him. And he ends up angry.

This inability to respect the attitudes and beliefs of others is a major relationship roadblock. Yet many otherwise intelligent men can't see their way around it. In fact, the more successful a man is the more convinced he is that he is "right" about everything.

4   "Personal problems can easily be solved with impersonal, logical solutions." Many men answer fears and problems with "willpower" or "self-control." They see their own relationship problems as isolated mistakes, rather than a serious misreading of people and situations.

These men believe that there are easy "how to" answers to personal problems. "Do this and you'll get her to spend the night at your place," or "Do that and she'll come crawling back to you." They don't realize that relationships are a lot more complex.

This blind spot prevents them from seeing that there may be a pattern to their problems, and so they are doomed to repeat the same painful patterns.

5   "My wife or partner is weak and vulnerable and needs to be protected." The many men who believe this feel responsible and guilty when problems arise, but hide their thoughts and feelings so they don't- "crush her." But this just makes things worse. The woman is "protected" from knowing what's going on with him, and the man becomes resentful for having to hold back, resulting in confusion and frustration.

(Ironically, when the relationship ends, it turns out that HE is the desperate, dependent one, whereas SHE has no trouble building a new life for herself)

6   "Great sexual performance is as important to a woman as it is to me." Many men believe that sexual performance is utmost in a woman's mind - and that she will seek a new lover if he has a performance problem. When she doesn't reject him for temporary impotence or other difficulties, he is both grateful and surprised.

In fact, one woman said she was actually GLAD when her husband became impotent.

"He started to kiss me more and he became more emotional and tender. Good sex for me is first and foremost being close. If I get that, whether or not he has erections is minor, except for the fact that it bothers him so much. I want to know he needs and loves me. That turns me on the most."

7   "Sex problems have to do with my body, not with my mind." Sexually, many men believe that any sexual problems they may have are mechanical failures - sort of like broken plumbing - rather than deeper reflections of feelings. He feels humiliated by his failure and, in desperation, may turn to an "instant" and often ineffective cure.

8   "Problem? What problem?" Because they often can't see the pain they cause in others, many men ignore problems till it's too late. When they finally do see a problem, they assume it's no big deal since they never noticed it before. So they reach for a quick fix, which further angers their loved ones. When things break down altogether, they tend to say: "Everything seemed to be going just fine. Oh, there were little things once in awhile, but they were just minor."

"We'll be fine in no time." Because they hadn't noticed the problem for so long, when men do notice, they figure it's no big deal. So they reach for a quick fix.

9   "If they don't hear me, I'll just talk louder." Many men believe that if he's not being listened to, speaking more forcefully will make others listen. By doing this, of course, he pushes people away.

10   "I am in complete control." Many men have such a need to be in control that they can't spot the difference between a woman who truly loves them and a manipulative woman. These men are certain that a woman's seemingly instant admiration means that she finds him irresistible. They haven't a clue that they could be making a serious misjudgment and falling victim to an act.

11 "Don't worry, be happy." When loved ones bring them their problems, many men hand out their favorite sayings, such as, "Put a smile on your face and you'll feel better," or "You can do anything you want - there's no such thing as `can't.'" These sorts of pat answers shows just how self-involved they really are and how little they actually know about the people they care about.

Tragically, many women see their men's behavior as simply self-centered and hurtful - rather than as a man's different way of loving. It all starts when boys and young men are applauded for their accomplishments. Sure, they're told to be loving, but competition and achievement always come first.

12 It's simply not fair to reject men for how they love and who they are. To truly love a man is to love him for who and what he is - and is not.

CHAPTER FOUR

HOW TO SPOT A MIDLIFE CRISIS

A midlife crisis doesn't come from out of nowhere. It's a logical link in a chain of experiences that may have made a man a great success in the world but that have also taken him light years away from his inner self.

Midlife is the time when all the typical male traits discussed in the previous chapter come home to roost. Sometime in his 40s, all of a man's built-up defensiveness and emotional distance paint him into a corner called CRISIS. His unfeeling behavior has finally made a mess of the relationships he cares about the most. He realizes that his desperate search for money and power has meant nothing. He discovers that no matter how much he's got, it's never enough.

At midlife, many a man concludes that the bad in his life far outweighs the good. The family he has slaved away for has shut him out. Said one 47-year-old man: "I've done my best, but it's all turning to garbage and I can't deny it any longer. The truth is, I have no relationship with my wife or my children."

We all know the man who "solves" such a crisis by buying a shiny new sports car, changing his hairstyle or finding a young girlfriend. But these are poor substitutes for getting to the heart of the problem. Instead of looking within himself to find out what went wrong, he tries to ease the pain with the very same "instant fix" behavior that created it. Worse yet, these latest demonstrations of childish behavior often destroy the last ties he has to the people closest to him.

THINK YOUR MAN MIGHT BE HAVING A MIDLIFE CRISIS? WATCH FOR THESE SYMPTOMS:

A sense of inner "deadness." No matter what he does, few things in life make him feel excited and optimistic.

A string of conflicts and fights with his wife or partner that never get resolved, leaving him hopeless and frustrated. He no longer believes that things will improve or that she will ever understand him.

Little or no interest in sex with his partner. No longer a source of pleasure, sex with his mate just makes him feel bad. "1 can't please her and I'm not getting anything from this either," he reasons.

The realization that no amount of financial security will satisfy him. Yet even if he could afford to retire, he wouldn't, because he no longer enjoys anything apart from work.

The awareness that his mate is always unhappy, tired, or feels ill. He gets the feeling that it's his fault - he has made her unhappy.

No closeness with his children, who have disappointed him. "They only talk to me when they want money," is a common complaint. What's more, he resents the fact that the kids are closer to their mother and seem ungrateful about his contribution. Ironically, it was a lifetime of his cold, controlling behavior that set him up for this rejection.

A sense of overall failure - he'd expected to have achieved a lot more by this point in his life. Life isn't turning out at all how it was supposed to.

The sad feeling that he betrayed himself because he never really did it "his way." Now, at midlife, he's desperately convinced that it's his last chance, if he's ever going to risk being "true to himself."

A sense of guilt and hopelessness - he sees how wrong he was to manipulate others to get his own way.

A feeling that his own life is one endless series of pressures and responsibilities. Instead of becoming easier, life has become harder. But he sees no point in struggling anymore.

A growing sense that his needs and feelings don't really matter to those close to him.

Learning to recognize the signs of a midlife crisis is an important step toward helping both men and the women they're involved with avoid its painful pitfalls.

Chapter Five

WHAT MEN DON'T TELL THE WOMEN THEY LOVE

It's natural for a man to close up. Remember: That's what he was taught to do as a child. His father was stern and silent. His heroes in action films and comic books were tough, tightlipped and triumphant.

These guys didn't know the meaning of small talk. When they did speak, it was only because they had something important to say.

One man I know can still hear his father saying things like, "Talk is cheap," "You sound like a gossipy woman" and "Silence is golden" when he "talked too much."

"When I would try to talk to Dad," this man recalls, "I could see his eyes glaze over. He'd look bored and distracted. Or he would start to lecture me about what I was saying before he heard me out.

"I never learned to listen because I was never listened to my- self. What we 'talked about' were impersonal or objective things, where it was a matter of having information and cor- rect answers. I never learned to discuss things without a pur- pose or a point to justify it."

A man may manage, despite what his male role models taught him, to open up in his relationships. Often, however, women's unpleasant reactions turn him off all over again. His attempts at being heard or understood having failed, little by little his conversation becomes more and more limited and eventu- ally he simply stops talking about anything personal altogether. Stephen, age 43, described his experience in trying to com- municate with several women he'd loved over the years.

"Women don't really want to know what I feel, like they seem to think they do," he explained. "At first, I believed them when they said they wanted me to share my feelings. I often regret- ted it later. Despite assurances that it was safe to risk and disclose what I felt, what I said was often judged 'not nice' or unloving.

"When I talked to her about the problems I was having with the relationship, I usually received an angry or tearful response. I learned that 'opening up' was dangerous and rarely worth the aggravation."

Men are often surprised by how seriously women take what was actually intended as a joke or tongue-in-cheek comment.

Most men end up believing that it wouldn't take much to hurt or disappoint their partner "if she really knew me." Instead, they make a point to keep their mouths shut rather than risk it. "You can't say that to a woman," men warn each other.

So, men don't talk to the women they love about their deep- est feelings. But don't think that means they don't have them!

WHY IT'S RISKY FOR MEN TO SHARE FEELINGS

When men try to speak up but get a negative response, they turn off:

"I've given up trying to tell a woman I'm involved with how I feel," says one man. *"She only really listens when I say `nice' or `loving' things. Whenever I try to communicate anything else, I can feel her getting defensive and upset."*

Says another: *"If I want to avoid a battle, lingering bad feelings, and back-and-forth dancing to reassure her that I really want to be with her, and that what I said didn't mean I didn't love her, it's best I talk about only upbeat, nonthreatening subjects. Since that gets to be a bore, I find myself having less and less to say."*

And another: *"She may not like the fact that I'm quiet, but at least I don't get into endless discussions about what I `really meant' and how I `really feel' about us."*

"When I go away on business for a few days, and she asks if I missed her," says another man, "and I don't answer in just the right way, she says things like: `Maybe you don't want to be with me any longer.' Then I have to reassure her that it doesn't mean I don't care about her."

WHY MEN FEAR GETTING CLOSE

It's easiest for a man to open up with a woman who accepts his feelings and is aware of how her reactions affect him. In particular, no man wants to be told that his innermost thoughts are unloving, rejecting or cruel.

"How can I be close to a woman when she doesn't admit her

part in the problems we have?" says one man. "How can I get close to someone who makes me the `bad guy' and sees herself as blameless?" Says another, "How can I feel close to someone who keeps telling me I'm not a caring or loving person? I couldn't be as limited and bad at love as she makes out. If I really am, how could she really love me as she says she does?"

An experienced bachelor who describes himself as having been around the relationship track many times says, "In all my years in and out of relationships, I have rarely been with a woman who, on a regular basis, could accept how her reactions and behavior affected me and contributed to the responses and behaviors of mine that bothered her.

"In relationships," he continues, "women seem to think that everything loving comes from them, and everything hurtful comes from the man. When I'm with a woman who sees herself as an equal ingredient, I start to feel close and act close, and I love it."

A woman who wants the love of her man needs to listen rather than interpret and accuse. She also needs to take a good look at the part she contributes to problems.

Some women make a big deal of a man "screwing up," yet they don't seem to notice when he's being caring and loving, many men tell me. But instead of expressing their frustration and anger, these men clam up, feeling rejected and misunderstood.

While it's true that the way men talk and behave may often make them seem unloving, most men see themselves as trying hard to be close in their relationships. Women who want to be close to their men need to give them credit for their efforts.

WHY MEN DON'T UNDERSTAND WOMEN

"Are all women crazy, or do I do something to make them irrational once we're involved?" one man asks. "They're rarely like that until after we get `serious."

Men don't understand how women's moods shift so quickly - or why they're blamed for it. And they don't know hove to respond.

The worst is when men try to be LOGICAL in the face of a woman's EMOTIONAL outburst, causing her to suddenly and "for no apparent reason" become even angrier or start to cry. When he asks her why, she'll answer in ways that make no sense to him.

A seasoned book publishing executive recounted the "nightmare" of "irrationality" that occurred in the last few years of his marriage.

"I got into a running argument that finally blew my `logical' mind," he told me. "I'd play golf on Saturday afternoon - my only recreation on my only full day off.

"I'd arrive home around 6:30. For some reason, my wife thought that I should be home by 6:00. I'd ask her, `Why? What's the difference? Why do you need me here at 6:00?'

"She wouldn't answer. She'd just get angrier. I couldn't give in to her without a sensible explanation, but I couldn't get an explanation at all."

WHY MEN LOVE LOGIC

A man's logic is very important to him. A woman may see logic as a weapon he uses to avoid emotions. At the same time, a man can end up feeling totally helpless and frustrated in the face of a woman's emotions.

The source of this difficulty is that men are taught to be problem-solvers rather than caring, emotional partners. If logic gets them nowhere in an argument, they tend to overreact and become defensive.

Don't criticize his "cold" approach to a problem - you'll end up not talking at all. Instead, remind yourself that this is his "male approach" to things, and see if you can work out a compromise between logic and emotion.

WHY MEN PUT WOMEN DOWN

Men don't often mean to put a woman down, even though they may come across that way.

"I don't feel or intend to be critical of a woman, even though I'm often told that I am," says one man. "I don't want to control a woman or use her, either, but I hear that a lot, too.

"If I seem to be that way, I wish I could get specific examples. The funny thing is, I usually get that criticism when I'm trying hardest to be supportive."

What a man may see as helpful, a woman may see as harmful. One man gave up trying to get close to a woman he was strongly attracted to when she accused him of belittling her by opening the car door for her and carrying her food tray to the table at a buffet.

And then there was Jim, age 34, who at first was very drawn to Kristin. Because they were both psychologists, he assumed that he could talk straight to her and that she'd let him know if any problems came up. He broke off the relationship six months after they met when she suddenly gave him a long list of ways he had been "critical" of her, when all along he thought things were going well.

Another man arranged a second honeymoon in Mexico, hoping it would bring the romance and passion back to his marriage. It wasn't until he and his wife returned home that he learned that his efforts to be thoughtful and affectionate had failed miserably. His wife accused him of cutting her off in the middle of her sentences while they socialized with two other couples and of seeming bored by her conversation.

Although this man admitted that he did have a bad habit of trying to be the center of attention, he felt terrible that all his wife had noticed were the bad things - his loving intentions were completely ignored.

Remember: Men don't set out to put women down. In fact, they may think they're doing just the opposite, being helpful and supportive. A man who comes across as emotionally cold probably doesn't mean it that way, and it's certainly nothing personal. A woman's best approach to handling this situation is to calmly tell her man how she feels, while also considering whether she's being too sensitive.

WHY MEN ARE NOT HONEST WITH WOMEN

"Sure I lie to the woman I'm involved with," a man will typically say when asked about honesty in relationships. "When I've been honest with any thoughts or feelings that aren't 100 percent nice or at least non-threatening, the women have always gotten upset. It's not worth it."

In intimate relationships, men may have feelings and thoughts that are "not nice" or are easily misunderstood. If a man's wife has a hard time making up her mind, for example, he may get irritated because he has learned to decide or act quickly, but he keeps his irritation to himself. When she wants a hug or kiss, he may feel uneasy because he was taught not to act that way. In bed, he may fantasize about other women because that's what he learned to do as a young man. But he certainly won't tell her about it.

Because they're afraid to hurt their mates, many men won't tell the truth. Soon, they become out-and-out dishonest, hiding every sort of thought, experience and feeling.

WHAT MEN NEED TO BE HONEST WITH A WOMAN

It's normal to have misunderstandings, especially at the beginning of a relationship. How a man and woman work out these misunderstandings can predict how healthy their relationship will be. Women who get angry and upset and make their man feel guilty when he tries to reveal "bad news" may win in the short run, but they're planting the seeds of dishonesty in their relationship. "I'll never make her understand me," said one man, "so I might as well say nothing at all."

Any man who is truly honest will, from time to time, say things that are hard to hear - things that women have to learn not to take personally. At best, a woman can react to what he shares as a glimpse into his soul. This will launch a cycle of trust and openness.

WHY MEN HAVE PROBLEMS WITH SELF-CENTERED WOMEN

Many women's idea of being loving is to give their man what they think he wants - whether or not he really does.

"So often women give you what you DON'T want and ignore

what you DO," observes one man. "Then they get upset when you're not thrilled!"

Eric, age 37 and married, described what happened when he was disappointed by a gift his wife bought him. "She said I was killing her enthusiasm and love and that she'd never go out of her way to give me a gift again."

Another man describes how his wife greets him at the door after work every day with lots of hugs and kisses. "I'm really too wired and preoccupied for that sort of thing when I first get home. But she's hurt if I don't respond. I mean, if she wants to love me, let her give me what I can handle. Or don't give me anything -at least that way I won't feel guilty and pressured."

Self-centered love means giving something that makes YOU happy instead of your loved one. (You can see how men are guilty of this when they claim to be working hard for their family - not admitting that they enjoy the work themselves - or when they offer "helpful advice" in hopes of a grateful response.) Women who give self-centered love are ignoring how the men in their lives would like to be loved.

Says one man: "On my 40th birthday, my wife threw me a surprise party. She knew I didn't like birthday parties, and she knew that I wasn't happy about turning 40. Just in case there was any question, I specifically asked her NOT to give me a party.

"Instead, she went all out with catered food -although I really needed to diet-and invited people I didn't want to see. During the party, she kept coming over and telling me to smile and not be a 'party pooper.' It was agony.

"Then I had to open the gifts. She told everybody to bring gag stuff. Most people brought something that had to do with my supposedly being over the hill sexually. I just didn't think they were funny.

"After the party, she was angry and hurt. She kept saying, 'At least you could have tried to be nice.' She was convinced that SHE was the victim here. According to her, I was the one who couldn't accept or give love!

"The problem was, she was 'loving me' HER way. It had nothing to do with how I felt or who I was."

WHAT MEN DON'T TELL WOMEN

When we get love that doesn't "fit" we feel bad that it doesn't make us happy even though it's supposed to. Until women learn to give men what they really want, neither side will know how well a man can love. He'll be too busy feeling guilty!

Women need to find out what their mates really need. This will take patience, since many men have no idea how to tell them. As part of this learning process, women need to regularly check back with their man to be sure they're giving the love they want, and to accept his response without criticizing or getting defensive.

Believe it or not, it's better to do nothing at all than to do something you THINK is loving but that actually ends up making him unhappy. Men try to express their love, but many women don't make it easy for them.

"No matter how much I tell her I love her, as soon as I utter one wrong word, she forgets everything else," one man laments.

"Out of nowhere, she'll ask, `Do you still love me?' or `Do you love me as much as ever?' It always catches me off guard. I get so rattled that she immediately takes it as a rejection.

"She'll tell me I never loved her in the first place, which is crazy. Why on earth would I be with her if I didn't love her in the first place? If she thinks I'm only with her because I'm afraid to be alone, or because I'm using her, then she couldn't think very much of me. After this happens a few times, I DO start to doubt my love - just because she keeps pressuring me to prove it!"

WHAT HE NEEDS TO MAKE HER FEEL LOVED

Because men show love differently from women, women often don't believe that a man's love is real. And because men have such trouble showing their affection, sometimes what they say from the heart comes out as hurtful - something they don't mean.

A man may hear from his partner, "My feelings don't go like yours - on again, off again. Even when you try and show me your love, it doesn't feel like love. Sometimes when you're with me, it doesn't feel like you're even here."

Men throw up their hands in frustration when they hear accusations that seem so unfair. And the longer men's loving feelings are doubted or misunderstood, the greater their confusion and anger.

HOW MEN HATE BEING TOLD THEY'RE NOT GOOD ENOUGH

"Once I commit myself," one man told me, "it turns into 'open season' for criticism. Suddenly I learn what a lousy partner I am. It gets to the point where I'm happy as long as she doesn't look unhappy and I'm not being told there's something wrong with me!"

Jerry, a divorced man in his 40s, remembered, "When we'd be with the children on weekends, nothing I did was ever right.

Either I was talking too much or I was too quiet. Or, I was told I was doing fine with the kids and ignoring my wife, or I wasn't giving them enough attention and was putting all the responsibility for the children on her and having a selfishly fun time. Or it was pointed out to me that I was just going through the motions - because I didn't really want to be there at all."

WHAT MEN NEED TO FEEL GOOD ABOUT THEM-SELVES

Constant criticism of your mate - especially if it makes no sense to him - can really put a damper on relationships, to say the least. Men often react to criticism by becoming more emotionally detached, because they start doubting their ability to love.

Remember: Men weren't raised to be intimate, but they do try. Accepting the way that they are, that they DO in fact express love in their own way, can bring out the best in them.

ABOUT GREAT BEGINNINGS AND TERRIBLE ENDINGS

"Don't first adore me, telling me how wonderful I am for all the wrong reasons, then hate me later on because I wasn't who you thought I was or who you wanted me to be in the first place. From start to finish, you never knew who I was," observed a man who had experienced many "wild" beginnings and painful endings.

The man a woman bitterly blames at the end of the relationship is pretty much the same man she described as wonderful, special, and "different from other men" at the beginning. This is because at the beginning, the woman isn't passionate about who the man really is - but who she WANTS him to be. It's not much different from a man falling in love with a beautiful face or body.

Few women actually know their mates - who are, in fact, neither as wonderful as they first thought nor as terrible as they describe them at the end. Actually, it's as if a real relationship never took place.

We've all heard about men who don't want to commit. Why is this? Because they know the dangers of being put up on a pedestal. They know they can't possibly live up to the image women have of them. So to protect themselves, they avoid getting too involved.

Don't get me wrong - men certainly enjoy being adored. But they pay the price by having to pretend to be someone they're not. In the end, they make their partners disappointed, betrayed and furious.

One man described how hard it was to get his wife to see him as he really was. "I tried to get Linda to appreciate the real me without turning her off."I1 failed miserably. Whenever I'd say to her, 'But this is who I am,' during an argument, she simply refused to believe me."

When a man says, "This is who I am," listen up. Then ask yourself whether you can love this person just as he is. The two of you are going to have some tough times while you learn to relate honestly with each other, but that's the basis for a solid relationship.

HOW MEN AND WOMEN USE EACH OTHER

"Let's not call this marriage a relationship. A husband is not a person, he's a responsibility object," one man says.

When a man gets in touch with his real feelings and with what's going on in his marriage, he often has the sense of being used as an "object," feeling like "a wallet" because he's expected to pay for things, or "the garbage man" because he has to do "the dirty work." (At the same time, many wives come to view themselves as "appliances" or "service stations.")

Men feel resentful when they catch on to how they're being used. They discover that they are being "loved" for their "usefulness," not for the person they really are.

WHAT MEN NEED TO FEEL LOVED, NOT USED

Let's face it: Women do tend to judge men as "marriage material," just as men judge women. Admitting that we all do this is a big step toward feeling less used.

The best antidote is to work at being FRIENDS. When we present ourselves honestly and communicate person-to-person instead of trying to impress or control each other as potential mates, the problems that inevitably come up are easier to solve. When people are busy playing rigid roles, conflicts can't be resolved in positive, productive ways, and things start to fall apart.

Listen to the comments of a number of men:

"When I hear the word 'husband,' I tighten up. I don't think it's because I'm afraid of commitment. It's that being a husband is a job - with never ending 'shoulds.' A husband is 'supposed to be' all sorts of great things, many of which I know I'm not very good at. So, in the end I'll be seen as the "lousy husband."

Said another, "Now I know what women mean when they say, 'I don't want to BE a wife - I NEED a wife.' That's how I feel. I don't want to be a husband - I need a husband. I feel used for what I can do, but never loved for who I am."

A young man considering marriage said: "I don't mind if she

loves me for what I do for her - if she'll admit that's what's going on and not cop this holier-than-thou attitude about how loving she is and how afraid to love or be loved I am.

"Why not begin with some honesty about how we need each other for our roles and take it from there? At least then I won't be the only one accused. 'Objects' don't get close. Hopefully, people can."

"I don't feel I'm being listened to," was the frustrated response of many men I interviewed.

A woman who has become accustomed to her man's inability to express his emotions often gives up and stops paying attention. Then, when he complains that she's not listening, she gets angry, thinking he's just trying to cover up his emotional flaws.

"When I talk to my wife, she acts bored or distracted. I get the feeling she's not really interested," says one man.

"When I tell her she's not listening, she answers, `You don't really want to talk to me - or about us, anyway. I could be anybody. So why should I pay attention?"

When men express themselves in their customary "logical" manner, women don't think it counts as caring conversation. But as far as he's concerned, he's doing his best to reach out - after all, this is how he learned he should communicate. Women need to accept that what men have to say is a loving attempt to express themselves. Women who succeed in this say men love them more easily because they feel "heard."

"I don't want that kind of power over a woman - to feel that I can destroy her with a wrong word or misbehavior," says one man. "I don't want a woman who's so helpless that I feel more powerful with her than I want to be."

When a woman is unhappy, many men feel that it's because of something he did or said. When sex isn't good, it must be his fault for not turning her on. When he says or does something without thinking and she gets so hurt, he's "spoiled" the day. Men don't want to be made to feel cruel and insensitive, but this is just what happens when women act helpless and fragile. Men's fear that they might do or say something to hurt their mate is a reason so many men resist attempts at honest communication.

ON BEING STRONG - OR SHOWING WEAKNESS

Just as women are a lot stronger than men think they are, men are a good deal weaker than they seem to be. In fact, at the end of many relationships, the "fragile" woman often does much better in her new life than the "tough" man.

Men and women both have strengths and weaknesses. Unfortunately, women don't show how strong and assertive they can be till they're ready to break off the relationship. At the same time, men don't show how dependent and afraid they can be until they're dumped.

Both sexes have areas of power and of helplessness in relationships. By revealing your own strengths and vulnerabilities and by recognizing them in your partner, you will both avoid ending up feeling controlled, manipulated or abused.

WHY 'NICE' DRIVES MEN CRAZY

"I know she wants things to be `nice,' but `nice' all the time is a bore," says one man. "It feels phony, and there's always that pressure on me to be nice in return if she's always that way. I don't feel nice all the time, which makes it even worse. I become the bad guy for not feeling something I see as phony and deadening."

"I like women better and I trust them more if they're direct and `not nice'," says another man. "`Nice' women always make me feel there's something wrong with me, which makes me feel manipulated.

"I want to shake `nice' women and say, `Stop it! This is boring and dead and unreal. One day you'll turn on me and give it to me with both barrels and say it's my fault because I didn't know how to be nice. If you love me, then stop being so damn nice and show me your other side.'"

A man with a long, unsuccessful track record in romance remarked, "In my relationships, the `nicer' the woman was at the beginning, the angrier she was in the end. Also, while you're involved with them, the really `nice' women always seem tired, sick, or they can't seem to make decisions. I guess they're just sitting on a lot of negative feelings that they deny even to themselves."

"Sex with a 'nice' woman isn't much fun. I mean, the kind where the woman ends up saying, 'That was very nice!' or 'Wasn't that nice?' and you know she hardly got anything out of it. She just wants to be NICE."

Men can't be as consistently nice as women, who would rather be "nice" than express what might be dangerous negative emotions. When a woman asks her man, "Why can't you at least try and be nice?" he may often feel beaten up for something he's incapable of. What's more, he's totally frustrated that they'll never get how they really feel out in the open.

The fact is, no one can keep up "nice" all the time without denying a lot of real emotions. A man who is not "nice" is not being uncaring or is not trying. A woman needs to accept that her man, their relationship and even she herself all have aspects that sometimes aren't so nice. When she does so, problems can finally be worked out - and genuine "niceness" can be expressed.

WHY MEN HAVE PROBLEMS BEING SUPPORTIVE OF WOMEN

"When a woman tells me her plans or dreams and I don't tell her right away how great they are, she thinks I'm putting her down," says one man. "But I'm always skeptical about `exciting ideas,' even my own, when they're new. A woman will announce a dream, such as opening a shop, or being an artist, and I'm supposed to immediately help make it happen or share her excitement. If I don't, it means that I must be against her.

"I can't always be her cheerleader, and I don't want to feel like I have to say her idea is great if I see the pitfalls. Then if I bring them up, I'm accused of raining on her parade. But if I nod and hold my tongue, I'm called `unenthusiastic.'"

One man said, "My wife told me she was going to take writing classes, buy a word processor, and write children's books and magazine articles to add to our income. I thought to myself, 'Does she know what it takes to break into publishing and how long it'll be before she makes any money' I had serious doubts, and I was a little angry, too, because we DID need extra income, but I decided not to say much of anything.

"Bam! Before I knew it, she was dropping her plans to go back to school and it was all my fault. She said I didn't want her to do it. I really felt manipulated. So now I tell her I don't want to hear her plans until she's already acted on them."

Another man added, "I'm pleased if she's pleased, but I resent the pressure to be excited if I don't automatically feel that way!"

WHAT MEN NEED TO BE SUPPORTIVE

True support means being honest with someone, not just blindly encouraging them. Men can get excited about a project, but often only when they're allowed to discuss "the realities" as they see them.

Men tend to focus on the downside of new situations. Why? Because they're naturally critical of themselves. A woman should be prepared for this when she decides to share her dreams with her partner. If he does offer her criticism, she needs to accept it and not take it personally. This is simply his way of being supportive. When she can finally listen to her man's comments without getting defensive, she has a very good shot at winning both his respect and his heartfelt support.

Men experience many things very differently than women. The surest way to "open up" a man is to understand and accept the person he really is. Don't put him down for what you consider to be his inability to be sensitive, loving or caring. Instead, try hard to understand him, letting him express his inner feelings without fear. In this way you can help your man to open up - and show you his love.

Chapter Six

QUESTIONS WOMEN ASK ABOUT MEN

Judy and Jim loved each other. But they couldn't talk about anything personal without getting angry and frustrated. If Jim said it was important to save money, Judy would criticize him for being "cheap like your father." Then Jim would explode: "You just don't get why I'm worried about money and the future, do you? You always think that somehow we won't have to worry about tomorrow. Well, I don't see life that way! I always need to feel prepared for the worst."

When they would go to the mall together, Judy sometimes caught Jim looking at a pretty girl. He might even comment about her "sexy walk." Judy would always get insulted, while Jim would try to explain that looking at girls was simply a way to pass time because shopping was dull. It had nothing at all to do with his feelings about Judy, he would insist.

As I said, Jim and Judy were in love. But the strain caused by these sorts of misunderstandings was starting to make them doubt that they were right for each other. How was it that they had been so close when they first met but now could hardly talk? And why did these intelligent people keep taking offense at what the other one said?

When men and women confuse and anger each other, it's often because they are speaking "different languages." This has been true since the beginning of their relationship, but they didn't notice it. Early on, they romantically believed that they knew each other so well they didn't need words. Now words fail them.

Because women almost always end up feeling that they're the victims of insensitive men, they rarely get around to understanding what these men are all about. They simply expect men to change - period. But that expectation makes real change impossible.

I hope that if you've read this far, you're beginning to understand that most men WANT to be sensitive and kind to the women they love. If their relationships have problems, they feel just as frustrated and helpless as women do.

The problem is that men and women have different ideas about what love is because of how they were raised. One sex might see something as an expression of love, while the other sex doesn't. For example, many women consider intense closeness absolutely necessary in a relationship, but a man may feel smothered and pressured by this. Or a man's loving desire to take responsibility for things may make a woman feel he is trying to control her.

Differences like these leave both partners hurt and angry. Each believes that they gave love but didn't get it back. What's more, each believes that the other could love "better" if only he or she really wanted to.

To understand why men react the way they do, women need to learn what men are really about. Study these answers to women's most frequently asked questions about men

Q   **Why are men so insensitive in their personal relationships?**

A   In a cruel twist of irony, the same personality traits that make a man seem so manly and attractive when a woman first meets him later seem to that same woman to be terrible flaws. Once committed to the relationship, Prince Charming seems to become Mr. Rat in his Cinderella's eyes.

Take his logical, cool and controlled manner, for instance. At first, his partner probably considered these traits to be very masculine. But now she sees them as signs of his coldness, lack of feeling and fear of intimacy.

And his decisive, take-charge manner that swept her off her feet? That now appears as an oppressive need to control her while not caring about what she wants or needs. What she was attracted to as his independent and self-sufficient style now looks like a permanently distant manner that makes her feel rejected and unneeded: The ambitious goals and com-petitiveness that made him seem so successful? They now make him seem selfish, aggressive and unloving as the rela-tionship evolves.

In other words, everything that was positive has become nega-tive. This is a hard concept for both women and men to grasp.

While women feel hurt, men are bewildered. What his partner once thought was so romantic about him becomes the source of intense criticism. He doesn't "get" how his partner seems to become so easily provoked and angry.

"I haven't changed, yet somehow everything she loved about me at first seems to enrage her now. I'm the same, but her so-called love for me certainly isn't," is how one man sadly summed it up.

Q   **What do men want in a relationship?**

A   Men's conflicting needs to be both independent and dependent create a push-pull, come here-go away mixed bag of messages.

When men are seeking a relationship, they want attention and intensity. But when they're involved, they may want just the opposite!

1. A woman who cries and accuses him of causing her pain; he doesn't understand and feels unfairly blamed.

2. A partner who criticizes his behavior while pressuring him to show he loves her.

3. A woman who accuses him of being selfish and unloving when he believes he is generous and loving.

4. A woman who criticizes him for the way he looks at the world; she doesn't understand that he sees things that way because he feels tremendous pressure to succeed.

5. A woman who accuses him of considering everything more important than the relationship.

THESE BRING OUT MEN'S BEST BEHAVIOR AND TRIGGER LOVING BEHAVIOR

1. A woman with interests of her own who stimulates and challenges him, making it "dangerous" for him to withdraw because she won't put up with being kept at arm's length.

2. A secure, self-confident woman who doesn't pressure him to say he loves her; she doesn't need him to fulfill her.

3. A competent, independent woman who lets him know that she can take care of herself; she loves him for who he is, not for what he can do for her.

4. A woman who understands what makes him tick; she can accept his sometimes puzzling ways instead of jumping to the conclusion that he's unloving or unfeeling.

5. An always-growing relationship that requires him to work at it instead of taking it for granted.

Q **Why do men fawn all over shallow, manipula-tive women and take the nice ones for granted?**

A Of all the male blind spots concerning women, the way he totally loses his senses when he meets an insincere and manipulative woman has got to be the worst.

"It's a snap to get a man to do what you want," says Sue Ellen, a blonde Texas beauty.

"Most men will do anything for a woman who makes him feel he's something special. In fact, successful men are so easy to wrap around your little finger that I don't know why some women have such a hard time. Maybe it's because those women take men too seriously. Just remember that they're mechanical, love-starved, defensive little boys and you can get almost any man."

Ironically, it is men's fear of closeness and their need to control that gets them into these relationships in the first place. They want the FEELING of love minus the demand of really being intimate. This is exactly what he gets from the woman who's not interested in a real relationship but just wants money or sex.

The manipulative woman knows just how to stroke the male ego, which is actually pretty shaky. The more of a typical, emotionally detached man he is, the easier he is to manipulate.

When a married man "escapes" from a traditional, boring marriage into the arms of such a woman, he feels as if he's getting an exciting, fresh start. Actually, just the opposite is happening. Soon he feels depressed and empty because the excitement - in fact, the whole "centerfold fantasy" - is unreal, leading to bitterness and anger.

As illogical and painful as it is to get involved with these women, many men do so again and again, especially men who are egotistic, immature, oversexed, self-centered, aggressive and desperate. If a man is lucky, the manipulative bimbo will hurt him so much that he will take a good look at himself and finally learn to love for real.

Q   **When we're together, I feel that he wants to be left alone. When I go away, he's mad. What's going on here and what should I do about it?**

A   Men give mixed messages because they were taught as kids that they should be totally independent, even though they have strong needs for their mate.

A woman trying to be close may make her man feel presured and smothered, so he pushes her away, pretending that he doesn't need her. Then when she leaves him alone -just like he told her to - he feels abandoned and pulls her back.

This crazy push-pull effect shows how much he needs you and how much he needs to pretend he DOESN'T need you!

I have told many women whose husbands act as if they don't care that the "cure" is to stop pursuing him - to even pull away for a while. The moment he senses that she may not be interested, she becomes much more appealing. While I'm not suggesting this as a permanent solution, I've found that a woman who keeps her distance from this kind of man stands the best chance of drawing him out.

There is no simple answer to this problem. On the one hand, a woman shouldn't "love too much," desperately pushing herself upon a man. On the other hand, I certainly don't recommend that she make herself scarce when her mate doesn't want her, and be at his beck and call when he gets lonely. That will only bring out the worst in him.

A woman has got to be her own person. This might make her man angry at first. But before long, he'll find himself more and more interested.

Q   **Why does he talk to me as if I were a child?**

A   Men are taught to be defensive and in control. They
         see life as a constant struggle for power, control,
         security and independence. (This is why even wealthy,
         powerful men never seem to get enough wealth or
         power.) Being softhearted and warm, open and
         trusting, afraid - these are all qualities they've

been taught to avoid at all costs. Women, of course, are quite comfortable having these qualities.

A man tends to take control of things, which can lead to him being protective, critical or impatient. Often he ends up feeling that, by comparison, the woman is immature and naive. So that's how he treats her.

Q   **Why does he forget personal events like birthdays and anniversaries and tease me about being sentimental?**

A   I've talked about how men focus on THINGS rather than FEELINGS. Forgetting these occasions shows just how out of touch a man has become. Many women write personal notes and make calls to their husband's family because somehow he doesn't get around to it. Sometimes men DO remember those things, but usually it's because he writes it down, knowing he'll hear about it if he forgets.

Because a man gets so caught up in the pressures of the "jungle out there," he thinks of personal events as distractions from the battle. To him, taking even a few minutes to make a phone call or mail a card is like falling asleep on guard duty.

Now this apparent insensitivity is bound to upset his partner. All I can tell you is that it's the price he pays for being a man and it isn't anything personal. You say he used to remember these events? That's because he had a goal - to win and keep your love. That doesn't mean that once you've been together awhile - and he starts forgetting - that he loves you less. All it means is that he's back to concentrating on "the battle."

Q **How do men really feel about the women they are involved with?**

A There are about as many answers to this question as there are relationships. Most men need a special woman to give meaning to lives that revolve around work and are often lonely. His partner thus becomes his "personal lifeline."

It may not seem that way when the two of you are in the middle of some problem, of course. He gets defensive, which makes it seem as though he doesn't care. He is frustrated and angry because he has such a hard time talking about his feelings and desires.

It's a vicious cycle. When he gets silent out of fear that she won't understand him, she gets frustrated and furious, which in turn enrages him and makes him feel more powerless and controlled so he withdraws even more.

A man also worries that he might say or do the wrong thing and his mate will fly off the handle. Instead, he hides his feelings. You know the cliche about the "big man" afraid of his "little wife"? This is where it comes from. He is the "bad boy" who is afraid of anyone finding out his feelings and fantasies. So, he clams up.

Another common problem is when a man gets bored because he needs outside challenges and new adventures - just the opposite of the female desire for a meaningful commitment based on just being together.

He's in a double bind. The more loving the woman acts, the less he's interested - even though he desperately needs her love. Before you start thinking he doesn't love you, remember, he's just being typically male - looking to new horizons without realizing that what's at home is really important to him, too.

Q   **Why does he seem to treat me like an object instead of a person?**

A   This is a common feeling among women, but men don't even realize what they're doing. A boy is taught to think of people in terms of how useful they are to him. He doesn't MEAN to see people as objects, but this is what he thinks being a man is all about. It's a mistake to take this personally.

Even his best friends are often just objects - they come along as sort of a package deal with the golf or tennis club or business ventures. In fact, he even thinks of himself the same way, like a machine that may or may not be in working order.

This is why many men can't deal with emotional problems, which they consider the result of irrational thinking or malfunctions in the machinery. They try to solve complex personal problems with mechanical, cut-and-dried solutions that often make matters worse.

When a man deals with problems at home by lecturing or giving advice to his wife or children, they may suspect that he doesn't really know who they are as individuals - or care to, for that matter. Instead of really getting to know them, he thinks he knows exactly how they SHOULD be.

Men like this look for impersonal, "logical" answers. They think that relationships are just like cars, able to be fixed up with mechanical solutions - if only he can find the right ones.

A man actually believes he's treating a woman as a person even when she accuses him of treating her as an object. He gets angry and frustrated because, as far as he's concerned, he's treating her the same way he treats anyone else in his life . . . which, for better or for worse, is absolutely true!

Q   **Why does he hate it when I tell him I love him or spontaneously touch him?**

A   A man can feel threatened by a woman's sudden attentions - he sees it as her demand that he be affectionate in return RIGHT NOW.

One man told me, "Her embraces often catch me offguard. While part of me thinks how nice it is that she wants to show how much she loves me, more than anything else I feel irritated by how suddenly she expects me to respond to her."

A married man said, "My wife's spontaneous hugs and kisses always feel like a test. Will I return it with enthusiasm? Do I really love her? Am I happy that she kissed me?"

Q   **Why does he hate it when I cry?**

A   A woman's tears turn off a man the same way a man's emotional coldness turns off a woman. A man who clams up when a woman cries may suggest that he doesn't care about her, but that's probably not the case. More likely, he feels helpless, afraid that their problems are hopelessly complicated.

He also might view tears as controlling and manipulative, a woman's trick to win hugs and kisses - and this makes him angry.

Q   **Why is he afraid to commit?**

A   This isn't always true. A man who doesn't feel threatened is HAPPY to commit to the woman he loves. But he doesn't want to be pressured into commitment just to satisfy his partner.

The woman who longs to get married should play close attention to the "commit-ability" of any man she gets involved with. A good possibility is a man who can be her friend, a man with whom she shares many interests and goals.

Commitment grows out of true love and caring. In a healthy relationship, it's not necessary to ask for commitment - it just develops because both partners want it. But it takes time. There's no guarantee that feelings of desire and commitment will appear in two people at the same time. Expecting a man to commit when he isn't ready is as unfair as pressuring a woman into having sex against her will. For sure, you can't force a commitment if your partner isn't ready. You'll just make him resent you - and that will end up destroying your relationship.

Just remember this: Men who feel loved and unpressured are happy to commit. If a man's not ready to do so, it means he's got some things to work out for himself - or with you.

Q   **If I am as important to him as he says I am, why does he take me for granted and treat me so insensitively**

A   Men do appreciate their partners, but they have the hardest time showing it - especially if a woman is pushing to get him to do so. Often, when a woman tries to get close to her man, he heads for the emotional hills, shutting down and withdrawing.

On the other hand, if she withdraws, he may suddenly wake up and start to show affection.

A man's "harshness" and "insensitivity" are his way of protecting himself. Women have an intense need for intimacy.

Men try to fulfill this need, but many discover that they can't measure up. The needier a woman gets, the more a man closes himself off emotionally, becoming impatient and irritated.

A woman may imagine what a man in this situation feels like if she has ever been involved with someone who at first seemed independent and strong, then became insecure, possessive and demanding. She will probably recall that her love dissolved, and she found herself acting cruelly and rejecting him.

This vicious cycle gets worse and worse, with the woman feeling rejected and the man feeling guilty and both feeling angry. This is a major blind spot in many relationships. Both partners need to pay close attention to what's going on and try to adjust their behavior - a woman may have to learn to be less needy, a man less quick to shut down.

Q   Why was he so eager for sex when we first met, but now that we're committed and I really enjoy and want it, he seems not to care or even want it at all?

A   Men's and women's roles in sex have changed. Our ideas about the natural "horniness" of men and the "frigidity" of women stem from a time in the past when men and women treated each other as sex objects.

In the old days, a man might be obsessed with sex, because each time he got it might be the last time. This isn't true anymore. Today, women aren't hard-to-get sex objects but are intelligent, independent persons who actively want to be emotionally close and sexually satisfied.

For many men, that's a lot of pressure. Sex is no longer an exciting challenge but a difficult demand. He has lost control of his woman and their sex life - a big loss, because it was that sense of control that used to bring him to a fever pitch of excitement. In response, he may lose interest in sex.

I know this makes men sound pretty bad, but remember, he suffers from his behavior as much as the woman does. Sex problems are something that BOTH partners have to work on. It won't do any good to blame one partner or the other. Keep in mind that these problems are often a symptom of a deeper problem in the relationship.

Q   **Why do men have extramarital affairs and should these relationships be taken seriously?**

A   Relationships are always in a delicate balance. If there is a serious imbalance, the partner suffering the most will look for an escape hatch. An affair can destroy a relationship, but it can also restore it - if you pay attention to the underlying message.

A woman who feels controlled and ignored may look to an affair for intimacy. In the same way, a man whose wife is over-dependent and insecure may feel resentful and suffocated. He may find it irresistible to have an affair with a woman who makes no demands and who keeps her emotional distance.

To leave a man who cheats or to force him to promise to be faithful misses the point. His affair isn't the real problem. It's only the natural reaction to a bigger problem in your relationship that needs to be corrected. If it isn't, he will end up cheating again. Keep in mind that a man's cheating usually doesn't mean he wants to end the marriage. The other woman may be very attractive to him, but only as long as she doesn't demand that he be close and commit.

Some women think they can get their man back by paying more attention to him or working harder on their relationship. To the contrary, the women least likely to be cheated on are those who focus more on THEIR OWN lives than on their relationship. They have their own identity and fulfill their own needs. They don't desperately hang onto their men or make impossible demands -behaviors that drive many a man into the arms of another woman.

Some fortunate men and women have used painful affairs to transform bad relationships into wonderful ones. The woman who understands male dynamics will focus on changing the way she relates to the man she loves instead of leaving him or punishing him for an affair. But the problem belongs to both of them. The goal is for both to look beyond the affair to the problems that caused it in the first place.

Q   **Why do men become so anxious, and even panic-stricken, when they can't perform sexually?**

A   Men tend to look at their sexuality in mechanical terms, without realizing that there are emotional aspects to their sexual performance. When a man's penis isn't cooperating with him, he panics because he feels out of control.

He can't understand that the problem might have something to do with deep feelings. Instead of looking inside himself, he may seek "instant cures," but in the long run these don't work.

Men feel helpless in the face of impotence. They want to control things by willpower, and when this backfires, they feel intensely threatened. As a therapist for many men who have had sexual dysfunction, I never talk with them about THE SEX PROBLEM.

Instead, we talk about who he is and what his relationships with women are all about. If he can open himself up to this, the so-called sexual problem automatically corrects itself (except in those cases where the cause is physical).

A man's "dysfunctional" penis is trying to tell him something. If he ignores the message, he may end up in a downward spiral of anxiety, desperate solutions, self-hate and depression. If he pays attention, he gets on a path to satisfying self-awareness.

Q   **Why does he fall asleep so soon after sex, and does that mean he doesn't love his partner, or that he's selfish?**

A   A man who usually falls asleep right after sex is exhibiting the mechanical, unemotional way he has of relating to his partner. Ejaculation means he got what he needed in the way of sexual release. Afterward, in his need to avoid being close, he conveniently falls asleep.

Keep in mind that he probably isn't even aware of this behavior. He probably doesn't intend to hurt his partner, though she may end up feeling that way. However, getting mad and accusing him of being selfish and unloving will just make him angry and guilty - and probably push him farther away.

This isn't to say that this and other problems shouldn't be dealt with. If a woman's needs are not being met by her partner, they need to discuss this. If he can't talk about it one-on-one with her, they may need to see a therapist. If that doesn't help, the woman needs to realize the relationship may never work and ask herself if she really wants to stay with him.

Q   **Why doesn't he like to go on vacations even though he works so hard?**

A   Vacations have the same "feel" for a man as shopping. As far as he is concerned, a vacation is a "distraction" from the "serious" pursuits of life that constantly preoccupy him.

What's more, the problems and conflicts of his relationship are harder to disguise on vacations. At home, he manages to avoid these problems by going to work, mowing the lawn - by taking care of his daily responsibilities. On vacation, it's just him and his partner face to face.

Vacations also magnify the differences between men and women. Couples who have balanced relationships have fun on vacations. But couples who have extreme differences are in agony. "Vacations are hell" is how one man described them.

Many men, if they had their way, might NEVER go on a vacation. When they do, they feel irritable and threatened, feelings that increase the longer they're away from home. They'll look for reasons to "escape" back into their usual routine - saying there's a crisis at work that they have to get back to deal with, for example. Remarked one man, "Vacations are exhausting. It's great to get back to work - and relax."

Q   **Why doesn't he like his father?**

A   Many men don't feel close to their fathers.

"I don't call my Dad when something good happens to me," stated a young man of 29. "I call Mom. If I tell my Dad, I don't sense any real joy or excitement on his part. Sometimes, he'll even make a cynical comment like, `You're finally getting somewhere,' or he'll say, `That's great, son!' and change the subject."

How does this come to be? Little boys bear the brunt of their father's negative and defensive perceptions of the world. In preparing their sons for a world they see as a hard, dangerous place, fathers emotionally drive away their sons, who instead grow closer to their mothers. The young boy doesn't want to be like the dad he fears and hates. He sees him as cold and critical. At the same time, the boy knows he has to try to live up to his father's high standards or be punished.

Many a father sees his job as that of turning his son into a high-performance, fearless machine. Rarely does he get to know who his son really is. Who hasn't heard about the father who pressured his son to excel in sports when the boy had absolutely no interest or skill in such an undertaking? The son just ends up resenting his father.

The more pressure a father puts on his son, the more the young boy will move away from him and toward his mother emotionally. She, in turn, may try to meet some of her own needs for closeness and affection through her relationship with her son, intimacy she isn't getting from Dad, either. If she feels controlled, frustrated, hurt and angry at his father, he will share these feelings and dislike his father even more.

Ironically, the harder a man pushes his son to "be a man," the less of a real man the boy is actually going to become. In extreme cases, the boy becomes a violent macho son, desperate to prove his masculinity instead of being a "sissy" clinging to his mother. This boy becomes uncontrollable. Many violent criminals have a tattoo with a heart and arrow that says MOM. Tearfully, he apologizes for the heartache he's caused her. Mention Dad, though, and he expresses hatred and even a wish to kill him "if I ever see him again." From his macho perspective, Mom was a saint and Dad a cold bastard.

Because of his intense closeness to his mother and distance from his father, a son here learns to understand or empathize with him. As an adult, it's often impossible for him to forge the slightest emotional relationship with his father.

Q   **Why doesn't he have any close friends?**

A   This is a common problem. Even when men seem to have real camaraderie and "buddyship" with other men, it's most often only skin-deep. Men have a hard time trusting each other. Why? Because unlike women, they rarely communicate in a truly personal way. This impersonal approach makes it unpleasant or unfulfilling for men to spend a lot of time together.

Most men have "activity friends" who share interests in things like watching football games or playing golf. If the activity disappears, however, the relationship probably will, too. Their connection was external, impersonal, impermanent. So much for "male bonding."

Typically, a man's failure to have close friends started when he was a boy, when he learned to interact with other people only for a purpose. If someone wasn't useful to him, he preferred to spend his time by himself. What's more, even as a boy he was often distracted by his efforts to prove himself by accomplishing something worthwhile - from building the best model airplane to getting good grades in school.

When a boy grows up and gets married, any friends he does have tend to fall by the wayside. Sometimes, his wife doesn't make it any easier. He may want to spend time with his buddies but feels guilty when his wife tells him that he rarely spends any leisure time with her. As men get older, they become even more withdrawn from personal relationships.

Q   **Why do men seem so negative and cynical about people and life once you get to know their real feelings?**

A   Men find it nearly impossible to believe that the world is a safe place. Even the cheerful, overall "nice guy" probably harbors some pretty darn negative attitudes deep down.

A Few Aspects Of A Typical Man's Upbringing And Personality Cast A particularly Dark Shadow Over His View Of The World

* He feels terribly alone. He thinks that no one really cares about him, knows him or can be depended on if he becomes sick or vulnerable. To protect himself, he becomes a fighter - ambitious and competitive.

* He sees the world as a jungle and most people as a threat. People can't get close to him, and he doesn't dare risk getting close to them.

* He feels driven to prove his worth and importance by achieving great things, from making a million bucks to working out at the gym until he looks like Arnold Schwarzenegger. Ironically, this behavior turns off the very people he's trying to impress. It also makes him a victim to "users" who want him to do things or buy things for them. If these users are people who claim they love him, he ends up feeling very cynical about love. He knows that when he stops achieving for them, they'll reject him.

* He needs to control everything and rebels against submitting to anyone else's will. People around him can't live with him, so he ends up lonely and loveless.

* He's convinced that he's right and everybody else is wrong. This includes his being right about what a rotten world this really is. He is sure that his is the correct viewpoint, and ev-

eryone else is wrong. Again, he ends up turning off people around him.

Q   **Why is he still so insecure even though he's so successful?**

A   In the same way that many women feel that they are never quite thin or beautiful enough, many men never feel secure, powerful or rich enough - even though it makes no logical sense to someone looking at him from the outside.

A man feels driven to be "successful" in the same way he feels the need to prove his masculinity. Deep down, he's awfully insecure. He can't just BE. He has to BE SOMEONE IMPORTANT. He has to prove himself constantly. After awhile, even the most successful man can't succeed enough. What happens is that with every triumph, he raises his standards, so "failure" by his impossibly high standards becomes much more likely the next time around.

A man's insecurities about himself also make him isolated and disconnected from others. He's so busy accomplishing things that he neglects or outright mistreats the people who try to be part of his life - the same people he says he's working so hard to succeed for! The older he gets, the worse this gets, and the less real contact he has with others - so the feeling grows in him that he has to have MORE to feel secure and to protect himself - more money, more power, more whatever.

As his lonely world gets 'colder', he tries to warm it up with an intense pursuit of MORE of the things that he believes will earn him love, respect and appreciation. However, they usually bring about just just the opposite: resentments, jealousy and hostility in people he's stepping on or over as he works his way to the top.

On the other hand, he may seem to enjoy life more without any "messy relationships" to muddle things up. He probably finds that worldly success becomes easier to achieve as he becomes less attached to others, since this leaves him more time to spend working. This endless work becomes a kind of tranquilizer for him that relaxes him and makes him feel safe. But he's really very unhappy underneath it all.

It's a vicious cycle: The man driven to succeed to prove himself to others just ends up pushing them away.

Q   **Why is he so moody: first high and happy and then suddenly in a bad mood, and for no apparent reason?**

A   The extreme ups and downs of some men's moods may make them seem like they're suffering from a form of mental illness. Actually, their moodiness is the result of their tendency to look outside of themselves to figure out how they're supposed to feel about themselves.

A typical man depends on events in the world to tell him whether he should feel good or bad. His favorite football team won today's game? He feels ecstatic. His boss wasn't pleased with a report he did? He feels miserable. His mood depends on what's happening around him and what he thinks other people are thinking about him. He doesn't have a handle on liking himself regardless of what's happening out there.

This man has an insecure "self" that readily "bounces off the walls." One moment he feels "I'm the greatest!" and the next, "I'm nobody." These shifts can occur quickly for seemingly insignificant reasons. An extreme example is the intensely competitive tennis player, euphoric after making a good shot, then soon after filled with disgust, rage and self-condemnation after he makes a few poor shots.

Then there's the man who experiences sexual impotence after years of a very satisfying sex life. His self-esteem hits the pits. "I'm not the man I was," he whines. He can be so despairing and self-loathing that one might think that never once did he have successful sex.

As a man gets older, his battles become more difficult because his capacities are diminishing. Adding to his troubles, he may readily give up endeavors, interests and pursuits he doesn't perform "perfectly." His ego is just too fragile.

Q   **If men want to be close to their families, why don't they make that a priority?**

A   Believe it or not, most men are convinced that they
      ARE making their families their priority. They simply
      don't realize that their behavior toward their families
      isn't earning them any points with the ones they love.

Remember: Men have learned that living means doing, earning, protecting, advising, making decisions and so forth - not being emotionally intimate.

When a man performs these functions, he expects to be loved and appreciated in return. However, in the process of doing all these things for his family, he ends up disconnecting himself. The wife and children he is working evenings and weekends for become strangers who resent him for not being with them. Even when he is with them, he may end up giving unwanted advice or being critical - when he thinks he's being helpful - or being distracted or cut off, because he doesn't have an intimate emotional connection with his family.

Q   **Why does he dislike shopping?**

A   Just as men and women love differently, they shop
     differently. Women shop for recreation and pleasure,
     whereas most men shop with a definite goal or
     purpose in mind. Men think about women and their
     shopping the same way women think about men and
     their work: "Oh, no! Not again!! What for?"

It all starts with the fact that men tend to deny their personal
needs. Although he may have no problem buying things for
someone else, a man often has a great difficulty buying something for himself unless it's absolutely necessary. He'd rather
wear the same pair of shoes until they fall apart, unless his
work demands otherwise.

<u>Chapter Seven</u>

Opposing Views

Timothy, a 39 yearold teacher, suffered from damaging patterns that destroyed his first two marriages - both of which began on high romantic notes and ended with bitterness and accusation.

Determined not to keep repeating these patterns, he began psychotherapy to understand what he was doing wrong. He wanted to learn how he could relate to a woman as a person rather than as a prize. Tim had always been drawn to "flashy, sexy, head-turning women."

Soon after he started counseling, he dated a woman and remained in the relationship even though, for the first time in his life, there was no initial romantic rush.

"She was easy to be with, someone who seemed to know how to be a friend and a good playmate," Tim said. "We laughed a lot on dates. When we spent weekends together, I didn't get bored; and I didn't feel I had to entertain her or do the usual - going to restaurants and movies. We didn't have to busy ourselves with entertainment to enjoy each other, so I knew that this might be special and new for me."

Nevertheless, Tim had to struggle to prevent the relationship from taking the usual destructive turn. One of his biggest challenges was letting go of his need to control -while a big challenge for her was to take responsibility.

"I had become much less interested in being in control and, in fact, had gotten to the point where I enjoyed being the passive receiver at least as much as being the initiator. Even though Allison was a strong person, I could feel the tension when I waited for her to make the decisions and let her lead the way. Other times she would take full responsibility and make the decisions, but I could feel myself resisting and pretending I was pleased even though I really felt pushed and irritated."

Sometimes, Tim admitted, change was so difficult that he longed for the "good old days." "I'd have to remind myself how boring and destructive they, were. I can understand why the old way is hard to give up, though. It's the line of least resistance, and it's nice to believe you might make it work "this time," just to get out of doing the hard work of dealing with the tensions and conflicts as they come up."

Opposites Attract

Whatever one sex struggles with, the other sex struggles with its opposite - and despite the old saying, opposites like this DON'T attract.

Both men and women trigger each other in a kind of dance of differences. This is painful to both, and both are responsible for the problems that erupt. Even though one partner might seem like the "good guy" and the other the "spoiler" or the "destructive one," both are partners in the same destructive dance.

Men and women experience many things quite differently. These differences contribute to confusion and conflict:

WOMEN experience a sense of powerlessness and feelings of being exploited and patronized in the competitive workplace, while they're generally comfortable in personal relationships.

MEN experience feelings of powerlessness, vulnerability and insecurity in their personal lives. It is not unusual to find adult men who have managed to alienate every single person who has ever been close to them, including their children. Men tend to misread and mismanage the personal relationships they depend on most. They seem unable to fully trust and share their feelings with anyone.

WOMEN are frustrated and turned off by men's fear of closeness and lack of warmth.

MEN are frustrated by and react negatively to women's apparently endless need for reassurance and warmth. They consider this behavior irrational and feel it's impossible to ever convince women that their love is for real.

WOMEN fear men's anger and violence.

MEN are turned off by women's tears, their resistance to discussing or negotiating problems, and their accusations that he is the cause of all their problems.

WOMEN are repelled by men's obsession with sex.

MEN feel manipulated by women's use of their sexuality as a form of control, rewarding men for being involved with or loving them.

WOMEN feel oppressed by men's defensive egos and need to control.

MEN despair over women's resistance to making decisions, clearly stating what they want, and reluctance to taking control. Men end up feeling responsible for women's well-being and happiness, and they resent this.

WOMEN feel rejected and alienated by men's preoccupation with work and the ways they withdraw from intimacy.

MEN are exasperated by women's unrealistic attitude toward money, their obsession with diets and shopping, and their relentless preoccupation with the relationship.

As you can see, every complaint of one sex is met with a counter complaint by the other. This is why men and women are engaged in a constant struggle to accept and respond positively to their differences.

As we've seen, when a man and a woman first meet, they often respond positively to the feminine or masculine qualities of the other - the man loves taking charge of their dates, the woman loves his "manly" emotional cool - but eventually they come to despise these very same qualities. Each accuses the other of deliberately undermining the relationship or refusing to change to make things better.

Only a cynic would believe that men and women enter relationships wanting to be abusive or hurtful. It's simply not the case. Yet that's often how each one ends up seeing the other. Two people who start out thrilled with each other, end up calling each other "uncaring" or even "crazy." The fact that so many relationships end in tears, anger and hurt tells us that something is seriously out of control.

Who Hurts Whom?

MEN hurt women with coldness and disconnection.
WOMEN hurt men with their "hot" emotionalizing and constant need for intimacy.

MEN hurt women with their need for control and their inability to be "wrong."
WOMEN hurt men by falsely going along with what he wants. Thus, she loses her identity and makes him feel responsible for everything.

MEN hurt women with their negativity, cynicism and distrust of people and emotions.
WOMEN hurt men with their relentless "niceness," "positive thinking" and naive optimism about people and problems. This makes him feel more insecure and responsible.

MEN hurt women with their aggressiveness and eruptions of anger.
WOMEN hurt men with their fears, tears, helplessness, anxiety and powerlessness.

MEN hurt women by looking at them as sex objects.
WOMEN hurt men by using sex for reward and control.

MEN hurt women with their resistance to making a commitment.
WOMEN hurt men by pressuring for intense involvement and commitment too early in the relationship, especially when they threaten to leave men if they don't get what they want.

MEN hurt women with their apparently insatiable greed for money and power..
WOMEN hurt men with their lack of planning and preparing for the future and their Pollyanna-ish belief that "everything

will work out for the best," which men see as making them responsible for everything.

MEN hurt women by harshly criticizing their competence.
WOMEN hurt men by viewing them as far stronger and more capable of dealing with life than they actually are, but later resenting them for not turning out that way.

MEN hurt women with their silences, lack of emotion and withdrawal when there is a problem.
WOMEN hurt men by constantly pressuring them for openness, closeness and involvement when they are least able to open up.

MEN hurt women with their analytic, logical and mechanical approach to personal problems.
WOMEN hurt men by making "irrational" assertions and wild accusations, and by making demands that seem unreasonable.

Men and women alike are victims of an unconscious destructive cycle. Unfortunately, few people are able to admit their part in contributing to a relationship's problems. Instead, they go from partner to partner, thinking that sooner or later things will get better.

But a person must become aware of the part he or she plays in creating their pain. Only then can they begin to personally change and improve their relationships.

Chapter Eight

How A Woman Can
Change Her Man

The best way for a woman to successfully change a relationship is to see it through the eyes of her man. Instead of focusing on her deep desire for intimacy and commitment, she needs to look at her man realistically and 'see what he's all about in their relationship

Sometimes a woman may discover that she really doesn't want to be involved with the guy after all. "Maybe I don't love him like I think I do," as one woman put it. "Maybe I should have some serious reservations about the degree of my involvement." On the other hand, she may realize that there's something worth working on here.

Listen to a man and try to get a true understanding of how he sees the relationship. The very act of listening can improve the relationship, because the man enjoys the sense that his partner is actually relating to him as a person, not just as an object to satisfy her own needs.

It is my belief that when a man "tunes out" or seems preoccupied when his partner is speaking to him, it is partly because he doesn't relate to what she's saying. Her words sound like a foreign language or a fairy tale she seems to have invented. He might not be consciously aware of this, but somehow he just can't concentrate on this mumbo jumbo.

THREE SECRETS BEHIND TRYING TO CHANGE HIM

(1) You can't "love" a man into changing. In fact, heaping a ton of attention and affection on him is more likely to drive him out the door. A woman who overdoes "love" makes a man see her as extremely needy. It also makes him feel guilty about his inability to give her what she wants. He may see her as being selfish and manipulative, giving only because she wants something in return. He turns off and pulls away.

The notion that most men are wounded little boys at heart who need to be loved in order to be "healed" may be partly true. But even wounded animals become distrusting and skittish when someone comes toward them too close and too fast.

(2) Changing a man has more to do with how a woman feels about herself than what she does in the relationship. "I trust a woman who likes herself and has a satisfying life she is committed to," is how one man expressed it.

When a woman has a healthy degree of self-esteem and enjoys her life with or without a man, a man she is involved with is more likely to feel interested in changing and improving their relationship. He doesn't feel pressured but really wants to be with her. He feels he can trust her to go through the difficulties that change involves and knows his efforts will be worth it.

(3) Identifying and changing the things you do to trigger negative responses in your partner are the most effective ways of changing him.

For example:
The woman who wants closeness with a man should think about what she does to push him away instead of thinking about "his problem" with intimacy.

The woman who feels controlled by a man should focus not on his controlling behavior but on what she's doing to give away her power.

The woman who feels a man is treating her like a child needs to think about the ways she is acting helpless.

The woman who "loves too much" needs to stop thinking about "his selfish ways" and start thinking about her intense dependence on him.

The woman whose partner becomes silent and withdrawn needs to learn what she does to trigger this silence rather than trying to coax him into opening up.

Bringing Out His Best

Women have a great ability to bring out the best or the worst in a man's behavior. Most men can become either Prince Charming or Mr. Rat, depending on how a woman approaches them. When a woman always comes to him with hurt feelings and frustration, he gets defensive and his worst traits emerge. When a woman is strong, independent and doesn't judge him - when she is the "best person" that SHE really is - he becomes the best that HE is.

Ironically, most women don't act their "best self" until after they end a relationship. A 35-year-old highly successful business-woman was married to a man who had become completely cold and detached. That was partly in reaction to the fact that when they were together she was fearful, cried easily, and was unable to express her needs clearly. Almost immediately after they divorced, however, she became the confident, assertive and humorous person her friends knew her to be. When she became involved with another man she vowed to keep being her best, and their relationship was a radical improvement over her marriage.

Five Ways To Make Sure He <u>Doesn't</u> Change

1. MAKE HIM FEEL GUILTY: Statements guaranteed to turn him off include, "You're so nice to everyone else, but all I get is your negativity and bad moods," "Every time you treat me this way, I can't do my work because I'm so upset," or "Everything is a priority in your life except me."

Guilt may sometimes induce a man to change temporarily or on the surface, but deep down he is angry and will resist real change.

2. PLAY THE BLAME GAME: Accuse him of being selfish and insensitive and only interested in taking care of himself. Or tell him, "You don't know what love is. All you know is how to take," or "I have to pay the price because you can't stand your mother."

Men have serious problems in their relationships, but beating them over the head drives them farther away.

3.INTERPRET HIS BEHAVIOR NEGATIVELY: See everything he does through dark glasses. Tell him, "You're afraid of intimacy," "You hate all women," or "You're just paying me back for what your mother did to you."

These interpretations might be accurate, but attacking a man with them is akin to a man's complaining to a woman, "You hate men," "You want to be taken care of like your dad did for your mom," or "Your love and niceness are a coverup for your anger."

The person hearing these kinds of statements takes them as an attack and backs off in self-defense.

4. KEEP TALKING TO HIM ABOUT THE RELATIONSHIP:

Many men feel about relationship talk the way many women feel about sports or business talk - a little goes a long way. Talking about a relationship tends to become repetitive, boring and irritating to a man, just as men's talk about mechanics or politics bores many women.

What's more, much of relationship talk is negative. The hidden message behind a woman's persistent talk is often something like, "Let's talk about what's wrong with you and why you're incapable of relating intimately." Some discussion is necessary in any relationship, but don't overdo it.

5. COMPARE HIM TO OTHER MEN:

Tell him, "Look at the way your friend Ted treats his wife. He has such respect and love for her. You're the only one of your friends who doesn't seem to care about involving himself with his wife and family."

Actually, he knows this kind of comparison isn't true, since everyone's situation is different, but it doesn't matter. He knows she is making comparisons as a way of expressing her disappointment and resentment. For sure, he views it as a hostile attack rather than a constructive effort to encourage closeness.

How To Tell If The Change Is For Real

Real change happens in a relationship only when both partners become aware of how they contribute to the problem and both are willing to work hard at changing themselves. Sometimes people change on the surface. After a short while, however, the old habits reappear and the problems return.

False change involves "trying" but failing to come to grips with the heart of the problem. Many women have trouble recognizing their anger and communicating it in a direct way. They prefer to be "nice" and avoid "negative" exchanges. What ends up happening is that they cry, accuse or act injured instead of directly expressing their anger. To "solve" this, her partner may end up walking on eggshells, afraid of her reactions.

Take the typical man who has trouble admitting he has personal needs and feels insecure. He ends up acting cold, withdrawn and angry instead of directly communicating his insecurity. To "solve" this, his partner acts like his mother, taking care of his needs before he realizes he has them, so he never needs to express them.

Becoming "sensitive" like this to each other helps for a while, but in the long run works only temporarily. Sometimes it makes things worse, because both partners are convinced they worked at it and now it's really hopeless.

Only when she can bluntly tell her man she's angry at him - and only when he can say he needs her love and reassurance - can deep -and lasting change begin.

Why 'How To' Techniques Backfire

Many people try to change by using "how to" techniques. They are doing something for effect, but they are actually insincere. This approach is always guaranteed to fail, like diet and exercise programs that don't address the deeper aspects underlying a person's overeating problem. The popularity of how-to answers to serious problems makes authors and publishers of instant self-help books wealthy.

Anna, for example, was a woman involved with a man she described as "cold and selfish." The members of her support group, who had similar problems of their own, told her that men abuse women who make themselves too available, and only become interested when a woman plays "hard to get."

Even though Anna was desperate for reassurance from her boyfriend, she began to pretend she didn't care. After awhile, he began to pay more attention and show greater interest and affection. But because she hadn't looked inside herself to see how dependent and needy she was, the instant he became more interested and involved, she clung to him even more than before. And sure enough, he pulled away again, this time seeing her as inconsistent, unpredictable and "crazy" because of her extreme, irrational shifts. "Nothing works with him," Anna despaired. "I give up."

The truth is, how-to strategies are essentially techniques for manipulating another person. When that person figures this out, as he always will, he will feel even more distrusting and distant.

Blaming Something 'Out There'

Men and women both make change nearly impossible when they blame their problems on an outside force instead of looking inside themselves.

Common blaming statements include, "He works too much," "She's let herself go," "He's always watching sports," "She's obsessed with soap operas and food," "He's not affection-ate," "She's insecure," and so on. The person coming up with these notions may feel reassured, telling himself that the problem is "out there" instead of inside himself. But blaming like this just makes real change and growth impossible.

Blaming One's Partner

Extremely harmful to a relationship and making change nearly impossible is the false idea that one person in the relation-ship is always better - or always worse - than the other. Women do this a lot.

It's never true that:

One partner really cares and knows how to be loving, and the other one doesn't. The truth is, both partners in a relationship are both loving and unloving in different degrees.

One person is primarily to blame for the problems in the rela-tionship, while the other is the healthy or the good one, val-iantly working to keep things going. This approach just makes one partner feel like a martyr while the other feels like the eternal bad guy.

One partner is always caring, the other always hostile. Once again, this simply isn't true. Both partners express both of these qualities in differing degrees. Clinging to ideas like these turn a relationship .into a fingerpointing nightmare. Each person sets out to make the other feel responsible for all the pain and problems of the relationship, while they see them-selves as patient and loving. Instead of looking at themselves, they lay blame until the bad feelings completely destroy their relationship.

Women As Martyrs

From my experience as a psychotherapist, the single greatest obstacle to change and genuine intimacy is this: Many women truly believe that they are the injured, loving partner in a relationship with a hopelessly selfish, unloving man.

If you feel this way, it may have a lot to do with the way you traditionally relate to men, including:

"Romantic relating," in which women merely REACT to men. In the very beginning, you probably wait for the man to invite you on a date and to take responsibility for where you'll go and what you'll do. Later, though, when the man takes responsibility for other aspects of your relationship, you end up feeling controlled, powerless and taken for granted.

A tendency to accommodate and adapt to a man's preferences, schedule, lifestyle and social interests. This is a woman's traditional role, the role of the giver. If you play it, though, eventually you'll feel used, taken for granted, or treated as a nobody.

Placing too big an emphasis on the relationship. Sure it's important, but a woman needs outside interests and friends. Otherwise, she becomes overly sensitive to the smallest upsets in her relationship. Meanwhile, men aren't usually as focused on relationships as women. So women end up feeling resentful that they are giving much more than they're getting, while seeing their man as selfish and disinterested.

A tendency to seek a closeness that your partner is incapable of giving. When you do this, feeling insecure, you may push for continual reassurance that he cares. He feels smothered and drained by the pressure to prove his love and responds with irritation, which you take as rejection. After

80

awhile, he may actually start believing that he is inferior and insensitive. He takes on the role of the "bad guy" and any hope for the relationship goes out the door.

A man can't change in the relationship by himself, no matter how much he tries. In order for him to change, his partner needs to become aware of the effect she has on him and make efforts to change herself as well. Then, the relationship can actually be repaired and improved fairly easily.

My general rules for predicting the likelihood of positive change are:

When one partner sees himself or herself as blameless, change is impossible.

When one partner sees the other as the cause of most of the problems, change is slowed.

When both partners focus on their own part in the problems, love can bloom once again.

What Doesn't Work

These Behaviors Are Sure Fire Turn-Offs.

Being extremely emotional. This has the same negative effect on a man that his cold, analytical- and detached attitude triggers in a woman.

Blaming him for all the problems in the relationship. This makes him feel misunderstood, bad about himself, and hopeless. It can also spark him to leave.

Pressuring for closeness and asking to be held in the midst of an angry confrontation. At the very time when he feels least capable of showing affection, this makes him feel even more resistant.

Being critical of his "doing" approach to the relationship. Doing things is a man's approach to a relationship. Saying "that's not real love" is rejecting him and will drive him away.

Accusing him of disliking or fearing women and closeness. He will feel falsely accused because he believes he loves his partner and is fond of women.

Suspecting him of not really wanting to change because his efforts seem forced. Men think and plan before they act, so they may seem mechanical.

Telling him that he hurts you because he just doesn't care. That will make him stop trying.

What Does Work

These behaviors will bring him closer:

Asking him to tell you what he feels and thinks about the relationship and listening without getting defensive. This will make him more willing to try to improve it.

Asking him to tell you exactly what you do that upsets him, discussing them, and working to make changes. This will reassure him that his feelings count.

Waiting for him to reach out without pressuring him for closeness. This is the quickest way to bring him out of himself.

Maintain your own identity and interests.

Signs Of A Poisoned Relationship

Sometimes, the problems have gone so far it may be hopeless.

Signs of this include:

Violence or the constant threat of a violent eruption at any moment.

Angry outbursts and coldness that lasts for days.

Extreme cases of "escape" behaviors, such as over-working, TV-watching, drinking and drugs.

An absence of affectionate, personal contact.

Spending time alone together is always boring, exhausting or painful.

Time apart is a "holiday" you look forward to.

Feeling that you are "dying" in the relationship.

In bed at night, your body tenses up and you can't stand touching your partner.

On weekend mornings, you get out of bed as early as possible to avoid contact.

When it is almost impossible to listen to your partner without becoming distracted or irritated.

Your partner's habits disgust you.

Feeling that the death of your partner by accident or illness would be the easiest solution.

Chapter Nine

Getting Intimate

Whether you're trying to change a relationship or just beginning one, becoming aware of the following gives the basis for genuine intimacy:

♥ **A traditional woman's intense intimacy needs cannot be fulfilled by any man.** Just as no woman can satisfy an insecure man's need to "feel like a man," a woman's intense needs for affection, reassurance and closeness will be unsatisfied by any man. Some men may try, but in the end they will always fail, because her needs stem from insecurity that he can't erase.

A man faced with an emotionally demanding woman will back off, even if he wishes he could get close. At the same time, he feels angry, because most likely the woman is on his case for not being what she wants him to be.

It's very important to realize that men don't intentionally frustrate women or withhold affection. Quite simply, many women want a lot more than most men can give- and they end up driving men away in the process.

A woman needs to recognize and accept the degree of emotional intimacy that her man can offer. At the same time, she has to take a close look at her insecurities and figure out what she can do to overcome them in healthy ways.

♥**Men do not hurt women intentionally. Like women, men do their best to make their relationship work.** They need love and fulfillment just like women. Problems arise when those negative behaviors that both sexes exhibit become exaggerated. Two people who started out as romantic, affectionate and sensitive end up seeming selfish and abusive because of misunderstandings that build upon each other. Men don't cause all the problems. Some women love to pin all the blame on their man - but that's anything but the thing to do if you're aiming for emotional intimacy.

Women need to realize that men do not enter love relationships planning to be hurtful. Abusive behavior is the symptom of a sick relationship, not of a selfish, destructive man.

♥**A man can't make a woman feel good about herself in a relationship**. A woman with low self-esteem hopes that her partner will help her like herself more, but it never works that way. This woman will eventually view her partner as being critical, unsupportive and unappreciative. Stemming from deep self-doubt, these feelings make a man feel pressured to give something that he can't. The only way a woman with low self-esteem can feel better about herself is by working on it as the personal problem that it is.

♥ **Men show love the way they have been taught to**. What they don't show, they can't show or never learned. For many men, "doing for" a woman rather than showing emotion and being close is how they express love. This way of expressing love is as crucial to the existence and survival of the relationship as is a woman's focus on emotional closeness. Being responsible and taking action feels like love to them. They get angry and frustrated when women complain they're not emotionally close enough. A man's love is expressed differently, but it is just as meaningful, real and intense.

♥ **Men are raised to perform and achieve in the world, making them seem unemotional and insensitive**. A "real man" pursues goals, is logical, cool and calm or aggressive when he needs to be, untouchable and invincible. It's tough on a man to be a "real man."

Women must realize that insensitive men were blocked in their emotional growth as boys. With work, they can develop emotionally as grown men, but only with women who don't put them down for their emotional shortcomings.

♥ **In times of arguments and conflicts, men tend to become defensive and detached**. This is their form of self-protection. The greater the stress, the more distant, uncaring, and cold a man may seem.

Trying to pressure him to get closer and to open up during these stressful moments will only upset him and drive him farther away. It makes intimacy even more difficult and can even make the relationship seem hopeless.

Women need to recognize men's tendency to back off during stress. They also need to be aware that as the stress lessens, men "bounce back." When they feel unpressured and safe, they can allow themselves to be warm and responsive again.

A man experiences his relationship differently from his partner and appreciates a woman who understands and accepts this. The woman who criticizes her man because he thinks or feels in ways that she doesn't isn't very loving. To love a man truly means creating an atmosphere where he feels safe to say what he really feels and thinks about the relationship - even though it may be much different from the woman's point of view.

♥ **A woman who focuses on her relationship at the expense of her own identity hurts herself and her relationship**. It makes her see herself as more giving and loving than the man, while she thinks he is being terribly self-centered and unappreciative of her.

Men are at their loving best when they feel stimulated and challenged by a woman who doesn't "sacrifice" herself to the relationship. Although a man may try to control his partner by demanding, for instance, that she be at his beck and call -he responds badly if he actually succeeds.

Women must realize that being over-intense is self-destructive. Men lose interest in women who lose their identities in a relationship. Men remain connected to the woman who maintains a strong, separate identity.

♥ **Men want and need love as much as women do.** Although men may not be able to put it into words, their need for a relationship with a woman is very strong, particularly because men are often emotionally isolated, without close friends. Once a man becomes involved in a good relationship, he commits himself quite firmly and becomes extremely dependent on it.

♥ **Real love between a man and woman builds slowly while both partners deal with the conflicts**. Real love is not "being nice" or always "getting along" without anger or an occasional fight. Being afraid of conflict, in fact, creates an obstacle to genuine closeness.

♥ **Differences exist in all relationships.** Women must let go of romantic notions that there should never be a problem. Problems will always arise. Relationships grow closer when men and women work together to solve them.

Getting Close: Men's Predictable Behaviors

There are behaviors and feelings all men seem to go through in a relationship:

CONFLICT: If you have an honest relationship, conflict will appear early on - and it will be intense. But it will decrease as you work together to solve problems, and you will understand each other better and feel closer.

In a highly romantic relationship, on the other hand, there will be little if any conflict in the beginning. Everything will seem magical and loving. This won't last forever, though. Suddenly things will seem to fall apart. A "real" relationship is beginning to form. At this point, the partners may break up or they will begin to work at it, creating a truly loving relationship.

FEAR OF INTIMACY. If a man is being real with you and not trying to play it smooth, he will have difficulty with and anxiety about emotional intimacy and openness at the beginning of your relationship. However, once he feels safe enough, not manipulated or used as an object to satisfy a woman's needs, he will give himself over to the relationship in a very involved and committed way.

If, on the other hand, he is a "magical man" arriving on the energy of a romantic fantasy, wonderful intimacy will seem to exist from the start. However, the magical closeness will disappear until the relationship finally evaporates.

RESISTANCE TO INTIMACY. When a relationship first hits troubled waters (as it always will), most men will fear making their feelings known, not wanting to be blamed for the trouble.

A woman who pressures a man to be open and intimate while he's struggling through this situation will make him feel threatened, causing him to withdraw even more. Men open up when they feel it's truly safe to do so.   A woman's best tool is patience.

NEGATIVITY. A map's negative, cynical or self-protective attitudes are the result of his seeing the world as a hard, dangerous place that he has to work hard to succeed in. A woman who tries to pressure him into seeing the world more positively just turns him off, because she doesn't try to understand why he feels the way he does.

As a relationship grows, his negative views will probably decrease because he doesn't feel so alone anymore. He may become less worried about work and money and pay more attention to the relationship.

RESENTMENT OF RESPONSIBILITY. A woman who makes her relationship and her partner responsible for her happiness creates an unhappy, resentful partner. He may withdraw and become silent. The only way around this is for a woman to take full responsibility for her own happiness.

NEGOTIATING. To negotiate a conflict with a man, give him specifics and stay on the subject while you're talking. Otherwise, most men give up in exasperation because of their need for things to be logical and "make sense."

THINGS THAT WOMEN DO THAT BRING OUT THE WORST IN A MAN

You're asking for trouble if you engage in any of the following:

♦ Refusing to make decisions or take action, then getting angry over feeling controlled when the man takes responsibility.

♦ Accusing a man, once he is committed to the relationship, of being hurtful and uncaring.

♦ Talking about the relationship when he is clearly thinking about something else, then accusing him of not caring.

♦ Asking him to be open and honest, then responding with tears and anger when he exposes true feelings.

♦ Asking a man to spend more time with you but not having any ideas on how to spend that time.

♦ Being attracted to a man for the work that he does, and then resenting him for the time and energy he spends working instead of being with you.

Do You Really Want A successful Man?

Many women should think seriously about this: Do you really want a relationship with a financially "successful" man? Many women believe that they do, then think twice when they discover what life with him is really like.

It is self-defeating for a woman to be attracted to a man because of his ambition, only to feel rejected and resentful later when she realizes that his main focus is on his job. The ambitious, driven man has great difficulty pursuing both a relationship and his goals. Many successful men try and fail.

Women attracted to successful men need to know that the habits of these men probably won't change. In fact, they will probably intensify. He may never be satisfied with how much money or power he has. What's more, aspects of such a man's personality make him very hard to get close to, from his egotistic style to his tendency to manipulate people and situations to get his way.

Many women believe that such a man could change if he "really wanted to" or "really cared." This simply isn't so and pressure to change just makes him feel angry and hurt.

Getting A Commitment

Expect the following from a man in the process of committing and becoming close:

♦ Being protective, taking responsibility and "doing" for his partner.

♦ Confusion between love and feeling responsible. At the same time that he feels love, he also feels pressured to be responsible for the relationship.

♦ Intense attachment and possessiveness.

Once your man is committed to a relationship, you have great potential power - both positive and negative.

You must be sensitive to your man's experience in a relationship. In this way you can use your power to cultivate a long-lasting, stable relationship that makes you both happy.

OTHER BOOKS BY
HERB GOLDBERG, Ph.D.

The following books can be ordered directly over the internet by going to our website: Selfhelpbooks.com.

The Hazards of Being Male: Surviving the Myth of Masculine Privilege
Author: Goldberg, Herb
Category: General - Men
 ISBN: 1587410133
List Price: $17.95   211 pages

Herb Goldberg's best seller *The Hazards of Being Male* is one of the best books written explaining the changing relationship between the sexes. It ranks as important to men as Betty Friedan's *The Feminine Mystique* was to women.

The Inner Male: Overcoming Roadblocks to Intimacy
Author: Goldberg, Herb
Category: Interpersonal Relations
ISBN: 1587410125
List Price: $22.95 316 pages

Herb Goldberg's many self-help books have made him literally an icon in popular psychology, interpreting the male experience in the wake of the confrontation with the Women's Movement. What Betty Friedan's *The Feminine Mystique* was for women, his *The Hazards of Being Male* was for men. In *The Inner Male*, Dr. Goldberg reevaluates today's couples offering compassion and enlightened insight to their problems. He helps with decoding couple's mixed messages to each other, and to newly-sensitive men (perhaps vulnerable for the first time in their "macho" lives) he offers healing without scarring.

The New Male: From Self-Destruction to Self-Care
Author: Goldberg, Herb
Category: Interpersonal Relations
ISBN: 1587410060
List Price: $22.95   328 pages

Herb Goldberg's best seller *The Hazards of Being Male* is one of the best books written explaining the changing relationship between the sexes. It ranks as important to men as Betty Friedan's *The Feminine Mystique* was to women. His next book, *The New Male* became a virtual bible to a whole generation of men coming to terms with the women's liberation movement. If you think men are "the stronger sex" or that they enjoy privileged status in American society, you are wrong, says Dr. Goldberg. In this groundbreaking and extraordinary book, *The New Male*, he examines the crises created by traditional notions of masculinity and reveals that men today are in a real Catch-22 position: programmed to be tough and independent, yet they're now supposed to help out at home and to be sensitive partners to their changing women. Dr. Goldberg probes the inner workings of these impossible binds and tells men that it's all right to spend the day in bed if they're sick, to say "no" to sex, to hug a good friend, or to ask for help. *The New Male* provides a clear and useful vision of the changes all men must go through toward becoming genuine persons, freed from destructive stereotypes.

The New Male-Female Relationship
Author: Goldberg, Herb
Category: Interpersonal Relations
ISBN: 1587410982
List Price: $20.95   276 pages

  T*he New Male-Female Relationship* is a continuation of his original and proactive theory that provides startling insights into the conflicts between the sexes. In this ground-breaking work, Goldberg shows how traditional relationships are doomed to fail - not because of personal inadequacies, but because of the psychological defense mechanisms that pro-gram men to behave like machines and women like children. Goldberg offers a total reevaluation of the war between the sexes in light of the enormous changes the women's libera-tion movement has brought about in the last several decades. Immensely hopeful in its outlook, the book gives us a vision of just how good a relationship can be when men and women are friends and companions as well as lovers.

Help Is But A Click Away -

A MESSAGE FROM THE PUBLISHER

In my troubled youth, I discovered the hope and knowledge available in self-help books. I subsequently became a psychologist and went on to write five self-help books. I was so impressed by the power of self-help books that when the Internet became so prevalent in our lives, I realized it was the ideal place for people to find help. *SelfHelpBooks.com* emerged and is readily available to anyone who is in need of help.

SelfHelpBooks.com publishes books by mental health professionals as well as by lay people who have coped with life's adversity and have valuable advice to pass on to the rest of us. The titles that can be found in *SelfHelpBooks.com*'s virtual bookstore have been carefully selected to provide help for a range of problems from addiction to depression, from fear to loneliness, and from problems of youth to problems of the elderly.

At *SelfHelpBooks.com* we think we have a book for almost every problem. If you need help immediately, you can download it as an E book. If you are in less of a hurry, you can order a print version and receive it within days.

If you visit SelfHelpBooks.com and don't find a book relating to your particular problem, contact us and we will immediately add books in that category. If you know of a particular self-help book that has helped you, let us know and we will add it to our list as well.

Harold H. Dawley, Jr., Ph.D., ABPP
Publisher

**Quality Self-Help Books From Wellness Institute, Inc.
Order NOW and Save 25%**

You can receive any of the following books within three days by simply calling the Wellness Institute, Inc. at 866-77BOOKS (26657) and stating the title of the book(s) you wish to order.

Akutagawa, Donald
  Mind Your Own Business: My Turf,
  Your Space, Our Place   0961720298   17.95
Allender, Julie A.
  Chronic Illness: Healing the
  Wounded Heart   1587410516   12.95
Allison, Maggie
  Getting Your Emotional ACT Together:
  It's Simple But It Ain't Easy   587410028   12.95
Alpern, Gerald D.
  Divorce Rights of Passage: A Guide
  Through the Emotional and Legal
  Realities   1587410281   20.95
Alsterberg, Eric
  Life is an Adventure: A Guide to the
  Path of Joy   1587410249   14.95
B. Paul
  On Sober Reflection   1587410842   14.95
Bach, George
  A Time For Caring   1587410656   22.95
Bach, George
  Creative Aggression: The Art of
  Assertive Living   1587410559   22.95
Bach, George
  The Inner Enemy: How to Fight
  Fair with Yourself   1587410575   25.95
Barbach, Lonnie
  Shared Intimacies: Women's Sexual
  Experiences   1587410087   23.95
Barbach, Lonnie
  The Intimate Male: Candid
  Discussions about Women, Sex, and
  Relationships   1587410397   23.95

Beaudry, Michelle
    The Slam Club   1587410818   14.94
Bilich, Marion
    Weight Loss from the Inside Out:
    Help for the Compulsive Eater   0961720239   17.95
Binder, Aaron M.
    Pumping Iron After 50:The Golden
    Thread to the Self   1587410788   16.95
Bishop, Russell
    Christ's Touch Changes Us:
    Embracing True Guilt and
    Breaking Free from False Guilt   1587410052   14.95
Block, Joel D.
    Friendship: How To Give It,
    How To Get It   1587410303   17.95
Block, Joel D.
    Love Recreated   1587410915   12.95
Block, Joel D.
    The Magic of Lasting Love   1587410273   20.95
Block, Joel D.
    The Other Man, the Other Woman:
    Understanding and Coping with
    Extramarital Affairs   158741015X   17.95
Block, Joel D.
    To Marry Again: A Psychologist's
    Sensitive Guide to the Problems and
    Joys of Remarriage and Stepparenting   1587410109   14.95
Bloom, Lynn Z.
    The New Assertive Woman   158741029X   17.95
Braudy, Susan
    Between Marriage and
    Divorce: A Woman's Diary   0961720220   17.95
Burgess, John H.
    Managing Stress: For a Healthier Life   1587410257   12.95
Dawley, Harold
    Freedom from Fear: A Guide to
    Conquering Your Fears and Phobias   158741046X   17.95
Dawley, Harold
    Friendship: How to Make & Keep
    Friends   0961720255   14.95
Dawley, Harold
    L'Amitie   1587410001   14.95
Dawley, Harold
    Smokefree - How to Stop Smoking in
    Nine Easy Steps   0961720204   12.95

DesRoches, Brian
    Reclaiming Your Self: The
    Codependent's Recovery Plan   1587410338   23.95
DesRoches, Brian
    Your Boss is Not Your Mother:
    Breaking Free from Emotional
    Politics to Achieve Independence
    and Success at Work   158741032X   17.95
Fontenelle, Don H.
    Are You Listening?: Attention Deficit
    Disorders, a Guide for Understanding
    and Managing Overactive, Attention
    Deficit and Impulsive Behavior   158741001X   20.95
Fontenelle, Don H.
    Changing Student Behaviors:
    A Positive Approach   1587410206   14.95
Fontenelle, Don H.
    How to be a Good Parent
    By Dealing Effectively With The
    Most Common Behavioral Problems
    of Children   1587410958   22.95
Fontenelle, Don H.
    How to Live with Your Children:
    A Guide for Parents Using a Positive
    Approach to Child Behavior   1587410451   31.95
Fontenelle, Don H.
    The Parent's Guide to Solving School
    Problems   1587410990   25.95
Foster, Virginia
    Out of Your Mind   1587410524   14.95
Foster, Virginia
    The Quest for Love & Money:
    Specific Strategies to Develop the
    Lifestyle You Want   0961720247   14.95
Gayton, Richard
    The Forgiving Place   1587410877   17.95
Giacalone, Kathleen
    The Road to Hell & Back - My
    Conquest of Panic, Fear & Drug
    Addiction   1587410699   12.95
Goldberg, Herb
    Money Madness, The Psychology of
    Saving, Spending, Loving, and Hating
    Money   1587410184   20.95

Goldberg, Herb		
The Hazards of Being Male: Surviving the Myth of Masculine Privilege	1587410133	17.95
Goldberg, Herb		
The Inner Male: Overcoming Roadblocks to Intimacy	1587410125	22.95
Goldberg, Herb		
The New Male: From Self-Destruction to Self-Care	1587410060	22.95
Goldberg, Herb		
The New Male-Female Relationship	1587410982	20.95
Harris, C.T.B.		
Our Lost Manhood-Loss And Rebuilding of Masculinity in America	1587411032	20.95
Hastings, Anne		
America's Sexual Crisis	158741080X	23.95
Hastings, Anne		
Discovering Sexuality That Will Satisfy You Both When Couples Want Differing Amounts & Kinds Of Sex	1587410222	14.95
Hastings, Anne		
From Generation to Generation: Understanding Sexual Attraction to Children	1587410214	22.95
Hastings, Anne		
Reclaiming Healthy Sexual Energy	1587410230	17.95
Hunter, Mic		
When Someone You Love Is Addicted To Sex	158741094X	12.95
Janda, Louis H.		
How to Live with an Imperfect Person	1587410079	23.95
Kelly, Reid J.		
Hypnosis	0961720263	20.95
Kidd-Madison, Nellie		
Living With John - Caring for a loved one with Alzheimer's Disease	1587410613	14.95
Komor, Christian R.		
OCD & Other Gods	1587410370	16.95
Komor, Christian R.		
OCD Meditation Book	1587410389	14.95
Komor, Christian R.		
The Power of Being: For People Who Do Too Much	1587410311	20.95

Labowitz, Fred		
Winning at Work: How to Succeed in Spite of Yourself	1587410192	17.95
Lasater, Lane		
Recovery From Compulsive Behavior	1587410826	12.95
Leite, John S.		
Successful Parenting	1587410850	14.95
Levick, Keith		
The Healthy Child Cookbook: 146 Healthy Snacks, Meals, and Desserts	1587410435	14.95
Levick, Keith		
Why Is My Child So Overweight	1587410745	12.95
Lewis, Robert T.		
A New Look at Growing Older: Reprogramming for the Years Ahead	1587410036	14.95
Lewis, Robert T.		
Taking Chances: The Psychology of Losing & How to Profit from It	1587410117	17.95
London, Bryan		
Life is One Damn Thing After Another	1587410680	14.95
Ludvigson, Gary		
Building A New Home for Your Inner Children: A Blueprint	1587410702	12.95
Mercurio, Nancy		
Escaping The Chaos Within	1587410885	14.95
Mercurio, Nancy		
Leadership With A Heart	1587410869	12.95
Mercurio, Nancy		
Mastering Individual Effectivenes	1587410907	12.95
Molineux, J. Bailey		
Loving Isn't Easy: A Complete Guide for Understanding, Improving, and Saving Your Marriage	1587410419	20.95
Nesto, Donald F.		
Agoraphobia: A Recovered Victim's Perspective	1587410427	12.95
Nicholson, Luree		
How to Fight Fair with Your Kids... and Win!	1587410710	14.95
O Connor, William J.		
Connecting: Working Together for Health and Happiness	1587410044	20.95

Olson, Harry A.
 The 8 Keys to Becoming Wildly
 Successful   1587410540 20.95
Olson, Harry A.
 The New Way To Compete: How
 to be a winner in your career and
 your life   1587410508 16.9
Orlosky, Michael
 Calming the Inner Storm: How to
 Treat Your Depression   1587410664 12.95
Remig, Anita
 Talk to Me, Mom & Dad:
 How to Talk to Your Children 1587410729 14.95
Rinaldi, Bill
 You can If You Think You Can 1587410834 14.95
Rosner, Stanley
 The Marriage Gap: A Psychologist
 Probes the Divorce Explosion and
 Comes Up with Some Surprising
 Thoughts about Why Marriages Are
 Breaking Up   1587410176 20.95
Scrignar, C B
 From Panic to Peace of Mind:
 Overcoming Panic & Agoraphobia 1587410591 22.95
Scrignar, C B
 Stress Strategies: The Treatment of
 the Anxiety Disorders   1587410605 20.95
Simon, Jerry
 Stop Headache Pain NOW 1587410796 20.95
Spellmann, Charles
 You Don't Have to Be Afraid of Your
 Children: Who's Minding the Store? 1587410621 12.95
Waldman, Larry
 Who's Raising Whom?: A Parent's
 Guide to Effective Child Discipline 1587410265 12.95
Williams, Teresa
 She Must Like It   1587410532 12.95

SO-ADT-712

The Bear Guardian

Northwoods Tales and Meditations

Peter M. Leschak

Illustrated by
Jessica Allen Johnson

North Star Press of St. Cloud, Inc.

To John and Neil and all the rest.
Like blame and beer,
adventure is better shared.

Design: Corinne Dwyer
Cover design: Rose Dwyer and Corinne Dwyer

Copyright © 1990 Peter M. Leschak

ISBN: 0-87839-061-8

All rights reserved. Printed in the United States of
America by Sentinel Printing, Inc., Sauk Rapids, Minnesota.

Published by:
North Star Press of St. Cloud, Inc.
P.O. Box 451
St. Cloud, Minnesota 56302

Contents

Introduction: A Way into the Universe

In late August 1988, I was summoned to Duluth, Minnesota by the US Government. At the National Guard Armory I was outfitted with the appropriate gear and mustered into a twenty-man Forest Service fire crew. Shortly before noon our six crews boarded a chartered 727 and flew to Jackson Hole, Wyoming. By sundown we were working a fire line just across the Snake River from the Grand Tetons. The next week found us in Yellowstone, battling the most notorious forest fires of the century.

It was heady stuff, and we spent much time in harm's way—in front of lodgepole pines a hundred feet tall that were flaring up like matchsticks, or literally exploding into awesome towers of flame. Some of us were hurt; all of us were scared.

But it wasn't always hardship and fury. One night our crew was on patrol duty, guarding a line that we'd back-burned a few hours before. We split up into four- or five-man squads and spread out through the forest. It was cold in the mountains, so we built small campfires inside the burn. We divided each hour into watches and took turns patrolling the line, so we had a lot of time to crouch around the fire, trading stories to stay alert. Most of us hadn't met before we gathered at Duluth, so our tales were revelations. The talk was fresh and sincere. A fireside promotes camaraderie, generating honesty and laughter, and by dawn we were cousins, a close-knit tribe for the duration of our tour. We'd been unexpectedly thrust together in the face of danger, with high adventure as our job description. In the modern industrial society of specialization and safe, routine production, there aren't many who enjoy such privilege.

In this book are many of the stories I offered to that fire and the soot-streaked faces within its circle. It's a fact of life that we can share our campfires with only a few. I suppose it's better that way—it keeps those people (and those fires) special. But this book is meant to be read at night, by firelight. If you have no fireside, then snuggle close to a single lamp. Imagine open sky and the murmuring of pine boughs. I'll tell you stories you may not believe, but they're all true. Imagine cold water lapping a rocky shore and how vividly you'll dream beneath the gleam of Polaris.

But keep in mind another star as well—a brilliant orange star called Arcturus—"bear guardian." It's the brightest star in the constellation of Bootes, next to Ursa Major, "The Great Bear." Arcturus shines behind the Bear, rising just after sunset in early spring, when the earthbound brethren of Ursa Major are emerging from their dens after long winter sleep. The Bear Guardian is there to watch over them.

There's a story in this book where Arcturus is taken at face value (at least for a while) as the protector of a particular black bear living near the Minnesota-Ontario border. But the reason I chose "The Bear Guardian" as the title of the book is because it suggests adventure, mystery, and the lure of the northwoods; it connotes wildness and wonder. All of that is to be found in these pages. If you share my fire you'll vicariously journey down the remote stretches of the Little Fork River, where rapids are many, portages few; you'll struggle to pack 14,000 pounds of cargo through trackless wilderness in the company of twentieth century swashbucklers; you'll face walls of flame clutching nothing more than a glorified squirt gun; you'll pass restless, enchanted nights bathed in the sheen of woodland stars; you'll learn what it's like to thrive as a predator in the realm of the bear. There is laughter and tears, terror and exaltation, science and magic. And of course there's philosophy. John Muir wrote that "The clearest way into the Universe is through a forest wilderness." Here is one route.

"Let us probe the silent places, let us seek what luck betides us;
    Let us journey to a lonely land I know.
There's a whisper on the night-wind, there's a star agleam to guide us,
    And the Wild is calling, calling . . . let us go."

ROBERT SERVICE

Smokechasers

I was armed for the fear and destruction, but I didn't expect the beauty.

We were racing north on Highway 73, closing in on a forest fire. As a Minnesota Department of Natural Resources (DNR) "smokechaser," it was my twenty-second fire in nineteen days, but the first one after sunset.

Ordinarily, the detection aircraft would've ended its daily patrol at 7:00 p.m., but two big fires were raging elsewhere in the region, and Aero-2 had been ordered to stay aloft. The spotter had discovered this fire on 73 just before 8:00 p.m., and she was now on the radio, requesting our ETA.

"We'll be there in about two minutes," said Bob. "Which side of the highway is the fire on?"

"West. We'll circle it till you get here."

"Ten-four."

In a few moments we saw it. A curling arm of smoke was rising into the yellow-banded sky. It was tinged with the glow of twilight, a luminous auburn cloud swelling out of the trees. Just below the jagged silhouettes of the spruce and balsams we saw flashes of orange. The forest was speckled with bright tongues of fire—peeking and darting through the woods. Suddenly one of the trees in the foreground burst into a dazzling fountain of sparks. They danced and twisted upward, thrust away by a column of flame.

It was terrible, pulse-quickening beauty. And over it all—a lonely star in the indigo sky of falling night—was Aero-2. The pilot had switched on his landing light, and it shone like a beacon over the storm. It was as if Venus had decided to swirl, to approach the earth and orbit the blaze as our guardian angel.

She spoke: "Is that you coming from the south?"

"Affirmative, Aero-2. We have the fire."

"Ten-four. Be careful."

Bob wheeled off the highway, bouncing down a narrow, two-track dirt road, and in a moment we were on the fireground. A Forest Service crew and a local volunteer fire department had just arrived, and we were quickly enmeshed in the confusion of initial attack. But this far into fire season it was our natural habitat. Chaos was a familiar, if not comfortable acquaintance. I felt the pleasing rush of adrenaline.

Firefighting is a form of combat, and the DNR smokechasers are the infantry in the annual war against wildfire. After the snowmelt, before spring rains turn field and forest green, northern Minnesota is a dry expanse of potential fuel. The battles usually begin around the first week in April, and blaze on into mid-May. It's common for carelessness, arson, or lightning to ignite dozens of fires per day. Regular DNR employees can't begin to handle the emergency load, so every year the state recruits hundreds of volunteers. Experience is preferred, but not necessary. By the end of fire season, many greenhorns have collected more savvy than they bargained for.

Assembling the smokechaser force is an interesting problem. Firefighters need to be hard workers who are available to put in long, odd hours for three to six weeks, or longer. They should be responsible, trainable people—physically fit, willing to take initiative, with basic mechanical skills, and a reserve of bravery. In short, they're "good" people, the kind who are usually gainfully and inextricably spliced into the economy, and unavailable for short-notice, low-paying danger. Where do you find enough people? Mostly, it's a chancy, pot-luck kind of operation, driven by word-of-mouth. It's a friends-of-friends network, energized by public awareness of the need. It's nebulous, haphazard, and seems to work.

For example, among the two dozen smokechasers I served with in the spring of 1988, there were two who'd just mustered out of the military and had no immediate plans. There was one teenager fresh out of high school. There was a guy who'd recently quit a job, and another who'd been laid off. We had one moonlighter trying to juggle smokechasing and his regular job, and one college student attempting the same with classes and exams. But the majority were freelancers—inveterate questers of temporary jobs and contracts. Some were hunters of construction work—roofing, painting, concrete. Some did tree-planting, tree-thinning, part-time logging. Others opted for seasonal maintenance work like mowing and snow removal. We had one farmer, and two guys supplemented their incomes via the National Guard. The average age was thirty-one.

As a freelance writer I fit right in. On the second day one of the freelance construction contractors asked me, "What do you do in the real world?"

"I write books and articles."

"Really, no kidding? Hey, I was on a tree-planting crew once and the guy working next to me was a metallurgist. A Metallurgist! You meet all kinds on these jobs—world's full of derelicts."

We laughed, tacitly acknowledging that as smokechasers we were anything but derelicts. In the context of the fire campaign, we were mercenaries. Many of the older hands have their own fire-resistant Nomex uniforms, and some of us have served on fire lines out West, on the big "project" fires in California, Idaho, Oregon. In the context of general life, I recognized fellow addicts—yearning for action, greedy for freedom. Like most addictions, the price of freedom is high. Usually: no security, low average income riding on a boom/bust cycle, risk, uncertainty, and stress. But no one was complaining. The crew was jovial, energetic, and primed to fight fire. Most were veterans of both the fireground and the freelance lifestyle. The only grumbling was the good-natured, recreational bitching common to any organized group of American males. (There are certainly female smokechasers working for the DNR, but none on our crews in 1988.)

A smokechaser is paid $8.80 an hour, straight time. There's no provision for overtime pay unless you surpass 106 hours in a two-week payroll period. It's a middling wage. When you're on standby at the station, doing light work (raking, washing vehicles, sweeping floors) it seems like good money. When you've got a fifty-pound pump can on your back, humping through the woods on the flank of a hot blaze, scaling ravines, slogging through swamps, and eating smoke, it seems a tad low. I prefer to think in terms of about $500 per seven-day week.

Still, some figure heroes are worth more. That's the cynical, inside joke at the DNR. For most of the year it is vilified as another fat, revenue-wasting government agency. But for the duration of fire season the DNR is a noble vanguard of dedicated warriors in alliance with Smokey Bear. The same taxpayer who offers blanket condemnations of the "bloated, ignorant DNR bureaucrats" (while enjoying hunting, fishing, wood-cutting, solitude, beauty, etc. on the public lands managed and protected by the same) will sing its praises (and telephone number) when a wall of fifteen-foot flame is surging toward his barn. Nothing's too good for the DNR then. In 1988 we even had school children donating soft drinks to Smokey's helpers.

Of course it's all part of the pleasant myth—the standard journalistic line and popular belief that fighting forest fires is nasty, brutish, deadly work that consumes bodies and minds. Certainly it's hard and dangerous, but the truth is that nobody on this planet is happier than a trained fire crew out on the line. Among the fondest wishes of smokechasers is the opportunity to battle a big fire that runs all night and pushes the pay sheets into overtime. To the cameras we appear "exhausted" or "weary" and undoubtedly "dirty"—in our minds we're joyous, content, and lusting for payday. Those who don't relish the struggle weed themselves out.

But it's a two-edged sword. When people are trained to do something, they usually want to do it. Soldiers dream of war, surgeons pounce on reasons to cut, firefighters long for "the big one." We have a built-in ambivalence about fire. It's both enemy and friend, antagonist and mentor. Smokechasers are not dismayed to hear of a fire; the satisfactions of the fireground are intense and immediate.

For example, on the first day of the season my crew and I were dispatched to a fire that Aero-2 reported was threatening structures. Our smokechaser contingent was organized into four three-man crews, each riding a pickup equipped with a pump and hose reel mounted on a one-hundred to two-hundred gallon tank, plus handtools and pump cans. The other three units were already committed, so as we sped out of the station we realized there was no back-up.

My firefighting education had progressed to the point where I was trusted with a portable radio, the symbol and tool of command. For the first time I was to be the "fire boss." It's local tradition that the boss is also the driver, but Darin had a keener knowledge of the territory, so I asked him to be the pilot while I concentrated on being nervous.

This is where the "smokechasing" comes in. The plane spots a smoke and calls in a legal description. Each truck has a plat book, and as we head in the general direction of the fire we pore over the maps to determine the best route. But a legal marked off from the air may or may not be accurate, so we scan the horizon for smoke. By the time we reach the neighborhood, any fire worthy of our attention is kicking up an obvious column, and we "chase" it, homing in like bugs to a light.

This one was easy. Aero-2 not only gave us a clean legal, but narrowed it down to a specific section of a specific road. The smoke was readily visible, and Darin turned into a private drive that led directly to the fire. Four-foot flames had just burst out of the woods and were licking the side of a garage. I leapt out of the truck, grabbed the hoseline, and sprinted for the garage. Karl started the pump, and I was spraying from the hip as I reached the seat of the fire. In a moment I'd twisted the nozzle into a semi-fog mode and knocked down a twenty-foot length of three- to four-foot flames. I doused the wall of the garage, then dropped the nozzle and grabbed my radio. Darin and Karl had donned pump cans and were hurrying into the field of tall grass and brush just beyond the house. The head of the fire was eating up the light fuels, sweeping toward a pine plantation only a few minutes away, with another homestead beyond. Three "civilians" were out there swatting at the fire with shovels.

I was about to report to base and request a helicopter, when Zero Papa Alpha, a Hughes 500, banked in from the south. He'd been working a fire a few miles away, and base had told him to take a swing over us. I tried to raise him but got no reply. Base broke in and reminded me to switch to the tactical frequency. In my excitement I'd forgotten that on the fireground we were supposed to go to a "working" frequency to avoid cluttering the main channel. But the pilot was already landing, easing into a field on the south flank of the fire, so I grabbed a pump can and joined the fray, vigorously knocking down fire.

Those who use a pump can in earnest for the first time are surprised by two things: 1) how much fire they can snuff, and 2) how strenuous it is. The can holds five gallons of water that is ejected by pumping a slide on a two-handled "trombone," hooked to the can via a short rubber hose. Essentially, it's a large, sturdy squirt gun. During an initial attack, you pump as fast as you're able while walking/trotting through forest or field in the teeth of smoke and flame. The most efficient way to utilize a can is to wade right in, spraying parallel to the fireline so all the water strikes flame. If possible, one firefighter can hurry along the line "hitting the big chunks," while a crewmate (or two) follows behind "mopping up."

I didn't have that luxury as I fought toward the pine plantation. We were spread thin, and I enlisted one of the civilians to back me up with his shovel. We hit it hard, but the fire kept springing up out of the black, protected by matted grass, and we'd have to backtrack and nail it again. The man pointed to a barn about 400 yards ahead of the fire.

"I've got horses in there," he gasped. "Should I move them?"

The question caught me off guard. In the heat of the struggle I'd forgotten I was an authority figure—complete with uniform and radio. For a moment my mind was in a lather. My first impulse was to spew unvarnished truth—say something like "damned if I know!" But when you're packing a radio such candor is forbidden. The man had posed a legitimate question, and it was my job to ponder it—for a second. With a conscious effort (but still pumping away) I focused on the problem. I noted the distance to the barn, the force of the wind, the condition of the fuels, and the fact that three smokechasers had just piled out of the helicopter and were hooking up a 100-gallon bucket.

"No," I replied, "they'll be fine. We're about to get a handle on this thing." I sounded glib and sure, or at least I tried to. In any case, he didn't run for the barn.

In a few minutes the helicopter was ready. It roared off with its dangling bucket, and the "helitac" foreman and his two firefighters were deploying along the line. They each carried a bladder bag, a rubber sack with hose and trombone that holds about as much water as a pump can, but is easier to carry in the confines of a small aircraft.

In Minnesota, helicopters are used as instruments of initial attack. There's almost always a body of water nearby, and in a matter of minutes (or even seconds) an experienced pilot can dip a bucket into a lake or pond and return to the fire with 800 pounds of water—the equivalent of twenty pump cans. It's like having a dozen extra firefighters.

Papa Alpha returned in a minute, and his first bucket-drop hit the burgeoning line of fire that was singeing the plantation. It looked like two more would quench it. Before he'd returned with a second load, the helitac crew had helped snuff the rest of the line I'd been working, and I hurried off to grab a fresh pump can and head for the north flank of the blaze.

The flames had entered a stand of hardwoods and slowed down considerably—there was less fuel and wind. The ground was also swampy, and I experienced the comic sensation of fighting a fire while wading in ankle-deep water. The flames were consuming the dry grass and brush above the waterline, creeping toward a dense stand of balsam fir. I radioed the helitac foreman and requested a drop at the earliest opportunity. Papa Alpha zoomed over two minutes later, his bucket whipping just above the treetops as he laid down a swath of water that wiped out thirty feet of flame. Two more passes and it was all over but the mop-up. Karl joined me, and we cleaned up the north flank with pump cans. Papa Alpha made a few more drops near the pines, where Darin and the helitac crew finished it off. The helicopter landed, and in five minutes the bucket was stowed, the crew was strapped in, and they lifted off for new adventures.

The fire had burned five to ten acres of mostly grass and brush, but in the forested area it had left behind a half-dozen smoldering snags—standing dead trees that were now burning inside and high up, and would have to be felled. I radioed base for a chain saw, and while we waited I chatted with the property owner. He and his son had pulled pump cans off our truck and helped battle the fire, but he was embarrassed. His son had inadvertently ignited the blaze while burning trash in a barrel, and apparently there'd been a similar mishap the year before. The man knew he'd be charged for suppression costs—that is, all smokechasers' wages, mileage on our truck, and the cost of the chopper. Fortunately for him, the operation had been relatively brief, and it looked like he'd get off with a bill of $250 or so. Though it goes for $300 an hour, the chopper probably saves people money in the long run. The bucket drops can shorten the life of a fire dramatically.

We returned to base less than two hours after we left, having saved a garage (there was an $8,000 boat inside) and most of a small pine plantation. We felt great—satisfied and a little high. But not all our battles were so quick and clean.

Several days (and fires) later, my crew was dispatched to a three- to four-acre blaze that was eating up a steep, wooded hillside. It was believed to be an incendiary fire started by thrill-seeking kids. We saw the smoke from two miles away, but being near town and on an old mining site, the area was crisscrossed with a tangle of roads and trails, many of them dead ends. Aero-2 was still over the fire, so I radioed for assistance and she guided us in, turn by turn, like a puppet on a string. ("No, wrong way. Back up and take a left.")

It was convoluted terrain, with valleys and ridges, and a brisk northwest wind was being funneled and shunted around the high points, as if driven through a maze. One moment it was blowing from the rear, pushing the fire uphill and flinging sparks and embers that ignited spot fires ahead of the advance. The next moment freak gusts tearing along the ridges had reversed, and were rubbing our noses in smoke and flame. Our main problem was water. Except for one small section near the road, the terrain made our engine useless, and the three of us were furiously jamming and cramming the trombones of our pump cans, expending them in a few minutes, then running/stumbling downhill to refill at the truck, and struggling back up. In the interim, the fire would regain momentum. After an hour of fighting, we were nearly spent, and the fire was still uncontrolled.

We needed help, but there was no way I could justify ordering a helicopter or an air tanker. There were no structures in danger, and no valuable timber was being threatened. With all the roads around to act as firebreaks, the fire would most likely be stopped before it reached any large tracts (say over 100 acres) of available fuel. It was dangerous terrain for a bulldozer, so I just radioed for another crew.

In fifteen minutes they were there, and we took a few mo-

ments to assess the situation. John, the crew boss of our reinforcements, noted that there was a dirt road completely circling
the burning hill, and suggested that we use it as a fireline and
backburn all the way around—the classic tactic of "fighting fire
with fire." That seemed to be the simplest, least hazardous solution, so we broke out a drip torch and some fusees.

A drip torch is a metal can that holds about a gallon of a fuel
oil/gasoline mixture. A nozzle and wick protrude from one end,
and when lit, you can tip the torch at various angles to release
drops or a small stream of flaming liquid. You can create a line
of fire as fast as you can walk. Fusees are simply a firefighting
version of a highway flare. They shoot out a couple inches of very
hot flame, and are used like giant matches.

With the rest of the crew alert for spotting across the road,
John and I girdled the hill with fire. The only problem was a half-
dozen wooden power poles that skirted the east flank. Before we
ignited our general backfire, we burned out a ten to twenty foot
circle around the base of each pole to serve as a buffer zone.

At first the variable winds were a concern, but as the backfire roared up the hillsides it induced its own monstrous draft,
sucking smoke and flame up toward the center of a hellish vortex.
It was a small firestorm, generating a mushroom cloud of smoke
that was seen from a fire tower thirty-five miles away. Over
twenty acres were consumed more or less at once.

But in a half-hour the fire died down to scattered hot spots,
and after we'd mopped up those that were close to the line, John
and his crew departed. We stayed behind for another half-hour
as insurance, and as we drove around the south edge of the burn
on our way to the main road, we saw a brand new fire—five foot
flames lashing through grass and brush on the *green* side of our
firebreak road. In the distance, running down a trail like startled
deer, were three kids. There was no time to give chase. We had
structures less than a quarter-mile away, with only a narrow
road between.

Our truck was out of water, so as Darin and Tony jumped
out to grab pump cans, I was on the radio calling for yet another
crew. When they arrived ten minutes later, we were down to the
dregs of two cans. With a fresh engine, the fire was quickly under
control, so we finally left for base, overdosed on smoke and heat,
and snorting bitterly about the pyromania so common among

adolescents. Some of us have first-hand knowledge of that, but it was a long time ago.

The frantic, irregular hours of fire season seem to blend into a single incident—one long battle summoned to recall via graphic, isolated images. Like the afternoon we sat at the station, riveted by the radio traffic. A fire boss had called for an ambulance—a chopper was down! Papa Alpha had crashed. Tense minutes passed, and finally the word: no fatalities. But it was a sobering mishap. For the first time in thirteen years Minnesota had lost a helicopter on fire duty. As the pilot was dipping his bucket into a beaver pond the cable somehow got wrapped around one of his landing struts. When he powered up with a full load, he was snapped back to earth in a twisting rush. A chunk of rotor blade rocketed through the plexiglass and gouged his flight helmet.

I recall the hot afternoon my crew was called as reinforcements to a rolling fire that was gobbling up whole balsam trees and had jumped across a twenty-acre lake. We were directed into a small rural cemetery where the fire boss had a vantage point, and was pondering the option of ordering an air tanker. Such a decision is not done lightly. Not only would he tie up the heaviest weapon in our arsenal, but the fire would instantly become expensive. The four-engine PB4Y2 carries 2,000 gallons of retardant at eighty cents a gallon, and that doesn't include the cost of pilot and plane.

The boss was delighted to see us, but it was as if we'd arrived late to a bizarre funeral. Two low-boy trailers with their attendant trucks were parked amidst the graves, like hearses for bulldozers. A helicopter was just rising to fetch water, swinging over the dead with its bucket trailing in a gentle arc as if beckoning them to heaven. Nothing so loud had ever disturbed their peace. How strange it would be, I thought, to see the fire sweep through the brown grass of the graveyard, incinerating dead flowers and scorching the monuments. It would be best to let it run, to purify the boneyard. After the first rain the new green grass would rise like the saints in Revelation.

The fire boss drew a map in the dirt with his finger. He wanted us to cut off the fire from the west flank before it jumped a narrow dirt road. In a moment we were winding down the two-track trail, alarms screaming in my brain. We were approaching the head of a fire down a one-way, dead-end road, with fuel all around us. It was a calculated risk, deemed justifiable by the threat to a wide tract of timber and the scattered residences within.

Suddenly the road bottomed out in a swampy ravine, and I hit the gas, flinging mud from the tires as I struggled out of the hole and up the other side. Four firefighters emerged from the smoke as we crested the ridge. We could hear the fire. It was a loud, hollow roar—like a charging tornado, or the end of the world. We scrambled to start our pump and deploy hose, but the fire beat us to the edge of the road, swallowing a half-dozen trees at a time, and leaping the trail as if it didn't exist. Ten-foot flames lunged at us, and we retreated. I slammed the truck into reverse, dragging hose as I went. I backed as carefully as fear would allow, but on the slope above the swamp a rear tire hit a greasy patch and slid off the road. I resisted the impulse to gun it and maybe bury the wheel. With the howl of the fire pressing in my ears, I jumped out to take a look. With caution (and luck) I might pull out. I eased out the clutch in low gear, trying to keep the tire from spinning. To my relief the truck slowly crawled out of the hole.

But there was no going back—I'd never get it through the swampy stretch in reverse. Fortunately, the head of the fire had passed, and a partial clearing below the crest of the ridge had tempered the fire on the flank. We re-advanced, knocked it down, and drove into the black. We were now behind the head, and would pursue it on foot. The chopper ripped out of the smoke, his bucket just ticking the tops of the aspens. As I donned a pump can, one of the dozers plowed across the road, churning up a fire-line. We followed it in, wading into the flames to slug it out tree by tree, stump by stump, ember by ember.

We found out later that one of the dozers had broken down and was overrun by fire. The operator had burned his arm while defending the machine as best he could. But the rest of us, more or less intact, straggled back to the cemetery a couple hours later, black and coughing but laughing about victory and wondering about supper. It wasn't the proper demeanor for a graveyard, but we were too much alive for solemnity. The chopper, crew and bucket stowed, made one last call to the dead and then sped out of sight, bound for the next little hell-born paradise.

And so it went for twenty-seven days, until a half-inch rain gave us a break. Our crews had dealt with eighty wildfires. One day in late April we had nine fires, hustling and fighting like zombies until long after dark. Through a pleasant haze of fatigue we shared a late, store-bought dinner at the station, rehashing the adventures of the day.

But my most vivid recollection is not of the fireground. One afternoon early in the season, we were out on the highway responding to a call from Aero-2. I was sitting on the passenger side of the cab, fiddling with the eyeglasses strap that I always attached enroute. As we passed a late-model sedan, I absently glanced out the window. In the driver's seat of the Mercedes was a middle-aged man in a suit. A lawyer? Some kind of executive? A very good salesman? He looked affluent, businesslike, and terribly bored. Perhaps he was only pensive, contemplating the minutae of the next deal. In any case, I contrasted his appearance with my charged-up state of mind, and I had a silly urge to roll down the window and yell. With boisterous sign language I would point to our engine, myself, and my companions, like a preacher waving a Bible, or a hawker at a carnival. "Smoke!" I'd shout. "Smoke!"

But no, it would be impolite to flaunt our good fortune and privilege. There was no sense to rub it in. That poor man was going to work. We were going to a fire.

The Bizarre and Brutal Ramshead Hose Mission

1.

I considered the seventeen wood ticks to be an omen. I'd been on the portage trail a scant twenty minutes, and that's how many ticks had latched onto my jeans—all crawling upward. I'd never had that many on me at one time, and I took it as a sign of approaching travail. I was right.

This operation would be like so many others: if you had a precisely lucid perception of what it was going to be like, you'd never do it in the first place. Especially this one. We were portaging into the Boundary Waters wilderness—not to explore and fish—but to work; for $100 a day and all we could eat.

There'd been a wild fire west of Ramshead Lake a month before, and the U.S. Forest Service had used helicopters and cargo nets to drop 14,000 pounds of firefighting gear into the wilderness. It was mostly one-and-a-half-inch hose—over 30,000 feet of it. But though the equipment had been airlifted in, it had to be carried out by hand; with backpacks and canoes. The Forest Service called for bids, and a guy named Ropey got it for $14,000— an even dollar per pound. He was given a seven-day deadline. After that the Forest Service would lop $2,000 a day off the bid. They figured that was how much they'd lose in ruined hose. Ropey was told that a certain fungus thrived in wet fire hose, and unless the hose was cleaned and dried, it rotted from the inside out.

13

Well, the Feds should know their hose, but $2,000 a day? It seemed an arbitrary figure, and we surmised it wasn't so much a scientific calculation of the fungal lifestyle as it was a psychological bullwhip. Once the bid was awarded, the Forest Service wanted to keep the awardees humping. And, if the Forest Service wasn't happy with the progress being made, they could terminate the contract at any time. I had never met Ropey. A friend of mine had also put in a bid—significantly higher—and when he lost, he and I left a few names with the Forest Service, expressing interest in helping out if the need arose. We suspected that whoever got the bid (especially a low one) might go in with too small a crew, trying to maximize profit, and fall into trouble. That's exactly what happened, but I'm getting ahead of myself.

Ropey signed the contract on a Friday afternoon, and the Forest Service countdown began. He hustled his crew into the bush immediately. The following Tuesday afternoon he called me. He'd come out of the woods to buy more provisions and enlist reinforcements. The Forest Service had given him referrals.

"We're running a military-style operation," Ropey told me. He mentioned walkie-talkies, "canoe teams," and map coordinates. It sounded efficient and well-organized. "Our deadline is Friday night," he said. "We'll be out by then; it's going well. Once we're on the river we're home free."

But, if things were so rosy, I wondered, why was he calling for help? Still, the confidence in his voice had the ring of sincerity. I told him I could round up two others besides myself, that we could work through Friday, and we'd bring our own canoes.

Ropey sounded happy. "Great. I'll meet you at the head of Meander Creek no later than 6:00 p.m."

Meander Creek worried me. It was what Ropey meant by "the river." It was the most direct route from the Ramshead area to the Echo Trail, a major forest road. But on the map I could see it was a narrow, winding, shallow stream—a glorified rivulet through a swamp. No doubt there were beaver dams, deadfalls, and mud flats. It was mid-June after a dry spring, and water levels were low.

"So, the Meander has enough water in it?" I asked.

There was hesitation. "Yes," Ropey replied. It was less confidence than curtness. Did he sound a little irritated? It was a distress signal, but I knew I was going anyway, so I said, "OK, see you at six."

It was already 2:00 p.m., and I had an hour-and-a-half drive to the rendezvous, so I had to hustle. Steve wanted to go, but he didn't have a phone; I left a message with one of his neighbors. I called Neil, but he was out fishing. I left another message, and then packed my gear.

After two decades of primitive-style camping, it's a smooth process—as automatic as the morning toilet. Assuming I have food ready to pack, it takes less than twenty minutes to prepare for a week in the woods. This was one of the few times it was actually necessary to be ready that fast, but it's comforting to know it can be done. If I ever turn outlaw, I can be on the lam in a hurry.

Steve pulled into the yard at 3:45. He had a four-wheel drive pickup with oversized tires, so we lashed my canoe onto his truck topper. Ropey had advised that the road into Meander Creek was "rugged," and that 4WD "would be nice."

We drove to Neil's, and he still wasn't around, so we left another message and a marked map, and Steve borrowed one of Neil's two canoes. We tied down the old seventeen-foot Aluma-craft without premonitions, but this canoe was destined for its own adventures. In the end, it would've been better if we'd left it there next to Neil's garage. But that was something else we didn't know yet.

Confident that Neil would follow us later, we graciously left him one of his own paddles and headed north.

2.

The Echo Trail is one of the exciting roads of the world. It's a fifty-six-mile stretch of gravel that runs through a section of the three-million-acre Superior National Forest. We got on at the western terminus, just a few miles north of the Vermilion River Tavern on County Road 23. The Echo is a narrow corridor through deep woods, an uneasy buffer between our new machines and the ancient heritage of primeval North America. It's winding and hilly, making all the necessary concessions to the terrain of the Canadian Shield. The builders didn't drill and blast through the bedrock, they went over and around, traversing the given contours like a wandering bear.

I get anxious on the Echo. In one sense it's like a river—you never know for sure what's going to be around the next bend—moose, deer, bear, wolf, deadfall, logging truck. You've got to be alert at the wheel. But the anxiousness also encompasses a child-like anticipation—the warm, excited sensation I felt at age eight when we were on the way to the circus, or walking to school on the last day of class before summer vacation. Heading down the Echo is a pilgrimage to freedom—a migration to the wild nesting grounds of wonder and adventure. That rough, corrugated, dirt road, shadowed by spruce and pine, and rimmed by glacial boulders, is a preamble to wilderness. It's an apt transition from asphalt to portage trails, and it gives me goose bumps.

I told Steve that we had a rare opportunity. We wouldn't be packing mere camping equipment over the old canoe routes, we'd be hauling *cargo*, just like the Ojibway and the French-Canadian Voyageurs. We were going to be *paid* canoeists, out for profit. Loaded down with the Forest Service's hose and pumps, we'd probably come as near as moderns could to the wilderness experience of the Voyageurs. We could re-live history. Singing in French would be appropriate.

Steve gave me a crooked, skeptical look. He was less interested in historical romance than cold, hard cash. Well, good! That was no doubt an authentic Voyageur attitude. Musing upon the glories of the canoe country was less important than surviving the journey and relishing the glories of payday.

We turned off the Echo Trail onto a Forest Service road that led to Meander Lake. We took the first side road, and Ropey was correct; "rugged" was the word. It was an old logging road across low ground. It was constricted, deeply rutted, and studded with large rocks. We were glad for the high clearance of the truck, and though we didn't need the 4WD on the way in, it was clear that a good rainfall would make it mandatory on the way out.

The road snaked through the brush for a bouncing, bucking mile, and then dead-ended at a tiny creek that fed the Meander. Ropey was supposed to meet us there, but it was after six, and no one was around. We could see some recent tire tracks, and some fresh-cut logs straddling a mudhole, so we figured it must be the right place. We pulled the truck off the road, hefted pack and canoes, and started down the portage trail to Meander Creek.

Ropey hadn't mentioned how long the first hike was, but we

were expecting something relatively short and direct—no reason, I guess we were just hoping. There was nothing on our map. But the trail stretched on and on, and twice I had to shove the prow of my canoe up into the limbs of some convenient jack pines, and come out from under the yoke for a breather. The first time I did, I noticed the battalion of wood ticks. It was June 9th, and I mused upon the fact that if you enjoyed the company of insects, this was the best time to be in the Boundary Waters. It was in its most jungle-like phase—lush, dense foliage crawling with ticks, horse flies, deer flies, black flies, chiggers, nosee'ems, and of course multiple billions of mosquitoes. The latter are usually at their suffocating worst around dusk, so it would be nice to be in camp by then.

Each rod of that portage enhanced my dread of future pain. Seven tons of cargo would have to come back over it, not to mention personal gear and several canoes. It was far too long, and I began to have grave doubts about the wisdom of this venture. I assumed the trail was bypassing one or more beaver dams on the extremely sinuous upper Meander, but was it worth it? Wouldn't it be better to be on the water, even if it was a longer route?

We finally reached the creek, and Steve and I agreed it was just over a mile back to the road. As we broke out of the woods onto the wide bank, we startled a large whitetail that was watering on the other side. In the luxuriant light of the setting sun, the deer's coat was a deep reddish brown, and every detail of its muscular body stood out in textural relief. The thick hair looked like the softest velour. The deer stood for a few moments and then bounded off into a thicket of young aspens. It was a calm, almost leisurely retreat—prudent, but not panicky. The whitetails know when it's not hunting season. I believe they've isolated and internalized the odor of gunpowder and brass.

The sight of the deer boosted my spirits a notch, until I got a good look at Meander Creek. It was indeed narrow—two to twenty feet wide—shallow, and almost stagnant. The bottom was black mud, and there was fifty yards of serious swamp on either side. It looked like wonderful territory for mergansers and muskrats, but no place for fully loaded canoes. There was no visible current, and we had to check the map to make sure which way was downstream. We'd be heading north toward a portage into Ramshead Lake, and Ropey said he'd left a bundle of fire hose on top of a big boulder to mark the spot. The portage was about one-hundred rods long, and was not shown on the contour map. We weren't sure when we were going to get there, but it'd better be some time before dark.

With a rueful, "Well, let's do it," we slid our canoes off the greasy bank into the dark water of Meander Creek. We were in a maze of tall grass, crowded by solid greenery. The stream was dotted with tiny "islands"—spongy hummocks of reeds—and they added to the confusion of switchback bends. For the first quarter-mile or so, we could never see more than two or three canoe lengths of open water at a time, and some of the turns were so sharp that we had to stop, and then backpaddle to get our prows headed in the right direction.

But Ropey was right, at least there was enough water. We hit a long, straight stretch, and my mood brightened considerably. There was a discernible current, no obstructions, and we were making good time. Meander Creek was going to be a decent route after all. There was still that mile plus portage up to the road, but . . . and then my heart sank. Just ahead was a massive beaver dam. Beyond its muddy brim the land seemed to drop away. No wonder there was water here—the dam appeared to be five or six feet high and the only thing keeping the upper Meander from being one long mud flat.

We eased up to the dam, and I mordantly chuckled and then cursed. Below the barrier, Meander Creek was a trickle—a sloppy, grass-choked tunnel through the swamp. And we were barely a quarter of the way to Ramshead.

I truly considered going home. Coming back upstream with heavily-laden canoes was going to be a miserable trial. And unless we got some significant rain, the creek would be dropping daily. We might end up dragging the canoes through a long quagmire at the peak of bug season, in blistering heat. I was possessed by sickening depression, by grim anticipation of suffering. It's how you feel during the two or three days before you enter a hospital for surgery. Pain is inevitable—its prospect overwhelming. I'd been down this road before.

I shook my head and turned to Steve. My demeanor was morose. "Hot damn." I said. "Look at *that* mess! And this is supposed to be the easy part."

Steve weakly grinned, and then shrugged. It was eloquent body language. It meant: we told the man we'd be there, so we will; it's not possible to do anything but proceed.

I offered a laughing snort in tribute to the power of our deeply ingrained male sensibilities. Even in this age of Mutual Assured Destruction, little boys are still raised to be warriors. We are taught, both overtly and subliminally, that it's more than okay to suffer and die, as long as we are loyal (to whatever) and don't chicken out. That's a bit overstated for Meander Creek, but the principle holds. And that principle would endure quite a workout by Friday evening.

All right, I told myself, we *are* committed, so that's that. Not a profound thought, but simple statements often lead to profound deeds. We pulled our canoes over the dam and slid them down a natural ramp on the other side. The lower Meander was as rotten as it looked. We used our paddles as poles, pushing our canoes through a fetid emulsion of half-water/half-mud—or "loon shit," as it's called in backwoods vernacular. For the next half-mile every yard was a struggle. Where we could actually paddle instead of shove, the blades got tangled in thick, stringy grass. There was another, smaller beaver dam, and then a spot where an ancient dam had been breached. The slot through the old obstruction was hard against the right bank, and looked like a small gorge. It was so narrow that when I laboriously pushed and pulled to squeeze through, chunks of dried mud and bits of decomposed wood were knocked loose and fell into the bottom of the canoe.

After about a mile, the creek widened and deepened a little— enough for real paddling—but now it was studded with sunken and half-sunken deadfalls. Our near-empty canoes got hung up five or six times. We were able to rock them off, but how would the going be with fully-loaded boats?

Fortunately, we came upon Ropey's boulder and bundle of hose sooner than expected, and that was encouraging. We estimated it was about two-and-a-half river-miles back up to the first portage. At the present water level it would be a tough haul, but feasible.

We pitched our tent on a small rise overlooking the creek, just off the portage trail. As the sun went down we walked the 100 rods over to the shore of Ramshead Lake. If we'd had more time, we would've searched for Ropey's base camp, and joined his crew for the night. But Ramshead is one-and-a-half miles long, a mile wide, and dotted with islands. It could be a long search. As it was, if Ropey was still coming in that evening, he'd have to pass right by our tent. We could link up then.

Back at the creek, we sat on the big boulder at the water's edge and did a tick check before settling into the tent. I found three or four already sucking blood out of my legs, and another half dozen crawling around inside my jeans and shirt. Steve had a similar inventory. Given the gross density of the local population, it didn't seem worth the trouble to grind the invaders into the rock. We flicked them off into the grass, satisfied that at least they wouldn't be spending the night with us.

Beyond the fringes of the swamp, the land on either side of Meander Creek rises to low, wooded bluffs and forms a compact valley. The full moon had risen as we paddled downstream, and now, as the evening sky deepened to indigo, the valley was charged with lunar radiation. The hard, white light transformed the creek into a vitreous ribbon of vespertine fire. As the air cooled, a mist formed on the surface of the water, and the stream, looping away into the distance, glowed and "steamed" like a river of cooling lava.

The surrounding forest grew shadowy and indistinct, and it was easy to imagine that we were perched not on a single boulder, but on a mountain peak—that we were gazing out over a great, wide river and a deep valley that was thirty miles across. I pulled my vision back, and for a moment I could see it. The world of Meander Creek expanded, dilating out to the horizon like an opening cosmic iris.

But I quickly refocused as the mosquitoes descended. Their combined humming was loud and intimidating. It's the ominous sound of a whistling artillery shell—still high and distant, but just beginning to arc toward its target. It's the sound of a programmed beast, heedless of death and homing in for the kill. We covered all but our hands and faces, and then shook and swatted constantly, determined to enjoy the dusk for a while longer.

The disturbing thing about a cloud of mosquitoes is that the individuals are not afraid of you. They may dodge a slap, but they're undeterred. They will press their suicide assault relentlessly, no matter how many are destroyed. Unlike many creatures, they aren't skittish, and they're deliberate hunters of human blood.

They swarmed over Steve and me, dozens at a time hitting our hands. I felt like I was pulling on a pair of prickly gloves. The hood of my sweatshirt kept all but a few off my face, and I batted one hand against the other for several minutes as we watched the moon rise and the shadows go black.

At the tent, we brushed, jumped, and danced before bolting through the door. Only a few got in, and we sat up, on guard, until we'd killed them all. I found three more ticks in my sleeping bag.

We laid there, listening: to crickets, frogs, mosquitoes, and a pair of loons over on Ramshead. Their florid duet was at once distressing and soothing. Distressing, because to my ear that night there seemed to be a tinge of hysteria in the wild cries. What had the loons seen? These intimates of wilderness, and wide, distant water lived on a different plane, in another dimension. What did they know? Fantasies about sapient backwoods birds came easily on the bank above Meander, with the valley inundated by the moon and sparkling with fireflies.

The loonsong was also soothing; simply because we could hear it. In northern Minnesota loons are rigorously counted, studied, protected, and cherished. But unfortunately, they don't stay. In the autumn they migrate south, and we begin to hear horror stories. The winter before, some 500 loons had died in Florida, the result of mercury contamination. There are only about 12,000 loons in Minnesota, so if the 500 were locals, then four percent of the population had been exterminated. It was comforting to know that the pair on Ramshead were home, and relatively safe.

I was at the edge of sleep when I heard faint human voices, and the muffled bang of a paddle against aluminum. I gave Steve a shake. "There's someone coming downriver," I whispered.

We'd been expecting Neil, but he'd be alone in a plastic canoe, so this had to be Ropey and the additional crew he said he was going to recruit in Ely. I pulled on my boots and jeans, and went out to stand on the boulder. The temperature had dropped, and the horde of mosquitoes had largely dispersed.

The paddling sounded close, but due to the twists and turns of the Meander, it took about fifteen minutes for someone to come into view. I saw the orange glow of a cigarette ease around the last bend, and then two canoes slipped into the moonlit stretch of creek below our tent. Two men in each, they were loaded down with bulging Duluth packs.

It was suddenly strange to see other humans on this mean little backwater route in the wilderness—at midnight. It crossed my mind that we were all dangerously crazy. But at least it wasn't necessary to query about our respective identities. We weren't likely to run into a troop of Cub Scouts from Des Moines.

"Good evening," I said as they drew abreast of the rock.

"Yo. How ya doin'?"

"Better, now that the skeeters have gone to bed."

"That ain't no lie!"

I grabbed the prow of the lead canoe and pulled it up on shore. The stern man got out and shook my hand. "I'm Ropey," he said.

He had long, blond hair and a full beard, and wore a pair of round, steel-rimmed glasses. He was dressed in camouflage fatigues, with combat boots and a jungle hat. He looked and sounded like Donald Sutherland in the movie "Kelly's Heroes." He appeared to be in his late thirties.

Steve came down, and we briefly discussed the whereabouts of Side Lake. Ropey was disappointed that there were only two of us, and we admitted that if he hadn't seen Neil on the way in, then he probably wasn't coming. It'd been short notice.

"We'll do okay," said Ropey. "Are either of you guys vets?"

"No."

"That's all right," he said quickly, excusing our lack. "A couple of us are—we're used to night missions."

As he pulled a walkie-talkie off his belt he added, "We've got some weed along for our heads. We're all pretty loose."

"Good," I replied, and grinned. It was nice to know that our co-workers were laid-back and tolerant. It was clear now that when Ropey had mentioned a "military-style operation," he wasn't referring to the parade ground at West Point, or an OCS drill at Quantico. We were talking Da Nang, circa 1969. And it looked as if a part of Ropey was still there.

He switched on the radio. "Ropey to Ramshead. Over."

"Go ahead, Rope."

"Yeah. The dudes from Side Lake are here. I was thinking of putting them on the river tomorrow."

"No way!" came the angry reply from the base camp. "We need *everybody* up in The Burn."

It didn't sound good. From the tone of the voice there was a morale problem, and we weren't ready to start moving cargo upriver as Ropey had led me to believe on the phone.

"I guess you'll see The Burn tomorrow," said Ropey.

"Well," I replied, "we didn't come here under any illusions." The first portage and Meander Creek had dispatched any of those. "We're ready to work wherever we're needed." Steve chimed in with an enthusiastic second. I reminded myself that he was ten years younger than I.

"Good," said Ropey. His reply was a bit fervent, as if he were hoping our assertions were true, but would wait and see.

We asked him how they expected to handle that mile plus portage, and he answered, "Horses." At first I thought he'd used the word as an euphemism for the grunts on the crew, but he explained that he'd arranged to hire a hay wagon and a team of horses to make that last haul.

"All right!" I said. It was an ingenious way to overcome the Forest Service prohibition of any motorized equipment in the Boundary Waters.

Ropey introduced his companions. There was Joe, a short, effusive guy who was wearing a baseball cap and sneakers. He looked to be in his mid-twenties. Buck was towering and husky, part Indian, with big hands and a wide, ready grin. Tommy, sporting a beard and an engineer's cap, had trouble clambering out of the canoe. Ropey made a comment about Tommy not allowing "his disability to stand in his way," but he didn't elaborate, and it seemed impolite to inquire at this stage.

They intended to make the 100-rod portage into Ramshead and paddle to the base camp. I hefted one of the Duluth packs, Steve lifted a canoe, and we set off into the blackness of the forest. We used averted vision and groping feet to pick our way down the narrow, rocky trail. There was enough moonlight to make it only moderately hazardous, and we too were used to "night missions."

On the way back, I ran into Tommy. He was struggling under one of the packs, and I asked him if I could give him a hand. I was afraid he might be offended, but he gave up the load readily enough, and I humped it down to the lake. It was too dark for me to see exactly what Tommy's disability was.

In a few minutes Ropey and his crew were ready to shove off. He got out a flashlight and a map to show us the location of the camp, and asked us to be there "first thing in the morning." We assured him we'd be there before daybreak, and then we pushed their canoes off into Ramshead.

3.

Next morning, Steve and I were in our canoes by 4:30 a.m. It was chilly, near frost, and the aluminum canoes were ice-cold. As we portaged from Meander to the lake, I kept my hands drawn up into the sleeves of my sweatshirt. I almost always fail to pack gloves. They seem so frivolous; until you need them. When the weather turns on me, I usually end up using extra socks as mittens. Once my wife, Pam, and I launched a canoe trip during the first week of May. The day we left the sun was shining and the temperature was in the 70s. Two days out, and a long way from civilization, we awoke to sub-freezing air and two inches of snow. It had come during the night, and the weight had almost collapsed our tent. I have a vivid recollection of cold, whitecapped lakes, and a paddle grasped tightly with wet wool socks.

But Ramshead was calm, as placid as a puddle. A large island loomed out of the orange-tinted mist, like a ship at anchor. The base camp was due north, in a small bay that opened just to the west of another island. We had to paddle out a couple hundred yards and penetrate the mist before we could see the dim outline of the far shore.

We eased our canoes up to the campsite just before sunrise, and the place was dead, as if the mist was a cloud of poison gas. The previous night's fire was still smoldering, so I stirred it up, dropped in some sticks, and blew it into flame. Steve and I warmed our hands and looked around, bemused.

There were two tents set up beneath a large tarp. One tent was crooked, on the verge of collapsing. A knobby, unpeeled stick served as one of the tent poles. Loud, ragged snores ripped through the open door.

Three sleeping bags were outside the tents. Somebody was curled into a wad within two feet of the fire, and the bag had been laid directly on the damp, heat-sapping ground. No head was

visible, but an engineer's cap was in the dirt beside it. Must be Tommy.

Just under the lip of the tarp was a faded, olive drab bag. It was threadbare from long use and appeared on the brink of mold. At the top was a camouflage hat and a shock of blond hair. Ropey. His body seemed frozen, like it hadn't budged all night. I couldn't even see him breathing, and the overall impression was of a misshapened, carelessly dumped body bag.

There was no mistaking Buck. He filled an undersized sleeping bag to bursting, a cap pulled low on his face. His skin had a greasy sheen—from a heavy coat of bug dope. He was nestled against a couple of large coolers, which were next to three cardboard boxes full of food.

Ropey had told us we'd be well-fed, and sure enough, we could see oranges, potatoes, dinner rolls, assorted candy, barbeque sauce, canned goods, etc. The coolers, we soon discovered, were packed with bacon, eggs, pork chops, and ground beef. We obviously wouldn't be slurping reconstituted trail food out of slimy foil bags. It looked good, but this was a black bear's dream—150 pounds of luscious, accessible treats, some of the best humans have to offer. There'd be no stopping a bear if it got wind of this feast. And there it was, generously displayed in wide-open boxes on the ground. I wondered why they didn't have it in packs hanging ten feet in the air. Then, I noticed a special camping accessory. Propped against one of the coolers was a twenty-gauge shotgun; nearby, a box of slugs. They were employing the Davy Crockett/ Rambo method of bear control. It was a battered old gun with a rusty barrel; a mean-looking weapon that fit the camp perfectly.

Scattered in the branches of surrounding trees, and drapped over the guy ropes of the tarp, was a shabby collection of socks, pants, shirts, and underwear. The clothes were muddy, wet, and torn, and spoke eloquently of some very tough days. Near the door of the leaning tent I could see a pair of torn and soggy running shoes that belonged in a garbage can. They looked as if a dog had mauled them, buried them, and then dug them up to chew some more. I couldn't believe someone was actually using such shoes.

We'd been there for about ten minutes when we heard a stirring in one of the tents. A partially bald head appeared at the door. The guy hawked, spat, and then coughed. He grunted in pain and rose to his feet. His arms were splashed with lurid tattoos—mainly swastikas and bloody skulls. He looked to be in his late thirties; lean, tough, and experienced.

"Good morning," he croaked, and then took a half-dozen steps from the food boxes. He pissed long and hard, and then without another word, crawled back into the tent. We heard a muffled groan as he lay back down.

What sort of man sports tattoos of Nazi symbols and death's heads, I wondered? (Well, a pretty good one, as it turned out. We found that Rod was personable and hard-working, with a lively sense of humor. Though you wouldn't necessarily want him courting your daughter, he was certainly an asset out in the bush. He was the other Vietnam vet Ropey had mentioned.)

After Rod returned to the sack, it was almost two hours before anyone else stirred. Steve and I laid in the dirt and tried to nap ourselves, but we were too hungry and restless. We'd assumed that this "military-style operation" would mobilize early, and we were anxious to get underway and help them complete the mission. My initial impression was that they must be confident of success if they were so casual about the morning. It would be the best time to work—it was cool, and there were few bugs.

Finally, Tommy poked his head out of his bag. "How long you guys been here?" he asked, surprised to see us.

"About two-and-a-half hours," Steve replied.

"No shit?" Tommy yawned. "I'm supposed to be the cook; I guess I better get up."

He zipped open the bag, and I stared. Tommy had only one leg. His right was a flesh-colored prosthesis that extended halfway past the knee. It was held onto his stub by some sort of suction method, and as he limped around the camp to get it adjusted, it snorted and popped as if he were emitting a volley of ripe flatulence. It was enough to wake Buck, who sat up grinning.

It was also Tommy's first morning in this compost pile of a camp, and he looked a tad bewildered. "What should I make for breakfast?" he asked me.

"Hell, Tommy, I don't know. Let's see what we've got."

Steve and I dug into the coolers and brought out some bacon and eggs. Tommy found the skillet at the edge of the woods. It was large, with a conveniently long handle, but it was caked with crud. The remains of the previous evening's supper—whatever it had been—were glued to the bottom with dirty grease. It looked like old vomit. Steve and I exchanged a sardonic glance. At that moment I made a conscious mental adjustment. If I was going to get along on this operation, I'd have to "go native," disremembering my personal code of camp cleanliness. I'd think of food as mere fuel—not as something that went into my mouth, but as an organic substance that entered my stomach and powered my muscles via simple caloric energy. I would de-personalize breakfast and not look too closely at the dishes. St. Ambrose had the right attitude: When on Ramshead, do as the Ramsheadians do.

We discovered this maxim would have to apply to drinking water as well. The Forest Service recommends that Boundary Waters visitors not drink lake water straight—for all the usual reasons—but Ropey had expressed disdain for that guideline. ("Nothing wrong with that lake, man; water's like wine.") Some of his crew were more fastidious, and five gallons of potable water had been hauled in. But under circumstances which were never clear to me, the jug was emptied and some nearby garbage had been stuffed inside. The crew claimed the Forest Service did it, and vowed revenge. The Feds denied it, but the upshot was that unless we boiled large quantities of water every day—in hot weather—we'd have to take the lake water as presented. Nobody had packed a filter. In the past few years I'd become a conscientious boiler of wilderness water (largely due to giardia), but I had to remind myself that for nearly twenty years I'd sipped directly out of the lakes with no ill effects. I decided to hold that thought and enjoy the cold, unsmoked water of Ramshead (collected out in deep water far from shore). Tommy did manage to get some boiled each day, but it was never enough.

I stoked the fire, scraped the skillet, and then let it cook by itself for awhile. It never did look clean, but maybe it'd been more or less sterilized. Steve fried the first batch of bacon and eggs, allowing Tommy to ease into his new responsibilities. The crisp sound of greasy pig meat over an open flame eventually roused the rest of the crew.

Dave was thirty-two, an ex-Forest Service Ranger who quit in 1979 after being "screwed out of a promotion." He had the hard, wiry look of a distance runner, or a lightweight boxer. It was clear he had the respect of the rest.

Chris said "good mornin" in a soft southern drawl. He was

from Kentucky, and the next day he was supposed to hear the result of a child custody case that had gone before the Kentucky Supreme court. "The story got thirty-two inches on the front page of the Louisville *Courier-Journal*," he told me later in the day. He'd won the original judgement, but it had been appealed all the way to the top. He was confident of victory. Rich, who appeared to be a full-blooded Ojibway, crawled out of one of the tents, and immediately went to work on his feet. They were a mess—puffy, blistered, and in some places red-raw. He was in obvious pain as he applied Band-Aids to the worst wounds, and I was astounded when he reached for the mangled, rotten shoes near the tent and pulled them on over his almost equally battered feet. He later explained that he'd brought along some boots, but his feet had swelled up after the first day, and he couldn't get them on.

Last to rise, struggling from the brink of an apparent, near-death state, was Ropey. He crouched near the fire, waiting for a dose of the mud-brown coffee that Dave had boiling over the flames. Ropey started telling Steve and me about the ash dust up in The Burn. As you hiked through the burned-over area, he said, you kicked up little clouds of black dust that seemed to hang in the air for hours. "You can see it in front of your face, man—little black sparkles. It's thick up there."

Ropey had a Marlboro in one hand and a joint in the other. Between sentences he'd take a puff on the cigarette and a long drag on the reefer. At one point he broke into a ragged, chest-heaving cough—the kind of wretched hacking that makes your own ribs hurt just to hear it.

"That damn ash dust!" swore Ropey. "It's killing me!"

I took a turn at cooking, and then we finally handed the culinary reins over to Tommy. He seemed nervous at first, and was obviously not used to cooking at all, much less for an entire hungry crew.

As they passed around the morning's toke of cannabis, the guys gave Tommy a hard time, comparing his efforts to jailhouse food. It turned out that half the crew had first-hand experience with prison cuisine. Rich, who mentioned a ninety-day stint in the Ramsey County Jail, summed up the government offerings in one phrase: "cold coffee and warm milk." I didn't ask anyone what they'd done time for, but they agreed that some jails were better than others.

We didn't have enough utensils and dishes to go around, so we shared. I used some hazel leaves to wipe a suspicious glob out of a cup, and then disinfected it with some of the black, gritty coffee. It's amazing how good everything tastes out in the bush. I declined the marijuana, but pulled out my own drug—a tin of Copenhagen snuff. I'd quit the delightful carcinogen two years before, but allowed myself a special dispensation for this operation (and other selected adventures). I suspected I might need a reliable chemical mood-elevator. It's a narrow, but deep gulf between survival and *graceful* survival, and as most primitive forest peoples knew, a mild narcotic is often just enough to bridge the chasm. For example: You're about to set up camp after hiking fourteen miles in the rain. You know that your sleeping bag is soaked. But before you unroll it, you have a dip of snuff, (or smoke a cigarette, light up a joint, chew on a cocoa leaf, etc.). A small chemical adjustment is made in your brain that slightly alters your perspective. What was a cosmic tragedy is now a cosmic joke. It's still painful, and you would've survived it in any case, but now the soggy bag elicits a sigh and a morbid chuckle, instead of a sigh and morbid curse. It may seem a subtle difference, but spread out over a long wilderness trip, strung together by a series of little hardships, it may allow you to remain even-tempered enough to avoid clashing and bickering with your companions. This can be critical, especially since you're all probably carrying knives.

Finally, around 8:30 a.m., the crew was ready to go. Ropey said something inspirational like, "It's late, so we've got to hump until dark." We each donned a packboard with two or three empty Duluth packs strapped onto it, and then followed Ropey and Dave into the woods, or "the jungle," as Ropey called it.

The hose and the other gear had been gathered into twelve caches scattered west of Ramshead—a few of them over a mile from the lake. One of the biggest problems had been simply finding the stuff. Not even the Forest Service was sure where it all was, and the guys had spent the first two days searching and blazing trails. The Forest Service had provided a marked contour map—each cache labeled with a number—and Ropey had used a compass to navigate to each pile. But the map wasn't an infallible guide, and the Forest Service dispatched a plane to pinpoint a couple of the caches. The crew had made some progress after that, hauling tons of gear down to the lakeshore near camp, and stockpiling it for the canoe haul over to the first portage.

There were four caches left to pick up, and the plan was to finish two of them that day—no. 6 and no. 7. We threaded our way through the forest in single file, pressed in by veritable walls of foliage. The underbrush was thick and tangled, a dense snarl of trunks, stalks, limbs, and roots. Dave had blazed this path, trying to make it as direct as possible, but numerous deadfalls and a lot of swampy ground had forced a meandering trajectory that worked up over a ridge and then down to a pair of mosquito-infested beaver ponds. The trail was alternately stony and spongy, a twisting obstacle course of fallen trunks and slippery, moss-covered rocks.

A small clearing opened up on the ponds, and we used an old beaver dam as a bridge between them. Just beyond the dam was no. 6. We were three-quarters of a mile from camp, but it was a scabrous, bully of a trail. I learned later that the route through the woods had been established over Ropey's strenuous objections. He insisted that the crew should follow the edge of The Burn—no matter which cache was being hauled—even though it meant significantly longer hikes. He said it would be too much trouble to hack a usable trail through "the jungle." They'd done it his way for a while, but Dave finally grabbed a Pulaski and a compass, and strode into the woods. The rest followed, cursing Ropey's stubbornness. They were convinced it was easier, and, of course, if you believe something is better, it usually is.

At no. 6 were ten oblong bundles of hose, called "watermelons" in the trade. Upon delivery to a fire scene, the hose is tightly wrapped in neat circular rolls—dry, light, and compact. After a fire, the hose is dirty, wet, and heavy. The fire crews quickly half-coil, half-fold the 100-foot lengths into the shape of giant eggs or watermelons. Some are tight, some aren't, and Ropey's crew had to dress up several bundles before they could be carried without unraveling. Some hose hadn't even been "watermeloned," and it had to be drained of excess water before it could be gathered up. It was time-consuming work.

After a brief rest, we pushed on toward no. 7. We planned to carry all of no. 7 down to no. 6, and then pack it all into camp. Just beyond the ponds we dropped into a swamp. If not for the dry spring, it would've been impassable. As it was, we were able to cut across with only wet feet—except for one pocket of knee-

deep mud about five yards across. That would be an energy-sapper with full loads on our backs.

In a few minutes we ascended a steep ridge and entered The Burn. While searching for the caches on Day One, Ropey had found a scribbled sign hanging on a scorched tree. Left there by an exhausted fire crew, it read: "Highway To Hell." Joe assured me it was an apt name.

The Burn was already hot. The coal-black ground was soaking up sunlight and radiating waves of heat. Every bit of foliage had been consumed, and the forest was now a charnel, thickly studded with the skeletons of pines. The dead limbs reached out into the simmering air, scratching my bare arms as we passed. They left a crooked pattern of long, sooty smudges on my skin, like the scars of a cruel whipping. The lush forest had become a desert, a harsh landscape of arid shadows, but no shade. Our trudging platoon kicked up a haze of ash dust, and the minute particles stayed risen—scattering sunlight and fouling the air.

We traversed the heart of The Burn, the only moving life forms in the midst of cindery desolation. There were two ravines, steep and rugged, but otherwise the walking was easier than in the constricted greenwood. Nevertheless, the atmosphere was oppressive. From behind I heard Rich spit dust and say, "I hate this damn place!"

We were headed westward and upward, and at the crest of a naked ridge we finally came to no. 7. We were about a mile-and-a-half from camp, and it was a depressing sight. There were forty watermelons, a large cargo net, a dozen shovels and Pulaskis, two pumps, three lengths of suction hose, a heavy bag of hose fittings, a chainsaw, three five-gallon gas cans, a half-dozen bladder bags with pump nozzles, and three or four lengths of water-filled hose that had yet to be bundled. I estimated it was just over 2,500 pounds worth. We had to haul it back to camp, plus pick up the 500 pounds or so that still waited at no. 6. Ropey said that caches no. 10 and no. 11, which were scheduled for the next day, held about the same amount of gear, and were even further from camp. It would require a full day to wrap up no. 6 and no. 7, and then probably another day for no. 10 and no. 11. That left only one day to move the entire seven tons over the 100-rod portage, up the creek, over the mile plus portage to the road, and the twenty-five miles by truck to Ely.

I realized that we weren't going to make it by Friday night. No way. I could see why the crew had wanted Steve and me out in the bush and not on the "river." I realized that the lackadaisical, late-rising morning scene was not confidence, but probably dread and resignation. Ropey was still talking about hurrying to meet the deadline, but if he still really believed it could be done, he was kidding himself.

We dropped our packboards and went to work. Two watermelons were stuffed into each Duluth pack, and two, sometimes three, were lashed to each packboard. In some cases, if a hose was wet and very heavy, it was tied to a packboard by itself. The average weight of a load was about seventy pounds.

Our tactic would be to move the cache in two stages. Each man would carry a load most of the way through The Burn, drop it, and go back for another. Once we had all of no. 7 to the halfway point, we'd start moving it to no. 6. Once it was all there, we'd do the last leg into camp.

Since Steve and I were "fresh meat," we were expected to work harder. It was never explicitly stated, but we knew we had to prove ourselves, that Ropey and the rest were watching to see if the Side Lake boys were going to "carry their ruck," and earn their pay.

For my first load I hoisted one of the bulkier Duluth packs and then picked up a gas can with each hand. Steve followed suit, filling his arms with shovels. We hurried through The Burn to the halfway point, then hustled back to no. 7 for another load. Some of the others were taking a break between hauls, but Steve and I paused only for a sip of water and kept humping. We always carried something in addition to a pack, and we stayed cheerful— at least through the morning.

The effect on morale was instant and obvious. The pace of the others gradually picked up. They could see that Steve and I were making a significant contribution to the speed of the operation, and that we were hauling several hundred pounds that they wouldn't have to touch.

"Excellent!" said Ropey, as I marched up the side of a ravine with a full packboard, and two lengths of suction hose draped around my neck.

"Are you guys trying to lap me?" kidded Rich, as we skipped away from where he was resting. He grinned, happy that it was true.

"We'll keep it up while we can," I called back. "Tomorrow we'll be as raggedy-ass as the rest of you." But we had a lot of respect for this crew. They'd been trudging through the woods for five days, and had transported several tons of gear down to the water. They knew every inch of the dreary, sweltering Burn, and had arduously cut trails through seemingly impenetrable forest. They kept at it in spite of pain and injury. Rich's feet were appalling, and I was certain his battered shoes wouldn't last the morning. Joe had struck his ankle with a Pulaski on the second day, and each morning he tightly wrapped his foot with an elastic bandage. The wound had caused an ugly swelling, and his skin was dangerously discolored, but he felt lucky he could still get his shoe on. "It's getting better," he said. "Besides, I figure I can handle anything for one lousy week. I need the money."

I learned that Rod was forty, and had a history of excruciating back trouble. "I suppose it'll blow out any minute," he said. "Then you guys'll have ME strapped onto one of those damn packboards." He was hoping his vertebra would endure; he also needed the money.

Dave was breaking in a pair of new boots and had over thirty blisters on his feet. Ropey was pale, and seemed to be on the verge of simple exhaustion. He also bore the burden of ultimate responsibility. It was his name on the Forest Service contract, and he stood to lose the most if the venture failed, or if the bid started dropping by a dearly-earned, heart-breaking $2,000 a day.

The heat rose steadily, and by early afternoon my brain was torpid. My T-shirt and jeans were soggy, heavy with sweat; my shoulders ached. I could feel a building soreness in the lower back, and couple of blisters were forming on my toes. My mouth was dry and gritty. We were rationing the five quarts of water we'd packed in, and soon it was hard to generate enough saliva to keep spitting out the ash dust.

No. 7 was close to completion, so some of us started the shuttle to no. 6. It was a relief to get off the Highway to Hell, but the mudhole in the swamp began to take its toll. We threw a few deadfalls across it to serve as a crude corduroy road, but the more traffic that passed, the soupier it got. I expended a lot of energy trying not to stumble in and sink past my knees. We certainly didn't care about being wet and muddy, but it was too easy to wrench your back, or slip and fall while wading through the ooze. And it kept getting deeper. Without the logs we were afraid it would soon be up to our waists.

At least The Burn had been relatively free of bugs. In the swampy woods they were as thick as molecules. The horse flies and deer flies savagely assaulted any exposed skin (and bit through T-shirts as well)—especially the backs of our necks and behind our ears. When strapped into a pack, it was hard to reach them, and guys were cursing, shaking their heads like harried dogs. The mosquitoes settled on forearms in tingling waves, and you could kill a half dozen at a crack, smearing them across your skin like snot. Nobody even bothered with the legions of wood ticks. Let them bore into the flesh and suck blood—you could tear them out at the end of the day. If it ever came.

As the gear piled up at no. 6, it seemed like we were going backwards. A ton of fire hose is a gloomy sight—especially when you've already picked it up and carried it twice. By 1:00 p.m. I figured I'd walked ten miles, and struggled beneath 500 pounds of cargo. I was still hustling, but it was weary, mechanical drudgery. The trail appeared to lengthen, with new obstacles rising from the muck. I began to trip over rocks and roots that I hadn't even realized were there. There was a minimum of banter among the crew. We mostly worked in silence, each absorbing the suffering in his own way. I started playing little mind games—reciting poetry or compiling lists of favorite books or songs.

By 2:00 p.m. there was only one full crew-load left at no. 7, and we'd put a dent in no. 6. We filtered back to camp one by one, dumping our loads on the shoreline, and then dumping ourselves near the campfire. Tommy had fried up a stack of hamburgers, and they seemed a gift from God. The original crew members were especially pleased. Until Tommy arrived, there'd been no cook. It was another important morale-booster to be able to stumble back to camp and have a decent meal ready and waiting. The value of a full-time cook, or campmaster, is incalculable on an operation like this, someone to prepare food for exhausted workers, clean dishes, procure and treat water, police the camp, and guard the provisions. Performing those duties for a crew of ten is easily a full-time job, and Ropey had finally seen the advantages of it. But he was paying Tommy only $50 a day. I later talked to a veteran of such work parties who said it's traditional for a good cook to be the highest-paid individual on the crew. That made sense to me. Those burgers (and a subsequent dip of snuff) lifted my spirits to a near-normal level.

Though I'd known these men for less than twenty-four hours, the common toil and common purpose was quick to breed an easy familiarity. People who share pain are much closer than people who share pleasure. It's easier to trust the man who is enduring the same stress as you. There is a tangible sense of mutual support and understanding. And the more brutal the conditions, the greater the mutual knowledge.

Steve and I had been accepted into the camp, and I felt comfortable enough to ask Tommy how he'd lost his leg. He immediately launched himself into the telling.

It had been a horrible motorcycle accident. He'd been broadsided by another bike, and his leg was mangled. He was already unconscious when he was rushed into surgery, and when he came to afterwards, his leg was gone.

Up to that point his delivery had been animated, almost excited. He seemed to enjoy the drama of his story, and relish my expression as I tried to imagine the trauma of the mishap. But then his demeanor changed. As he recalled that awakening nightmare in the hospital, his tone became mournful and bitter. He was on the verge of tears, and his voice was hot and fervent as he said, "I wish they'd never woke me up!"

Oh, oh, I thought. I'd stirred some deep waters. I was sorry I'd brought it up. But then Rich, who was busy patching his feet again, looked up and said, "Shit, Tommy. If they'd taken you to Duluth you'd still have your leg. Those local butchers cut it off for nothing!"

"That's right," said Ropey.

Tommy bristled. He defended his misfortune with a clinically detailed account of his injuries. It was a gruesome recitation of torn flesh and crushed bone.

Rich was unmoved. "They should've taken you to Duluth, man."

Anger replaced Tommy's sorrow. He was sullen for a few minutes, but then Buck lit up a joint and passed it around. What was done was done.

The crew seemed to have crossed a threshold that morning. It was apparent from the lunchtime talk that everyone acknowledged it was impossible to meet the original deadline. We new grunts had arrived, and though we were making a difference, it wasn't enough. Ropey continued to drop gung-ho, can-do cliches, but there was no conviction in his voice. We needed an extension from the Forest Service. If the welfare of the hose was indeed their primary concern, then it would be wise to keep the present crew on the job. We knew where it all was, and had already moved the best part of it to the shore of Ramshead, stockpiling it under tarps. Ropey said he'd ask for more time.

4.

After lunch we headed back up to no. 7 to resume our cycle of humping and shuttling. Dark clouds were closing in from the northwest, and we picked up a Forest Service weather forecast on one of the radios; it guaranteed rain.

With the sun gone it was much cooler in The Burn, and spirits were relatively high as we picked up the last of the cargo at no. 7. The canteens were full of boiled water—warm, but doctored with instant lemonade mix—and new blisters had been padded with Band-Aids. But the mood was fragile, easily undermined by the staggering heap of gear spilling into the brush at no. 6. The final leg into camp was long, hilly, and teeming with hostile insects. By the time everyone made two circuits, we were back on auto-pilot, re-immersed in misery.

It began to drizzle, and it felt good at first—a soothing, bug-banishing shower. But then the breeze picked up, throwing cold rain at us, and whenever I stopped to rest I started shivering. It was a typical northeastern Minnesota experience: wet and frying for half a day, then wet and freezing for the other half.

We'd all made about five runs to and from no. 6, when it began to pour. Parts of the trail were churned to mud, and it was all slick. Most of the afternoon was gone, so we huddled under the tarp back in camp and watched Tommy finish cooking a batch of pork chops and potatoes. All except Ropey. Once no. 7 was carried off, he'd disappeared into the jungle with his compass, scouting out a trail to no. 10 and no. 11. He'd been gone for hours, and some of the crew were irritated that he wasn't humping cargo with the rest of us.

After supper the rain eased up, and Dave and I tried to fire up the men for a final assault on no. 6. There were thirteen packs left to haul in, and it would be a psychological boost if we could say that it was done. But the guys were wasted. On average, each man had hiked nearly twenty miles since morning, and moved about 1,000 pounds of goods—over wicked, chastising terrain. Tomorrow would be more of the same, and the Friday deadline was history.

Finally, Dave, Steve, and I made one more run out to no. 6. Dave was apparently indestructible. This was his fifth day of hellacious struggle, and despite his abused feet, he appeared as fit as we were.

By the time we'd made one haul, it was getting dark. The overcast was low and misting, and full night would arrive early. Steve and I were about to shove off for our tent when Ropey finally returned. He was carrying a load of hose and was soaked to the skin. He hovered over the fire, shivering violently.

"Damn hypothermia!" he spat. "That's all I need." He said he'd checked out no. 10 and no. 11, and a route from those caches back to camp. He confirmed that there was as much to haul as we had today, but over a greater distance. The gloomy silence was the sound of hearts sinking. Ropey looked sick. His skin was chalky, his eyes were drawn into his head. His teeth chattered as he spoke, and he was coughing. He needed food, and lots of rest. I assumed he had spare dry clothes.

Steve and I pushed our canoes into the lake and paddled back to the portage. We each had a load of hose. The breeze had freshened into a bona fide southeasterly wind, and we struggled through steel-gray whitecaps—torn black clouds just overhead.

Our tent had been damp in the morning, so we'd left the rain fly open to facilitate air circulation. It was a stupid, rookie-like mistake. We'd counted on sunshine all day, something we had no right to expect. There was a half-inch of water in the tent—a cold, ugly puddle. The bottoms of our sleeping bags were wet. It was a fitting conclusion to our first day on the Great Ramshead Hose Mission. Actually, we were too tired to be very upset. It was just pleasant to lie down—wet or dry.

Sometime during the night—in a steady rain—Chris paddled back up the Meander and slogged to the trailhead. His wife was supposed to meet him there with the results of his case before the Kentucky Supreme Court. We heard him pass our tent on his way over the portage, but we didn't hear him return. It was a black, chilly night, and I was amazed at his determination and stamina. He had only the flimsiest of raingear, and he was probably soaked within ten minutes of setting out.

5.

By morning the rain stopped, but the overcast was still low, and the forest was dripping. Down at the lakeshore we saw that Neil's canoe was gone. We both got into mine, paddled over to the base camp, and found the Alumacraft there. Over breakfast we learned that Chris had used it to get back to camp. His trip to the trailhead had been a disaster. At one point he'd fallen out of the canoe while trying to negotiate a deadfall, and he'd arrived too late to meet his wife. On the way back downriver he'd tried to rest by crawling under the canoe and lying on the soggy ground. He'd gotten back to camp just before daybreak, and was still "crashed out" in one of the tents. He hoped to hear his news via radio sometime during the day, but in the meantime he was completely exhausted, and useless as a cargo hauler. Ropey was irritated. In effect, Chris was a casualty; just when all hands were needed most.

Nevertheless, it was another slow morning. By the time we hit the trail it was after 8:00 a.m. and Ropey was fantasizing about working until long after sunset—another "night mission" as he put it. Nobody was listening. The allusions to combat were wearing thin, and if everyone could just put out normal effort for the whole day, it would probably be all we could handle.

We loaded up all the empty packs and hiked out to no. 7. By then, any dry socks were clammy, any blisters numbed. We took a short break and Ropey used his map and compass to establish a bearing. He'd been to no. 10 and no. 11 only several hours before, but it was confusing territory and utterly wild. It would be easy to get lost, and we could waste a lot of precious time stumbling around in circles.

"This way," he said, pointing, and we confidently struck off, our route confirmed by an occasional blaze mark made by the firefighters.

But an hour later we were lost. The blazes petered out and somewhere we took a wrong turn. Ropey made several map checks and course corrections, but we were wandering. The brush was thick, the going tough, and we didn't even have any cargo to justify it. Tempers began to smolder.

Finally we broke out of the woods onto a wide outcrop of ledgerock. There was a vertical drop to a small clearing, twenty feet below.

"Shit!" said Rich. "That's no. 8!"

Dave agreed. It was a cache they'd worked two days before, and we were completely across The Burn from no. 10 and no. 11. We'd gone in the opposite direction, and were well over a mile from our destination. The whole crew broke into loud complaints spiced with bitter obscenities. For a moment it sounded like we were going to have a mutiny.

Ropey was crestfallen, as disgusted as the rest. He could see now where we'd gone astray. It had been a simple, but costly mistake—a crucial little zig instead of a crucial little zag. We hurried back through the woods, retracing part of our earlier course. In less than an hour we were standing next to a large pile of watermelons at no. 10, and we were almost glad to see it. (No. 11 was just down the hill—only a few hundred yards away.) But it was after 10:00 a.m.—we'd lost over two hours.

We started packing up the hose immediately, and Ropey said we'd follow the edge of The Burn back to camp. It would be a two-mile haul—one way. The crew rebelled. No. 10 had to be only a half-mile from the lakeshore. Why not blaze a trail directly to the water? We could make another stockpile wherever we came out on the shore. Picking it up later, via canoe, would be the easiest part of the job.

Ropey resisted. It would take too long to scout a new trail, he argued, and require too much work to blaze it and clear obstructions. He was adamant about the longer route being shorter in the long run, or something to that effect.

But in the meantime Dave had broken out a map and a compass. Due to his unassuming toughness, he possessed a high level of natural authority. He didn't say much, especially out on the trail, so when he talked, we listened.

He pointed to the southeast and said, "The lake is that way, and that's where I'm going." He hoisted a pack, picked up a Pulaski, and cut into the woods. Steve and I were right behind. There were grunts and nods of approval, and the rest joined us. Ropey had no choice but to heft a load and follow.

We tried to strike a compromise between a straight line and the path of least resistance, hacking at brush and tree limbs only where absolutely necessary. Most obstructions could be pushed aside, stepped over, or broken with bare hands. We made rapid progress for about a hundred yards, and then we came upon a huge white spruce deadfall, a tangled, impenetrable barrier. It would've taken us a half-hour to clear the way with Pulaskis.

"See!" called Ropey from the rear. "It'll be shit like that all the way down to the lake."

But Dave had already started to circle around it, and we marched on, undeterred. What we couldn't breach, we'd skirt.

"Anything's better than two miles in The Burn," said Rich.

"Damn right!" came a chorus of assent.

After a quarter-mile or so we dropped our packs. It was decided that Dave, Steve, and Ropey would move ahead—scouting, blazing, and clearing. The rest of us would transfer no. 10 to this drop-off. By then, our point men should have a trail to the lake, and we could start the next leg of the shuttle.

Ropey radioed back to camp and told Tommy to take a canoe and the shotgun, and paddle north up the lakeshore. He was to go about a quarter-mile from camp, determine a decent landing spot, and then fire a couple of shots. Between that and the compass, we should be able to find a convenient place to punch out of the brush. We hoped we were already halfway there.

Joe, Rod, Rich, Buck, and I returned to no. 10 and started hauling. The overcast was breaking up and patches of blue were visible through the trees. We were sorry to see it. It was going to be a scorcher. The morning had been cool, the bugs more or less dormant. But now a loathesome, buzzing/humming was rising out of the foliage. We were meat on the hoof—radiating seductive, full-blooded body heat. By 1:00 p.m. the sun was blazing at its zenith, and the thirsty hordes were diving at our faces.

Ropey briefly appeared on the trail. "I got bad news, man," he said.

My first thought was that the Forest Service had canceled the contract, "What's the deal?"

Ropey shook his head and sighed. "I just talked to the damn Forest Service. They said we can use the team of horses, but we can't bring a wagon in—it's the wheels, man, they'll make ruts."

I had to laugh. At least the Forest Service was being consistent about its goal of keeping the Boundary Waters a primitive area. "We could fix the ruts," I said. Ropey shrugged and moved on to tell the others. That mile plus portage was going to be a nightmare.

6.

It's exquisite torture to be driven and slaving in the heat. The worst part is being in control. I wasn't lashed onward by an external, corporeal taskmaster, but by my own mind. Out of pride, loyalty, and financial need, I was forcing myself to carry load after miserable load, stumbling along a partially marked, partially cleared "trail" that was barely sufficient for a rabbit.

The afternoon turned muggy, with the temperature at ninety degrees, and the heat seemed to be steaming my blood, causing my brain to swell against the inside of my skull. As usual, water was in short supply, and it required a fierce, angry self-control to take only a sip from the canteen. I felt prickly and shriveled from the inside out, and weary to the core of every abused muscle.

I slipped into a defensive, time-eating mode, a detached awareness that keeps the physical at a distance. It's part mind-game, part chemistry, and I used poetry as my pain-killing mantra. Unfortunately, Kipling came aboard, and I had an unpleasant daydream about "chawin' up the ground" with Gunga Din. You have to be careful what you memorize. For what seemed like an entire hour I could hear the lines in my head:

> You may talk o' gin and beer
> When you're quartered safe out 'ere,
> An' you're sent to penny-fights an' Aldershot it;
> But when it comes to slaughter
> You will do your work on water,
> An' you'll lick the bloomin' boots of 'im that's got it!

Our work was slaughter all right—a collective self-assasination of feet, knees, and lower backs. You dared not stop to consider that you were damaging yourself for the sake of six miles of canvas hose—it was too ludicrous, too bizarre. I focused on the "hundred dollars a day (and all you can eat)." It sounded substantial. There was an air of frontier romance about it—a free-wheeling, free enterprise bounty for rough-'n'-ready exploits. I was a hired gun: "Have canoe; will travel." I reminded myself of the Voyageur motif, about the mystique of *cargo*. I realized that I'd feel much better if I was portaging a bale of beaver pelts. But, fire hose! That's the twentieth century for you. We were toiling to rescue and preserve something we couldn't eat, wear, or use for fuel. Somewhere between my fifth or sixth trip from no. 10, I was briefly convinced that the most righteous course would be to let the fungus eat the damn hose—from coupling to shining coupling.

As we started the next leg of the shuttle, we heard three gun-shots. They sounded close, but the new trail went on for a quarter-mile then ended. Steve met us in a thick stand of young balsams and told us we should start another stockpile. They hadn't found the lake yet. Ropey had taken off ahead and disappeared while Steve and Dave were busy making the trail passable. They'd heard him shouting, but they couldn't find him. Steve figured it was at least another half-mile to the lake, if not more, and there was some wicked terrain.

"Still better than The Burn," said Rich, but his voice carried an edge of exasperation. If this trail got much longer, it would be only a marginal improvement.

We worked until mid-afternoon, transferring most of no. 10 to the next drop-off point. We'd yet to touch no. 11, but our canteens were dry, and we needed food. There were only four of us left who were actually hauling cargo. Joe had joined the trail crew.

There was a path blazed out of the balsam thicket, and we could hear hard chopping off toward the lake. So Rich, Rod, Buck, and I each hoisted a pack and set off toward the noise. Surely they'd found Ramshead by now.

A hundred yards down the trail Steve had just finished build-ing a "bridge." He'd dropped an eight-inch balsam across a deep mudhole, then lopped off its limbs. At the center he'd stuck an aspen pole into the quagmire. The stick could be grasped and used to steady yourself. With a pack on your back, the tapering balsam trunk was like a wobbly tightrope, and the pole was a welcome handrail. The mud, said Steve, was waist-deep.

We moved on for a half-mile, following a crooked, rocky trail through dense forest. Dave had routed it around a high ridge that reared out of a swamp, choosing to go north toward a creek that flowed into Ramshead. We found him blazing trees on the flank of the ridge, and he said that Joe was up ahead, pushing for the lake. Ropey was gone—apparently back in camp after hitching a canoe ride with Tommy. It seemed he'd been summoned by a Forest Service Ranger who was waiting at our base.

Steve and I skirted the ridge, dropped back into an ash swamp, and caught up with Joe. He hadn't reached the lake yet. He'd heard Ropey yell from the shore, but Ropey hadn't blazed a path; he'd left us all behind. Joe had spent the last half-hour trying to pick up Ropey's trail. He and Steve were furious. I dropped my pack and sat on it. Was Ropey punishing us for overruling his desire to hump through The Burn?

The rest of the crew caught up. Rich was livid. "That son-of-a-bitch!" he thundered. Only hours before, when Ropey first got the call from the Ranger, he'd said, "Let him wait. I don't desert my team, man."

We stewed for a while, donating hot blood to the mosquitoes, and then regrouped for a final drive to the lake. Joe found an old beaver dam that spanned the worst part of the ash swamp. It was breached in a couple spots, but we could easily step over the rushing water, and the top of the dam was firm—transformed into solid ground after decades of weathering.

From there it was up a small ridge and down a steep, stony grade to the shore of Ramshead. At the first sparkle of blue between pine trunks, Joe let out a joyous whoop, and we stumbled happily to the water's edge.

I figured that from no. 10 down to the lake was just over a mile-and-a-half via our rude trail. Ropey probably felt vindicated, but I turned to Rich and executed an orchestra conductor's flourish. He instantly picked up his cue:

"It's still better than the damn Burn!" There was an off key chorus of assent.

Tommy paddled up a few minutes after we emerged from the woods. Ropey had sent him back with a pot of coffee and eight Polish sausages. He wanted us to eat lunch on the shore and then return to the caches.

"Bullshit!" said Dave. "He sends us one sausage apiece and no canteen, and we're supposed to go back up to 11?" He shook his head, sincerely astonished. Tommy looked a little embarrassed to have delivered such a message.

We devoured the Polish and then Rich, Buck, and Joe got into the canoe and went back to camp to fetch another. They set Tommy to work on a decent meal, and soon we were all lying in the shade under the tarp, stuffed.

The anger toward Ropey had largely dissipated. First there was the food, water, and rest, and then his two pieces of good news: the Forest Service had granted a two-day extension, and Chris had returned to civilization to round up more grunts. Joints were lit, and a sense of well-being and good humor settled over the camp.

The benevolent vibrations reminded Ropey of his one experience with native, hallucinogenic mushrooms. I guess it was by way of contrast. He said he was working as temporary labor on a Forest Service trail crew when he came upon some Angel of Death mushrooms poking out of the forest floor. He ate three of them. There was quite a rush, he said, and then the agony set in. By means of an excruciating crawl through the brush—highlighted by violent vomiting and gut-ripping cramps, he managed to reach a road before he slipped into a coma. A passing motorist retrieved him, and at the local hospital they pumped him full of adrenaline and wrote him off as dead. Nevertheless, he came to; weak, but ravenously hungry.

As we snorted in mild wonder, Ropey took a long drag on a joint. In a tight, squeaky, marijuana-voice, he summed it all up: "Bad scene, man. Bad scene."

And then, as if part of the program, the walkie-talkie crackled, squawked, and came to life. A hard voice—a male baritone reeking of authority, barked: "Ely Police Department calling Ramshead."

The camp froze. Forks halted in mid-air, lungs stopped in mid-drag, and every pair of eyes darted from face to face. The common thought was obvious: who among this bunch of wild asses, derelicts, and jail-food connoisseurs, was the Ely P.D. after? It was one of those rare moments when nine people are thinking exactly the same thing, and all instantly know that all of them know. There was a moment of dead silence, and then we all broke up—raucously hooting at the irony of our communal self-knowledge. But Ely P.D. merely relayed a personal message for Chris.

That reminded Ropey: "Oh yeah. Chris heard that he lost the court case."

Chris had told all of us about it in detail, and was obviously proud that the case had gained front page newspaper coverage. He'd had no doubt that the judgement would be in his favor. Ropey said Chris was "pretty bummed."

An argument ensued.

"It's a shame he lost, but I hope he doesn't spend a lot of time crying about it."

"Hey, give him a break; we're talking about the custody of his kid."

"Well, there's no sense worrying about something you can't do anything about, and he shouldn't let it take away from this operation."

"He's been working hard."

"Yeah, when he's been here."

Chris' ill-considered venture back upriver the night before, and his subsequent incapacitation in the morning, had aroused some bitterness. He was missing a grueling stretch of work, and shared suffering was the bond that held this gang together. No matter that he had personal problems, or that he was now off for reinforcements; the focus of the job had shifted. The hose had become an abstraction; we would be paid not for cargo delivered, but for pain endured. The quality of mercy had been strained. The crew was no longer fulfilling a commercial contract, they were satisfying the demands of Purgatory. The efforts of body and soul were concentrated on survival and personal redemption, and you couldn't be credited with full survivor status if you weren't around to garner the full measure of misery. Chris would have to reestablish himself, perform some sort of penance to retain his original niche on the crew. For instance, he should've hauled in the rest of no. 6 before he left.

It was late afternoon when we all headed back into the bush. Ropey was rattling on about the fresh crew we'd have the next day and how he didn't want them to "get the glory" of hauling in no. 11, the last of the caches. He tried to psyche us up, but he also had some penance to do, and he knew it. He made sure that as we finished off no. 10, he always grabbed the heaviest-looking load.

It was a little cooler, and though the bugs were still vicious, we moved a lot of cargo. We transferred all of no. 10, plus the last of the stockpile at the first drop-off point, down to the lake, and we put a significant hole in the mound at the second drop-off. For the sake of "glory," Ropey led one assault on no. 11, picking up a pump and some heavy packs, and running them all the way to the water.

By sundown, we figured there was one morning's worth of cache-hauling left. A half-dozen guys could finish no. 11 the next day. The crew was beat, and there would be no "night mission." The trail was enough of a challenge in daylight.

Steve and I paddled back to our tent, too tired to wait for a late supper. Tommy had been hauling cargo, and there was nothing ready to eat. Out on the lake, we met Chris and seven new recruits coming in. There were two older men and five teenagers. Nobody looked especially eager, but they were alive and able-bodied, and probably deceived about the nature of the outing. Ignorance is indeed bliss—at least in the short run.

7.

The sky was clear in the morning, and by 7:00 a.m. the sun was already hot. The Forest Service forecast promised sunny, dry weather for the next few days, and that was a mixed blessing. The hose wouldn't be getting wet, and that would keep it relatively light and manageable. Wet hose can easily weigh twice as much as dry stuff. On the other hand, tiny Meander Creek was sensitive to short term weather. A dry spell of even two or three days would drop the water level significantly, and it was already a mess. We were grateful for the precipitation and consequent runoff that we'd had on Wednesday night.

There were sixteen guys in camp and an air of anticipation. Maybe we finally had this job by the throat. We enjoyed a lot of good-natured banter over breakfast. Three of the teenagers were hungover, and Chris was accused of a shanghai operation at an Ely tavern. The boys didn't look happy, and were sobering up rapidly as we discussed our plans for the day.

The priority item was no. 11. It would be the worst, the last of the gear to be humped out of the jungle.

"So who wants to go up there?" asked Ropey. "Who wants the glory?"

"Fuck the glory!"

"Yeah," said Ropey, "Yeah, but it's got to be done."

Silence.

"Dave?" Ropey arched an eyebrow and offered a tentative grin.

Dave actually turned his head away. I was surprised. He was the toughest nut in the bunch, always the first in line with a heavy pack. But of course this was his seventh hard day in the woods; he'd carried several tons for many rugged miles. He mumbled something, paused, and spoke aloud.

"I'll finish no. 6," he said.

"OK," replied Ropey.

There was another long, uncomfortable silence. It was too much.

"Tell you what, Ropey," I said. "You give me these five young bucks, and I'll go back up to no. 11."

"All right, man, all right!" His sense of relief, and that of the entire original crew, was palpable. It made the teenagers nervous.

Dave's demurral had inspired me. I was fresher, so why shouldn't I take on no. 11? It was partly a sense of duty, but mostly, I had to admit, I wanted "the glory." I had the highest respect for Dave, and even he wouldn't go up there. It was the average life's little chance for heroism. How often do you have the opportunity to make a dramatic, noble gesture—in public, before a group of your peers? I went for it.

The rest of the crew was divided between the canoes and the portage, and while we all got ready, Tommy said his goodbyes. He'd had enough fun. His prosthesis was a real trial in the woods, and a relative was paddling in to take him out. But he'd served us well, and before he left he gave Rich his boots to use for the rest of the job.

With two canoes—three of us in each—I led my skeptical young platoon over to the trail that snaked off to no. 11. On the way I assured them this would probably be the hardest work they'd have to perform on this job, and that we could finish it by noon. It was a mean haul, I said, but it was the last mean haul. Once everything was down to the lakeshore, drying in the sunshine, life would be easier.

We paddled up to the stockpile and pulled the canoes ashore. My recruits stared at the jumble of watermelons, pumps, and handtools, and their mood was not improved. That gear looked just as heavy and unwieldy as it indeed was.

We emptied enough packs to handle what cargo remained at no. 11, and then headed into the woods. I set a fast pace, anxious to see these guys strapped into loaded packs. I discovered that I took a perverse pride in showing them our wretched little trail. In a few months only an acute observer would be able to follow it, and by next summer it would've all but vanished. And I was glad of that; this was, after all, a wilderness area. But for now that trail was an achievement. We'd blazed a working path through trackless forest, and I understood the satisfaction of pioneers and frontiersmen. Once they had a trail (and mapped it), the land was truly open. Navigating and blazing, that was the hardest part. After that, civilization was inevitable—anyone could come.

We paused at the drop-off point in the balsam thicket and counted the packs on the ground. It would be two trips apiece from there to the lake. Everyone had broken a streaming sweat.

"This is ah . . . quite a trail," said one of the youngsters.

"We're about halfway there," I replied.

"It's not so bad," said another. His tone was timid, hopeful—as if he was lamely comforting a friend who was seriously injured.

"This'll be the last of it," I repeated.

After a swig from the canteens, we pushed on to no. 11. The cache was seventy yards out into a swamp, at the edge of a beaver pond. In wet weather the gear probably would've been underwater. As it was, the soup was only ankle-deep, and it felt good to cool our feet. We quietly packed up the watermelons and miscellaneous tools, and ended up with one load per man.

We humped them all the way down to Ramshead, and then started shuttling the gear from the drop-off point. A couple of the recruits hefted two packs each, and I made some manly noises of approval and appreciation. It was great to have fresh meat on board, and I could see how encouraging it had been to the original crew when Steve and I arrived.

I didn't plan it that way, but shortly after noon I was the last man out of the woods, with the last load on my back. My feet hurt, my shoulders ached, and I was drenched with sweat and harried by insects, but I was incomparably happy.

It was the sensation of control—the awareness of personal power that infuses the spirit of a volunteer. I had freely chosen the difficult road, and, at least for a while, I could savor my mastery over it. Using Ropey's military motif, the whole job had been like a mission behind enemy lines. We'd been in hostile territory, forced to play by rules that were slanted against us. The brutal trails and intimidating tons of cargo (not to mention the bugs and the heat) had been tangible, merciless adversaries capable of inflicting genuine pain, injury, and defeat. They were personal enemies—we'd named them, cursed them, and now beaten them. Through bitter, wrenching acts of naked will, we'd "destroyed" cache after cache, stronghold after stronghold.

And on the final run from no. 11 I felt like a champion, like a knight in muddy, bloody armor. I was thriving in the midst of opposition and hostility, brazenly striding across the domain of potent antagonists. I was glad to be there.

But if feelings like that lasted, I guess we would self-destruct out of sheer audacity, burned up by our own furious energy. Triumph is a dangerous drug. Its heady secretions easily stimulate overconfidence and hubris that can lead to disaster. But on the shore of Ramshead there was no chance of an overdose. First, I reminded myself, there was a lot of work left, and second, when I got down to the stockpile I found that three of the five recruits had already had enough. They'd finish out the day, they said, but then they were going home. So much for fresh troops.

Actually, they didn't say it—not to me. The information was quietly relayed by one of the kids who was staying. He waited until we were back in the canoes and had established some discreet distance from the rest. It's interesting how we all pick up the techniques of saving face, or allowing others to save face. And I did the same; I never acknowledged to the three that I was aware they were quitting.

The whole crew had assembled back at camp for lunch, and as we paddled up I could see Ropey squatting by the fire.

"Hey, Rope!" I yelled. "I got the glory! I got the glory!"

He laughed. "You earned it, man."

And that was my benediction—the sword touched to each shoulder. I'd been christened with the approval of "my leader." The camp laughed; I laughed; but yes, I *had* earned it. I would accept my $100 a day (as little as it seemed now for the effort required), but this was the reward I'd really been seeking.

8.

After lunch we got all six of our canoes on the water, and started hauling our camp stockpile, and the stuff from no. 10 and no. 11, over to the 100-rod portage out of Ramshead. Compared to backpacking, this water work was a delight. With every canoe filled, we could move about seventy watermelons at a time. In a mere three hours we had all the gear it had taken four days to pull out of the woods stacked in one huge heap at the start of the portage. Everyone was amazed at how rapidly it was accomplished.

But there should've been one more canoe. The first thing in the morning Steve and I had looked for Neil's Alumacraft at the base camp. It was missing for a second time, and we assumed Chris had it back upriver. He'd gone out again; this time for more provisions to feed the expanded crew. It was irritating, but we figured we could catch up with it later. We had to leave the job that evening, and if nothing else, we could pick it up on the way out.

In the meantime, we had fifteen people on the portage, all moving cargo. Despite blistering heat, the first couple of hours were spirited and bustling. Doing some rough calculations, I estimated we were transporting 2,000 pounds per hour. The mound on the bank of Meander—the threshold of the home stretch—grew quickly.

The original crew was fired up. After a long, terrible week, they could finally see the beginning of the end. Joe's ankle felt better, and he was almost trotting over the 100 rods. Rich, tortured feet and all, seemed to have found his second (or third) wind. Tommy's boots also helped, though an hour or so after we began the portage, I saw him limping. He abruptly sat down by the side of the trail, and removed the right boot.

"What's the matter? I asked. "You should be feeling good with a decent pair of boots."

"Shit!" he replied. "The one that Tommy wears on his fake foot and leg has never been broken in. It's as stiff as that damn prosthesis! Hell on my blisters."

As I passed him he was violently folding and twisting the boot, trying to work some life into it. Here's a bit of arcana, I thought. Remember: Beware the boots of a one-legged man. If I ever write a book about wilderness survival, I'll work that into a footnote about footgear.

We carried on, but by late afternoon, even the young bucks had slowed down, and it was a struggle to get the last of the cargo from the lake to the creek. Ropey looked particularly worn. It took him nearly a half hour to portage one of the canoes, and he had to drop it twice. He was ashen-faced and weak, and seemed to stagger a little as he walked. He was making only one haul to our three, and he felt bad. He overloaded a packboard to try to make it up, but that only punished him further.

"It's chemistry, man," he told me. "My chemistry is screwed up."

He got little sympathy from the crew. No one chided him openly, but guys were angry that he wasn't humping his share. And then he almost drove off all the new workers. Ropey had promised the fresh guys only seven dollars an hour. They knew the rest of us were in for $100 a day, and apparently they could live with that; we had seniority. But then Ropey either told one of them, or was overheard to remark to someone else, that he'd pay them only $100 apiece for the whole time they were on the job. Word spread quickly, and the new recruits turned bitter. They complained to Dave and Joe, threatening to leave the crew. With Steve and I having to pull out that evening, only the original six would remain, and they'd never make the new deadline.

Dave was angry. "It's $100 a day for *everyone*," he stated. "I don't care what Ropey says; if you stay, that's what you'll make. Period." Joe and Rich backed him up, and that mollified the crew. Besides, Ropey had no bargaining position. He had the most to lose if the job didn't get done. Along with the two-day extension, he'd received a new set of ground rules. If the new deadline was missed, Ropey would be fined $3,000, and be denied any compensation whatsoever. The recruits would lose a day's wages; Ropey would lose his ass. Dave and the rest had invested too much sweat to allow that to happen.

The camp on Ramshead had been taken down, and it was decided to establish a final base on the mile plus portage at the start of Meander Creek. Steve and I loaded up my canoe with camp gear; Rich and Dave filled another, and we headed upriver to find a site. The rest of the crew would follow later, bringing up the first load of cargo.

We were almost to the first beaver dam when we met Chris.

He was paddling one canoe, and towing another loaded with fresh food. Neither boat was Neil's Alumacraft. He passed us each an orange as we told him of the new plan. He was pleasantly surprised at the progress that'd been made, and gladly turned back upriver. Steve asked him if Neil's canoe was up there. Chris said it was.

With two of us in a loaded canoe, we got hung up on deadfalls in four spots, but we found that the large beaver dam which was holding back most of the creek wasn't as formidable an obstacle as I'd feared. The downstream side had a long, sloping "ramp" on the left. A trickle of water flowed down it, like an automatic lubrication system, and the muddy sticks were conveniently slippery. Steve and I hopped out and dragged the canoe to the top of the dam with surprisingly little effort. After that, we were in the wider, deeper length of the creek, and it was a joyride to the start of the portage.

There was a canoe stashed there, but it wasn't Neil's either. So while I stayed to help Rich and Dave haul the camp gear up to a wide spot in the trail, Steve portaged our personal pack to the truck. We assumed Neil's canoe was up there.

We were just starting to set up camp when I saw Steve striding back down the trail. His face was red and tight with rage.

"It's not up there!" he said darkly. "Neil's canoe is gone."

Damn! In a moment the whole aspect of the day was transformed. Steve and I had been satisfied. We'd put in our promised three days, and earned the respect of the crew. The job would be finished, and we would be paid. And of course we were happy to be heading for home.

But not without Neil's canoe. My stomach turned over. How in the hell do you lose a canoe? That would be the legitimate taunt. And it wasn't even our own property; Neil had been paddling that canoe since he was a kid. I felt ill.

However, neither Steve nor I had lost the Alumacraft. It was immediately obvious to all present that Chris had used the canoe at least once, and that Steve hadn't had actual possession of the boat for almost forty-eight hours.

"We came in with two canoes," said Steve, "and we'll leave with two canoes." He was smoldering. He stalked off toward the creek.

Chris had arrived at the portage, and I asked him when he'd

last seen the canoe. He immediately bristled. "Are you accusing me of something?"

No, no, I hastened to clarify. I just wanted to sit down and try to figure out what happened, try to trace the journeys the canoe had made without us. Who would want to steal a canoe? Especially with all the effort it involved to get it out of the bush—everyone had had more than enough weight to haul around, and paddle around. As we discussed the matter I realized that one of my paddles was also missing—a brand new one as it happened.

It was sad, because even the hint of trouble had instantly soured the atmosphere of camaraderie. We were all inadvertently reminded that Steve and I were, after all, outsiders. At root, this had been a commercial arrangement, a business relationship. My disappointment and Steve's anger had contaminated the atmosphere of good feeling.

In a moment the situation looked very bad, potentially explosive. Steve came stiffly up the trail, carrying one of the canoes that Ropey had rented from an outfitter in Ely.

Rich looked at me. "Is he going to steal that canoe?" I couldn't read his voice. It was unnaturally flat, as if Rich were being too deliberately calm. Was there a background of menace to his tone? As I had seen, these were some pretty tough guys. Before I could reply, Rich said to Steve, "You steal that canoe, and you're in deep shit, man." It wasn't a personal threat. Now I could hear the resignation. Rich wouldn't fight him for it—he wouldn't hassle a man who'd paid his dues like Steve had. But the crew wouldn't pick up the cost of a canoe either, and they'd have to report the theft to the police—as repugnant as that might be.

Steve had stopped in front of us. Dave and Chris were staring at him, genuinely sorry, I think, that this had happened.

"You can't take that canoe, Steve," I said, trying to keep my voice even, but supportive.

"I know," he replied, and his fierceness dissipated. He shoved the prow into a tree. I heaved a sigh of relief, and we all started to talk about it. Where was the canoe? It was conceivable that it had drifted away from the base camp during the night, but it didn't seem likely. Besides, Ramshead wasn't that big, and we'd probably have seen it.

Dave had one of the radios, and he called back to Ropey downriver. Would they double check to see if the Alumacraft was down there? It wasn't. But we'd been sure of that anyway. We hadn't seen it since the day before. Apparently no one knew where it was. We hashed over every possibility and came up with nothing. There didn't seem to be anything else to do for the moment.

I shook hands all around—firmly, warmly—trying to rekindle the comradeship. "It was good working with you guys," I said; and it had been. But it was over. I realized that only in the heat of the struggle, only in the very midst of the shared pain and laughter, was our sense of alliance and fellowship a living, affecting force. We'd been buddies for only a while, and I'd probably never see these people again.

I hefted my canoe and moved slowly up the trail toward the truck. Already I could see a dozen wood ticks crawling up my jeans. I waited until I was seated comfortably in the cab of the pickup, and then I plucked them off my legs and killed them one by one.

9.

The next day I called the Forest Service, explained the situation, and asked if they'd keep an eye out for a stray canoe in the Ramshead area. They called back the day after. Yes, they'd seen the Alumacraft. It was sitting at the mouth of Meander Creek, tucked back into a small bay on Ramshead Lake. It was pulled up on the bank, and I couldn't imagine how it got there, or who had taken it. In any case, the Forest Service said they'd notified Ropey, and he'd haul the canoe out and take it to Ely. We could pick it up there later. Fine.

Three days later Ropey called from Ely and said: "Hey, man, we found the canoe." He told me he'd found it at the mouth of Meander creek and that it was still there.

"The Forest Service told me you were bringing it out," I said.

"Oh no, man, we couldn't. We were truckin' cargo."

I said I understood, and Ropey offered to go back in and pick it up—"to tie up any loose ends on the job."

But I said, no, Steve and I would make a quick trip into Ramshead and retrieve it. Ropey sounded relieved.

"You know," he said, "the damn Forest Service took that canoe. They're the ones who left it there."

The next morning Steve and I portaged down to the Meander just after daybreak. We slipped my canoe into the creek and eased quietly downstream. Around the first bend we flushed two American bitterns out of the reeds. We were only a few yards from them when the huge birds shot straight up for four or five feet, and then flew laboriously away, looking like chopped-off herons. It was the first loudness of the morning, a startling ambush of sound.

Well-camouflaged and shy, bitterns are an uncommon sight, and I felt privileged. I was now also fully alert. But I was still surprised when we swung around the next bend and almost collided with a bull moose. The creek was only twenty feet wide, and the moose was standing in it, so we were basically prow to snout with the huge beast, less than ten feet away.

For an instant we froze, and he froze, and I saw that just fifty feet beyond the moose was a whitetail deer, which was also tensed and still. A photographer could've caught them both in the same frame. The deer, it's sleek, reddish coat seeming to effervesce in the dawn light, was just to the left and a little above the moose, standing in the tall grass on the bank. Their heads were both turned at the same angle, looking at us.

And then with a flurry of muddy splashing, the moose lumbered out of the creek and trotted off into the alderbrush. The deer leaped around and bolted into the trees. In less than fifteen seconds Steve and I were alone on the river, grinning at each other. It was morning rush hour on the Meander.

It hadn't rained for a week, and below the big beaver dam the creek had dropped to almost nothing. It was a lucky thing Ropey and Company had been able to come out when they did. Loaded canoes would've been dragging bottom for long stretches.

By 8:30 a.m. we'd portaged into Ramshead and paddled over to the mouth of the creek. Neil's canoe was there, sitting upright on the bank, completely out of the water. We expected to find paddles with it—perhaps my new one that was missing—but there were none. That was odd. Whoever had paddled the Alumacraft to that spot had taken the paddle(s) with them when they left.

Had a thief cached the canoe, intending to pick it up later? Had someone taken it there for some legitimate purpose and then forgotten it? Had it indeed drifted away, been found, and then left for the owner to recover? Had the Forest Service used it for some reason, as Ropey suggested? None of the above seemed particularly likely, and I guess we'll never know for sure.

We didn't ponder long. The heat was rising, and the bugs had found us. Steve launched the Alumacraft and we paddled out of Ramshead. Sometime, he said, he'd like to return to do some fishing.

No Stopping

It's good to begin a trek in the rain. It toughens the mind and ensures watertight packing. If you grow acclimated to foul weather by noon of the first day, there's little more to fear from the sky.

It didn't take us till noon. My friends Neil and John and I slipped our three canoes into the Little Fork River at 9:00 a.m., and by 10:00 a.m. the cold drizzle had tested our packs and our spirits and found them secured. It would've required exceptionally vile weather to dampen more than our raingear. We were psyched up, anxiously facing the length of the Little Fork. We'd charted a journey of 116 river-miles, and our map showed eighteen stretches of rapids. However, a disclaimer on the back of the map read: "Beware of hazards that may have been omitted . . ." There was probably a lot more whitewater than indicated, and much depended upon the water level. As the map also noted: "High water may cover up a Class I pitch entirely, but make another pitch much more difficult—changing a Class II to a Class IV, for example."

About these classes. The International Scale of River Difficulty consists of six general categories of whitewater, from Class I—"Easy. Small waves, few obstructions," to Class VI— "Great risk to life" (or in less polite language, suicidal). Niagara Falls, for instance, is a Class VI. Most of the recorded rapids on the

59

Little Fork are Class II—"Waves up to three feet. Some maneuvering required." But it's a subjective determination. One canoeist's II might be somebody else's III, which is considered to be the limit "for an experienced paddler in an open canoe." (Classes IV and V are treacherous runs—for decked canoes and kayaks only.)

Aside from a place called Hannine Falls, which was labeled Class VI, we intended to shoot every rapids. The main thing was, no matter what the official rating of a given rapids, they all had to be treated with respect. The river would lead us through long stretches of wild country where help would be far away. In the case of a serious misadventure, far enough away to be irrelevant.

The Little Fork begins in Lost Lake Swamp, just south of Lake Vermilion in northeastern Minnesota. (About twenty-five miles northeast of Side Lake.) From where it meanders out of marshland and bog and becomes a navigable stream—just west of the small town of Cook—to where it flows into the Rainy River on the Ontario border, is about 145 river-miles. Sixty miles as the raven flies. Its course takes it on a wide arc to the northwest, through the Koochiching State Forest and the Nett Lake Indian Reservation. It drains 1,850 square miles, and drops 225 feet from Cook to the mouth.

It's a dark river. Widespread clay deposits keep the water cloudy with fine suspended solids. When it's churned up at the rapids, the river looks like a great surge of foaming root beer. Its width varies from fifty to two hundred feet, and in the old days, when the water was high in the spring, it was used for log drives. The Department of Natural Resources says that "the last major drive in the region" was on the Little Fork in 1937. But I know an oldtimer who says he was on the last one, and it was in 1933. Maybe they're quibbling over the word "major." The oldtimer says that sometimes it'd take them an entire week to squeeze their raft of logs around a single sharp bend. That would be one way to get intimate with the river. In any case, the Little Fork isn't a logging tool anymore. There are enough roads now, and certainly enough trucks.

We got to know the river quickly. Aside from an occasional farm—usually gone to seed—and an even more occasional bridge, the Little Fork flowed through thick forest. For the entire 116 miles we likely wouldn't see one other boat or canoe on the river.

And this in mid-June. We had it to ourselves, and almost immediately we encountered a couple of stretches of Class I rapids that weren't on the map.

You'll hear it from whitewater runners—"I feel so *alive* in the rapids." They experience an amplification of reality, an attuned and altered state of mind. There's a sense of renewal and stalwart invigoration. Part of it is the adrenaline. While one level of your brain treats whitewater as "recreation," there are other neural circuits that shall always consider the approach of rapids as an emergency. They and the adrenal glands aren't fooled by conscious rationalizations about fun and sport. Hormones aren't ambivalent about jeopardy. So you get an automatic dose of chemicals that prolongs natural reactions such as increased heart rate and blood pressure, and there's nothing livelier and more vital than a briskly thumping heart.

But there's more to the altered state than the influence of wise chemicals. There's also a calculated, deliberate alertness. More than usual, you're paying attention. You must *concentrate*, intently focusing on the hazardous obstacle course and mapping a route through it. Amid the sparkling turmoil you have to pick out rocks and ledges—above water and below. You must estimate the height of waves and determine the strength of flows, eddies, and backrollers. It's a dynamic, quickening vigilence, and it's required for survival. Hormones can make you excited, swift, and strong, but they don't ensure that you'll make the right moves. Only tense concentration can do that. And curiously, though it's part of the aliveness, it's not automatic. It's an acquired technique, like learning how to use a paddle. And even in the rapids your attention can slip.

One time up on the Sturgeon, a tributary of the Little Fork, we were running a rocky stretch of complicated Class II. A lot of maneuvering was required, and there were some brawny waves, but even so I had a lapse of concentration. As I steered around a rough, white bend, I caught sight of a bridge about 200 yards downstream. There were three or four people standing on it, fishing. For just a moment I was distracted, idly wondering if I recognized any of them. I never saw the rock that got me. It was large, just below the surface, and the canoe heaved up onto it. The current spun the boat around and flipped it into the waves. I swam—that is, bobbed, bounced, and ricocheted—the rest of the way. I was bruised, ego included, but not seriously. I lucked out. The canoe could've been severely damaged, but wasn't. It was an effective remedial course on the value of alertness and aliveness in whitewater. "Swimming" rapids is conducive to a perky presence of mind.

And these first stretches of Class I perked us up. They were simple, float-through runs, but they inspired an edgy expectation that would help prepare us for the wilder water to come. We laughed and hooted with the simple pleasure of paddling down through waves, but it was also an opportunity to adjust the eyes for deciphering the codes of swift water. I don't know about my buddies, but even these friendly Class Is primed the faithful adrenaline pump.

Just over an hour into the journey we came upon the first Class II, and all sensory systems went to full alert. At the top of the rapids was a narrow chute, a fifteen-foot gap in a mass of ledgerock. The river poured through and then dropped three or four feet in a short, steep slide. At the bottom it fanned back out to its full width (about fifty feet), leaping and roiling over a boulder bed. There were some two-foot waves in there, and the rapids made a quick bend to the left. The whole stretch was about seventy yards long. Below the chute and slide it didn't look too bad, but that narrow gap scared me; there was no room for error.

We each had an aluminum canoe, and they're not the best for whitewater running. There's no forgiveness in the metal keels and hulls. Even when merely grazing a rock, they tend to hang up, latching onto wet stone like leeches. Then they pivot in the flow and you're at the mercy of the current. And wild rivers aren't known for clemency.

I immediately looked around for a portage, but the woods along the banks were undisturbed. With only a few exceptions, there are no portages on the Little Fork. When you come to a rapids, you run it. Nevertheless, there's an old rule of thumb for whitewater paddlers: "Don't run anything you're not willing to swim." It's a pleasing aphorism—prudent and even a little poetic. But it's usually ignored. I wouldn't willingly "swim" anything but a low Class I on a very hot day. A "naked" ride through anything more can be painful and dangerous.

So when you hit Class II and above, you do little things to make yourself brave. I zipped my life jacket and made sure it was snug. I strapped my eyeglasses to my head with an elastic band. We had our packs lashed to the thwarts with bungee cords, and I checked to make sure mine were secure. I took a couple of deep breaths and told myself to concentrate—on Neil. Acknowledged as the best paddler, he was going first. John and I pulled over to the right bank, just out of reach of the current, and stood up in our canoes to watch.

It looked like most of the water was at the center of the gap, and Neil approached it with an air of authority. His bow was slightly up. All three of us prefer to run whitewater solo, using our packs as adjustable ballast. When entering rapids it's nice to have the bow high and out of the stream—you can take bigger waves without shipping a lot of water. So we had our cargo tied in aft. My pack was right in front of me as I sat in the stern. Neil's gear wasn't as far back, so his bow wasn't quite as high as it could've been. It might have made a difference when he rammed that boulder.

It was directly in front of the chute, and he didn't see it. Maybe it was a trick of lighting, or maybe he'd been focused too much on the slide beyond. It was a flat rock a few inches below the surface—a bona fide canoe trap. Neil ran aground with a sickening screech. We couldn't hear his words over the roar of rapids, but we could see his lips form something like "Oh, damn!" He was hung up near the bow. If you get caught at the stern where your weight is, there's a chance. It takes more force to spin you around, and you are often very stable while working yourself off the rock. But if you're caught at the bow, the water pushing from behind will whip the canoe around instantly, shoving it sideways and off balance into the flow. If the rock doesn't tip you, and if you're not firmly stuck, and if you've got room to maneuver, maybe you can pivot right off and spin the boat the rest of the way around and be on your way. Maybe.

But Neil never had a chance. Perhaps if he'd hit the rock farther back—even at the middle of his canoe—he could've pried himself out of the jam. As it was, the stern swung around fast and hard, and even if the rock had let go instantly, there was no room to turn. The canoe flipped and Neil went over the side. From our vantage point he just disappeared. We knew he got thrust through the gap and flushed down that slide. Bottom up, his canoe followed immediately. For a moment it appeared as if it was going to be wedged between the ledges and crushed, but then the current twisted it around and the boat rushed down the slide. It was half-full of water, weighing several hundred pounds. Was Neil under it?

But then Neil popped up. He was scrambling onto a rock at the base of the slide, with one hand on the gunwale of his canoe. He yanked the boat, gear and all, partway out of the water and the grasp of the strongest current. Then he turned to us, shrugged, and grinned sheepishly.

While Neil emptied his canoe and checked his gear, John and I found a route around the chute. It was too early in the trip to take on an obstacle that had nailed our best paddler. There was a shallow, narrow stream hugging the right bank—a rivulet really—and we half-paddled, half-dragged our canoes down it to the base of the ledgerock. We launched back into the main rapids just below Neil and dodged our way through the rest of the bouldery Class II.

Neil was soaked and had lost his head band, but the canoe and pack were undamaged. We had potential tragedy to laugh about around the campfire. It's a thin line between disaster and slapstick. I just hoped we kept toeing the right side of that line.

A few hours later we rounded a wide curve in the river and heard Hannine Falls. The ominous thundering was like a weight on my arms and paddle. When you're an actual part of the flow, the sound of a collapsing, plunging river slows you down instantly. Even when you're a half-mile away you catch yourself creeping. Somewhere ahead there's a point of no return. If you follow the current too near to the lip of the falls, it'll drag you over no matter how tenaciously you struggle. With a falls like Hannine, you'd have to approach awfully close to lose control, but you still think about it. Especially when you finally ease around the last bend and see the edge of the world.

The top of the falls was punctuated by black slabs of angular bedrock. Here and there a battered log was wedged into the outcrops, but for long stretches between these obstacles the rim of the falls was a smooth line of clear water—deceptively unruffled. The river just dropped away. The abyss opened suddenly and the careening water had no time to froth and foam. Far beyond the lip we could see the tops of trees—a canopy of aspen and Norway pine that seemed a long way below. Literal tons of water smashed into solid stone at the base of Hannine, and the shattered waves expelled a cloud of fine mist that rose into view over the top of the falls. If there'd been sunshine, the vapor would've been suffused with an earthbound rainbow, a swath of benign color to lure you to destruction.

But pulling aside to the left bank was no problem for us that day, and we lifted our canoes onto ledgerock right next to the falls. There was even a portage trail. Hannine is about a fifteen-foot drop, but it's not perpendicular. It's more of a precipitous slope, like a very steep stairway over and around large, jagged rocks. It's rated as Class VI, but the author of our map's commentary qualified that by saying it was "conceivably runnable at low water levels by an expert in a decked boat . . ." Neil was scandalized. "No way! No way!" he huffed. "It's a friggin' kamikaze run!" And that from a man who enjoys living on the edge—of everything. So we looked at the falls, judging the possibilities; or the impossibilities.

And I think we saw it. I mean we really *saw* this natural system called Hannine Falls. We were satisfied with it. There was nothing in our way—no signs, railings, guided tours, or postcards. There were no tourists from Illinois hanging around taking pictures. I thought of our stop at Niagara Falls the previous autumn. My wife, Pam, and I drove through Buffalo on the way to Washington, D.C., and pulled into the parking lot at Niagara early one morning. But there's a certain fuzziness to the memory of that visit. When I summon up my personal recollections of the falls they're all entangled with movie scenes, calendar photographs, and lingering preconceived notions dating back to childhood. My actual experience of Niagara is attenuated by the photographically (and otherwise) expressed experiences of others. It's as if I saw the whole thing through a cultural and social filter.

Despite the obvious difference in scale, I was more impressed with Hannine than Niagara. There'd been too much hype about Niagara. What could live up to the expectations generated by a lifetime of advance billing? And the place was definitely congested. Walker Percy wrote: "Is looking like sucking: the more lookers the less there is to see?" I must admit that the inevitable busload of Japanese sightseers, with Nikons and Mamiyas clicking and whirring, was more than a little distracting. With hundreds of other humans leaning over the railings, or gazing down from the restaurants and hotels, the sense of being some place special was thoroughly diluted. We weren't explorers ("Discover Niagara Falls!"), or even travelers; we were spectators. The feeling was of being in a crowd in front of a widescreen television. It was nice, and I'm glad we stopped, but there were no goose bumps, no vivid remembrances. (Except maybe the Japanese tourists.) Perhaps if we'd approached Niagara from Lake Erie in a canoe, and then pulled out at the last second . . . (It's only a Class II right up to the edge.)

But I remember Hannine. It was ours. It wasn't a destination—something to gawk at and then say, "Gee, it looks just like in the pictures." It was an obstacle, something we had to get around. We studied it; not as mere scenery, but as "conceivably runnable." Hannine is vivid to me because experiencing it was a spontaneous, unstructured event. It wasn't filtered or "edited" by someone else. There are no brochures. It isn't showcased for consumption by tourists. I didn't set out to be impressed by Hannine Falls, and, therefore, I was. A real nightmare would be to paddle up there one day and find a parking lot with picnic tables and a fenced-in overlook. It was sufficient that about a quarter-mile upstream of the falls the State of Minnesota had posted a sign. It read "Danger" over a stylized image of a broken canoe. If there must be a sign I guess that one's fairly unobtrusive. Our tastes would've mandated a simple skull and crossbones; anyone paddling the Little Fork would be savvy enough to figure it out.

After Hannine there's 150 yards of Class II, a fairly steep pitch with some big waves. We re-entered the river below the falls, and with its swelling roar as a truly live soundtrack, we left it behind in style—spray shooting over our prows.

2.

We'd bunch up after a rapids, the first man through waiting around to see that the rest made it intact. Then for a while we'd cruise downriver three-abreast, in a confident little fleet. But soon we'd spread out, each paddling at his own speed, reaching his own compromise between progress and peace of mind. We weren't in a race, and we didn't have to push it, but on the other hand we carried food only for four, perhaps five days, and we had to keep traveling.

We were also packing about two gallons of water apiece. The

Little Fork isn't a polluted stream. Particularly in its middle reaches, it's about as pristine as a river can be in this day and age. But it is surface water, and therefore subject to natural contaminants such as giardia.

Boiling is an effective way to kill giardia and other living contaminants, but not always convenient, and sometimes it's impossible, so we were hauling a good supply of potable water. I had mine in two plastic milk jugs, lashed under the front seat of the canoe. I'd sealed the caps with duct tape in case I went over in a rapids, and I thought my water reserve was secure. But I hadn't counted on an attack by a hostile "native."

Three or four miles after Hannine, Neil and I were still within hailing distance, but John had pulled ahead. He'd disappeared around a bend a half-hour before, and that was the last we'd seen of him. The overcast had started to thin, and occasionally a shaft of sunlight would break through and shimmer on the ripples. I suppose it gave John a dose of inspiration, and he chose to express his good humor with some earnest paddling. But apparently hard traveling wasn't enough of an outlet for his sudden exuberance. Staging an ambush was more like it.

I was in a pleasant daze, lulled into a semi-hypnotic state by constant, rythmic paddling. The canoe and I were a unit, merged into a gentle but relentless river-eating amphibian. I saw and heard everything, but I was in touch from a distance, looking out from somewhere at the back of my head. It was a different level, perhaps a notch above routine, work-a-day consciousness.

So I was all the more shocked when I heard a loud shriek in the woods on the right bank. There was a splash next to the canoe. My head jerked around and I saw John hurling his second missile—another chunk of dead wood. He was yelling something incoherent about sacred ground and cannibalism. I was just starting to laugh when the chunk of wood hit the canoe. It bounced off the inside hull on the left and punctured one of my water jugs. The container bled profusely.

I was cursing as I crawled over my pack to the bow and tried to staunch the flow. I lost half of a precious gallon and vowed obscene revenge. But I've yet to fulfill my promise; the perfect ambush takes time. I've been toying with the idea of a sabotaged paddle in the middle of Class III . . . For a moment I was genuinely angry—we were talking water supply in the wilds—but John was just as genuinely contrite, and the moment passed. It was another mishap to chuckle about around the campfire; more fate-tempting slapstick.

Like our last Class II of the day. It was a mile above the confluence of the Sturgeon, and my heart bucked against my ribs when I saw it. That stretch was the kind of run I would never attempt for the first time alone. I wouldn't be able to work up the nerve. The map described it thus: "A big, flat outcrop on the right pinches the river, forming two-foot waves in high water." The author was being conservative. The "outcrop" is a massive escarpment of bedrock. It crimps the river against the stony bank on the left side, and the maddened current crashes against it. The rock is a solid vertical wall that reaches six or eight feet above the waves for a fifteen-yard stretch. Ram your canoe into that and it's all over but the crying. It's a fortress battlement—impervious to the storming river and contemptuous of aluminum and flesh.

I was intimidated, not sure how the current at the base of that wall was behaving. And we'd have to skirt the wall. There was a cluster of boulders to the left, and the effective passage was narrowed to perhaps one canoe length. There was also some big waves. The river dropped steeply, and we could only clearly see the first half of the rapids. The rest was partially obscured by the foamy tops of whitecaps. I scanned the banks for a portage. Nope. Well, I thought, I could always drag the canoe through the woods. It looked to be a little over a hundred yards.

But my supply of spare courage was near to hand. For Neil and John, portaging a Class II was simply unthinkable. They studied only the river. Whether or not a footpath cut around this rapids was irrelevant. I'm sure neither of them even noticed. I would draw confidence from that.

Neil went first. We watched intently as he paddled and ruddered alongside that wall. It looked like he was only inches away, nearly grazing it with his gunwale. But he didn't appear to be struggling, and his bow wasn't jumping too violently. In moments he was past the revetment and into the more open rapids beyond. A few more seconds of deft maneuvering and he was out of sight, apparently in control.

John immediately steered into the current and started his run. Just before he took on the first waves, he half turned his head toward me and shouted what had become our tongue-in-cheek prohibition before hitting whitewater: "No stopping!" he yelled. "No stopping!" And then he was into it, shooting past the escarpment and disappearing down the rapids.

Whenever we shouted that rueful slogan I thought of my friend Mike. He doesn't do a lot of whitewater, but one day he decided to give his wife Barb a taste of what it was all about. With her hanging on, tense and white-knuckled in the bow, he whipped their canoe into a stretch of Class I-II. Shortly after entering, he hit something and the canoe made a 180-degree spin. They were bouncing through the waves backwards. Mike is a competent, capable fellow in most areas, and Barb apparently had a lot of confidence in him. As they swept down the rapids out of control, she turned, and in an authoritative, wifely way said simply, "Michael, stop." At this point in the tale Mike breaks into an eloquent chuckle.

"No stopping!" I shouted after John. He and Neil had administered my injection of instant, face-saving bravery. The run was obviously not as hairy as it appeared, and I breached it like I knew what I was doing. The trick was to go calmly with the flow as it pulled you directly at the wall, and then dig in with the paddle and swerve away just before the water did. Though the current was swift, it was a surprisingly easy move. In a moment I was parallel to the rock, about two feet away, and picking up speed. There would be no collision. I was buzzed on adrenaline and the euphoria of survival. I'd made it! And then my heart froze. Directly ahead, right before the river broke away from the wall and spread out into a wide boulder pitch, was a waterfall.

OK, we're not talking Niagara here—not even Hannine. In fact, it was only about a two-foot vertical drop, maybe less. But after my anxiety about this run, it scared the hell out of me. There were two facets to my sudden terror. First, the "falls" was unavoidable. The last of the wall was on the right, a jumble of boulders on the left. Even if I'd been an expert paddler there was no place to expertly paddle to. I was committed. Second, it looked like the "falls" was created by the current plunging suddenly over the sharp rim of a ledge. The rushing water appeared to be very shallow, only a few inches deep. I was certain I was going to hang up, my keel grinding into the stone. Then I'd flip and/or be swamped. The canoe would wedge and be crushed into junk, and I'd be slammed into solid rock.

These horrors flashed through my mind, and it never oc-cured to me that if this spot was so deadly, then why weren't Neil and John and their canoes pasted all over the place? But in a second I was at the top of the "falls," just ruddering and hang-ing on. I braced myself for inevitable disaster, and then I was over it. My hull touched nothing—there was nary a scratch of metal on rock. I flew over the drop and into a big wave. The bow kicked up, and spray showered the seats. I was into the open rapids, and the rest was routine dodging and "deeking." John and Neil were at the bottom, grinning, and gesturing with their paddles to show me the best route.

I finally floated into calm water, still on my knees. It's good to keep the center of gravity low when running rapids, so I always ease my butt off the seat and transfer the weight to the kneecaps. It's also a good position for fervent prayer. I was certainly in an attitude of thanksgiving and joy after that ride. I believe my pulse rate stayed up over a hundred for a half hour. I was definitely alive.

3.

The sky was a featureless, dirty-gray overcast, and the late-afternoon light was flat and murky. More rain appeared immi-nent. So about five miles beyond the "pinched" rapids (and one more decent Class I) we made our first camp.

Our map indicated that along the entire length of the Little Fork there were only three officially established campsites, so we were on our own when it came to snuggling in somewhere for the night. Aside from the exposed rock at the rapids, the banks of the river are almost exclusively clay—a slippery, oozing, clinging kind of muddy clay. Your shoe sucks out of it with three or four inches of goop sticking to the sole. It's as if someone threw together a giant batch of wet cement, soggy oatmeal, and 90-weight gear lube, and then stirred vigorously. That sounds like the start of a viable Paul Bunyan tale. Perhaps the Little Fork clay is really the accumulated droppings of giardiasis-stricken Babe the Blue Ox. It does resemble fecal material more than anything else, and that was our standard label for it—though we employed a more colloquial term.

I can't find any way to wax poetic about it; the clay was a

stinking nuisance, especially when you tracked globs of it into your canoe. So when it came to a campsite, the idea was to find a bank with a healthy growth of long grass to serve as a "doormat." After we decided to make camp, we ended up drifting another mile before we found an acceptable spot. But then, all three of us are picky about where we pitch tents and throw down bedrolls. The ambience has to be right.

Of course a campfire covers a multitude of sins, and while Neil and I cleared away debris for a couple of tent sites, John kindled a blaze. Although the forest was damp and spongy, we were nestled into a thick stand of balsam fir and had a guaranteed supply of drier fuel. The lowest tiers of limbs on the big balsams are almost always dead and bone dry—sheltered from the rain by the dense foliage above. There was also a dead birch nearby, and balsam twigs and birch bark are a highly flammable combination.

The reassuring thing about campfires is that they always look and feel the same. Whether the evening sky is a dusky, fading blue, spangled with the first brightest stars, or as it was this day—opaque, low, and threatening—the flames jump and snap regardless. In its elemental, consuming nature, each campfire is a link to the ones before. In that portion of the memory that cherishes personal archives of sentiment, all the campfires of your life are arranged in a long winking line that reaches back years and miles. Sometimes the faces of old friends that are remembered most vividly are summoned up as they were seen in firelight.

I recall a campfire made by children, in a patch of woods just outside a northern Minnesota mining town. There were four of us huddled around it, flushed with the excitement of one of our first outings. We were telling ghost stories—heavy, bloody tales which amplified the calls of owls and lengthened the reach of shadows. With no warning, Bob plucked a cherry bomb from his pocket and dropped it into the middle of the fire. For a long moment we stared stupidly at the flames, not believing our eyes. Even Bob seemed surprised by what he'd done. Then as we all finally reacted and dove away, the campfire exploded like an erupting volcano—pelting us with hot coals and firey debris. Spot fires broke out in the forest all around and we scurried madly about, stomping on them. Nobody was hurt, so we laughed uproariously; but no one ever did it again.

I recall a campfire in the East Texas woods. A gang of college buddies lounged around it passing bottles of Jack Daniels and Southern Comfort. At first, the stories were loud and boisterous, spiced with the trade of affectionate insults. But slowly the youths mellowed as the flames died to embers. Easily, like the transformation of green wood to charcoal, the lively jesters became contemplative, introspective, and drunk. Graduation would cast them to the winds, but they'd never forget each others' names.

I recall a fire in November—on the icy banks of the Sturgeon. There'd been a mistake out in the rapids and Casey, a friend of mine, had to drag himself out of the river. He was shivering violently, his teeth chattering like the sound of an angry raccoon. His face was pinched and chalky. It was a hasty, feverish fire. I tore at bark and twigs and heaped them into a pyre as fast as I could. In ten minutes we had a bonfire, entire spruce boughs igniting in bursts of orange sparks. By the time the blaze was back to campfire size, Casey was resurrected. Color returned to his face—and to his speech as he scathingly reprimanded the paddler who'd messed up. But the terrifying plunge into swirling icewater would soon be a fond memory. The fire ensured it.

There's an Ojibway proverb that says: "Yesterday is wood, tomorrow is ashes; only today does the fire burn brightly"—a comforting observation about the nature of time that must've grown out of the frigid, interminable January nights inside lodges or tipis that were mere specks in a world that was all wilderness. The fire represented life, a continuity from ancestors to generations yet unborn. It was the night-time sun, the source of all good. It lit the "stage" for the presentation of tales, legends, and traditions which knit the people together. We moderns, who don't associate around fires on a daily basis, nor often depend upon them for survival, can only appreciate their qualities when we put distance between ourselves and the demands of civilization. The essence of campfires, the source of their universal appeal, is sharing. Sharing light and warmth, sharing the stories that seem to spring naturally to the lips whenever people gather around flames.

I recall hundreds of old fires. Some warmed hands, some cooked walleyes, some sterilized knives for minor "surgery," and some dried underwear. But all were shared. Even when you're out there alone, surrounded by vast, untamed darkness, you may share your fire with those past. There is that elemental link. By invoking the power of memory and rekindling the confidence of past adventures, the amiable flames ensure that you won't go off screaming into the night. There is power in that.

On the Little Fork, that evening's blaze was focused first on wet socks and canned chili. Dry clothes and hot food are potent narcotics out in the bush. Pulling on a pair of fresh socks is like a glimpse of the Promised Land. The first spoonful of anything that's even remotely palatable is an ambrosial offering. We'd come twenty-seven miles and run sixteen rapids—we deserved these luxurious rewards.

4.

At dawn the river was quilted with mist. Tendrils rose from the surface, curling into a cushion of fog. The atmosphere was still, as if treasuring the fragile burden of water vapor. The quiet morning would have its way for a while, but looking straight up we could see the cloud thinned quickly, that it was backlit with pale blue. Unless my local weather sense was off, the sky should be clear by 9:00 a.m., the fog ripped away by rising heat and a strong northwest wind.

But for an hour we slipped downriver through mist, easing paddles into the water, carefully lifting them out. It was proper for our passage to be muted. We floated past swamp-bound ash trees, moving only a little faster than wayward driftwood. Eyesight was good for about a hundred feet, and from the middle of the river we could see the first few ranks of dark trunks fading to nebulous invisibility. The forest was temporarily veiled. Wet, jungle-like shadows hinted at an ulterior vibrancy, as if the mist concealed some secret force of awakening and rejuvenation. It was spooky—in a reverent kind of way. The world was hushed, expectant.

And if visibility was limited, hearing was excellent. Our ears were hollow with silence, anxious to be filled with the sound of whitewater. On such a tranquil morning it was unlikely we'd be caught by surprise. Any rapids worthy of the name would signal its presence with a steady, pulse-quickening roar that we'd hear from a mile away.

What did surprise us that morning was the sight of Samuelson Park. The name is deceptive. It conjures up a cityscape—a quaint urban commons, or a sedate college quadrangle. And if a small woodland clearing with a privy and a single rustic picnic table is a park, then that's what Samuelson is. But what was so arresting was the volume of the rapids. The park sits on the right bank of what our map called, "Class II rapids, a four-foot sloping ledge with a well-formed backroller." It sits in the middle of a bend, hemmed in by high banks. The vibrations of its rampage bounce off the left bank and echo back upriver. As you paddle down a long straight stretch of calm water toward Samuelson, you have no doubt a beast lies ahead.

We beached our canoes and studied the run. The river narrowed and then swept down over an expansive outcrop of bedrock. The main current was like a smooth, high-velocity tidal wave. The surface of the wave seemed undisturbed as it plunged down the face of the slide. If you focused on any given point, the facade of the flow was placid. But as soon as you drew back to take it all in, the unbroken surface washed past in a plummeting cascade. At the bottom the wave exploded. A deposit of large boulders threw up a chaotic turbulence of whitecaps and spray— and the backroller. That's where the river seemed to hurtle straight down at the base of the slide, bash into the boulders, and then rear up and curl back on itself. If you approached the slide from downstream and inched up to the base (at a point where the whitecaps weren't too high and strong), the backroller could suck your canoe into the plunging tidal wave and bury you in an instant. It might keep the canoe—and you—indefinitely.

So the extent of the run would be one quick dive into five yards of wild wave action. There was at least one three-footer in there. Neil figured the best tactic was to come sailing right down the center of the slide, paddling vigorously to build up momentum. He wanted to hit that backroller hard, flying over it as quickly as possible and shooting into the waves beyond.

Actually, John and I had run Samuelson before. The previous summer we'd spent an afternoon on a fishing/scouting mission (good scouting, poor fishing), and ended up at the "park." With both of us in the canoe we'd charged down the slide twice. The first time, we hit the waves hard and wallowed a little "on top" of that backroller. I was up front, and I got a lapful of river as two or three whitecaps broke over the bow and swamped us. We barely stayed upright. Convinced we could do better, we emptied the canoe and made a second run. The first must've been lucky, because we hit the base of the drop and were eaten alive. The canoe was taken from us. I was dragged underwater for a moment, and my shoulder blades skipped against two large rocks. There was a brief sensation of being in the grasp of an awesome, unsympathetic power. And I guess there was luck the second time too. A minor change in the dynamics of the situation, and my skull could've been pounded instead of my back. It was a scenario worthy of meditation.

That had been in August, when the river is low and relatively tame. Samuelson was much fiercer now. The median flow of the Little Fork in August is about 400 cubic feet/second; in June, about 2,000. And that increase was being used to great effect—storming over the drop and thrashing into a white frenzy among the boulders. It was a different rapids than the one we'd played in last summer, and I had doubts about the wisdom of swimming there again.

Neil paddled back upstream for about thirty yards, and then spun his canoe around to face the rapids. As planned, he "gunned" it, churning up a wake with hard, quick strokes. His face had That Look. When a novelist describes a character's face as "glowing," this is what he means. Neil's eyes were set; they were focused, zoomed in, and, therefore, lit up. It was that spark of aliveness arcing round inside his brain. His chin and cheeks were taut, gathered up and streamlined by concentration. His mouth was braced —not tight, but snug. The lips were thin and a little stretched, but not locked. They were poised on the verge of shouting—either in triumph or in pain. Taken whole, his expression was a blend of absorption and determination, tinged with honest fear. He was interested in what lay ahead. Samuelson was the future (albeit short term) and Neil was facing it. To *face* a challenge; it's an apt phrase.

He powered over the brink and dashed down the slide. His bow kicked up high when he hit the backroller, spewing a shower of spray. In a flash he was amidst the waves, rolling and yawing and shipping water. And then he was through. But there was an inch of water sloshing around his feet. He pulled up to the opposite bank to empty it.

His run had been quick and neat, but it convinced me I should portage. Just as he'd passed over the backroller, I'd heard his stern slam against rock. It was a solid, apparently unavoidable impact. I did some fast figuring and estimated that between me and my canoe, I'd be carrying about seventy-five more pounds into that rock. I'd ram it with much greater force. Presuming I survived that, I also had to consider I had less freeboard than Neil. If he'd shipped that much water in the big waves, I'd probably take on enough to capsize. John reached a similar decision, and we dragged our canoes over the ledgerock and into the flat water beyond.

On the other side of the river Neil talked with two fishermen who'd watched his run. We'd seen these guys before, fishing from the banks of the Sturgeon. You hear a lot of stories about the colorful characters living back in the bush, tucked into places you thought belonged only to bears. There's no collective name for the small, rough-edged population of loners, homesteaders, and sometime loggers/sometime trappers who lived in these remote woods. Out East they'd call them hillbillies.

For this pair at Samuelson, that moniker might not be too far off the mark. They're a father and son who fled Tennessee five or six years ago for purposes of tax evasion, or so the story goes. I guess the southern "revenuers" weren't interested in pursuing them to the Little Fork-Sturgeon country. Here they sell logs, do a lot of fishing, and avoid the Minnesota game wardens. A friend tells me these two were pegged as chronic poachers long ago, and one of the local conservation officers has made nabbing them red-handed a personal crusade. My friend says that as a result, the Tennesseans have taken to crawling into culverts on the smaller streams and going after walleyes with fabricated rods that allow them to cast straight off the tips without a backswing. I'm surprised they just don't go in for "DuPont spinners"; but I suppose dynamite attracts too much attention— even out here. Though they haunt the banks of the river all summer, they're afraid of the river itself. Anyone who takes a boat or canoe out on the water is crazy as far as they're concerned. And rapids! To them, Neil was a madman. (And don't necessarily look to me for a debate.)

5.

Three miles beyond Samuelson we came to the Highway 65 bridge. It's the threshold of the really wild country. From here to the next bridge it's forty river-miles—one of the longest stretches of stream without a bridge in the entire state, and some of the "emptiest" territory around. Our map said, "Access is difficult from here downstream to [the next bridge]. The river is flanked by deep woods and few houses." Actually, for a twenty-five mile segment it was *no* houses.

There is contentment in voyaging through untrammeled terrain. To know that dense, uninhabited timberland extends for miles in every direction is a metaphysical kind of awareness. It's why prophets and hermits are traditionally drawn into the wilderness to dream their dreams and see their visions. A wide tract of virgin country is a great reservoir of natural quietness, a convivial form of solitary confinement. It's not that this tranquility is silent. A forest can be a very loud place, resonant with the voices of animals, the melodies of wind in the trees, and the polyphonous course of water from sky to land and off to the sea.

But these sounds aren't disturbances, they aren't harbingers or warnings. They denote or promise nothing but the rustic, unrefined primitive order. A person can rest in the midst of a forest and have his head filled with the chirping of warblers, the drumming of a woodpecker, the chattering of squirrels, the scurrying of field mice, the gurgling of a creek, and the low sighing of a breeze through pine boughs, then turn to a companion and say, "Isn't it amazing how quiet it is out here?" It's the difference between music and noise—a symphony is not oppressive. The music of the wilderness forms a psychic loop in your mind. The outside sounds draw your awareness inward. It's like listening to your favorite records and letting the measures escort you deep into memories and speculations. The quietness of the forest is natural habitat for the vibrations of thought.

And this tone is established by simple distance—by a significant separation from highways, railroads, billboards, and shopping malls. Unlike birdsong or rainfall, the brazen dissonance of internal combustion engines is a disturbance. It's not so much the sound itself, for most of us can appreciate the qualities of a "purring" engine; rather it's what the noise portends: development, exploitation, dense habitation. Engines, and the powerful steel tools we attach to them, are a threat. It's hard to consider engines without considering blades, rams, plows, and buckets. The roar of motors draws your awareness outward—to the material desiderata of modern civilization—to roads and bridges, mines and sawmills, dams and airports. These are not evil, loathesome things. It's just that they, through us, don't seem to know their place. When you're paddling down the Little Fork, channeled by wild banks, you know they don't belong there. And when you see the contrail of a jet high overhead, a B-52 headed west for Grand Forks, you're reminded that for 300 years the North American wilderness has been treated as an enemy—as an obstacle to Progress. The land is to be ruled and subdued, indelibly branded with the identity of its conquerers. Some of the evidence of our occupation, like radioactivity, chemical hazardous waste, and acid rain, will still be testifying to our hegemony thousands of years from now.

We need to live and thrive. We need our electricity and sewer pipes, we need our hospitals and theaters. But, at least in North America, isn't there enough? Does our conquest need to be utterly complete? Haven't there been a sufficient number of lupicides, vulpicides, and "terracides"? When you've traveled that simple distance, put those miles between yourself and civilization by means of your own quiet, unmechanical effort, you're jealous of the space and stillness. Even if you're an admirer of engines, you don't want one roaring up on you while out in the bush.

When surrounded by wildness, I'm endowed with a strong feeling of individual worth. I'm not just another worker or soldier in the teeming anthill of collective, interdependent society. The sense of belonging to the human race, to the rat race, to various social, economic, political, and ethnic families is beneficially diluted. With quietness and elbow room it's easier to see the boundaries between yourself and others; it's easier to hear the humming and fussing of your own mind, and listen to it—unimpeded by the insistent distractions and seductions of civilization. It's good to be singular. It's wise to be a little separate and apart. Humans have wreaked far less havoc as contemplative individuals than as habitual members of crowds. Hordes, mobs, and inquisitions aren't made up of people who've just emerged from a week (or a life) in the woods. Or so I believe when I'm out there.

For better or for worse, the reality of late 20th century North America is that most humans are compelled to live in places that have long since been redeemed from the grip of the primeval. Some people blossom in the tamed, upholstered environment, and some do not. But as long as we don't complete our violent subjugation of the wild places, we'll have sanctuary. There'll be a way to paddle or hike into regions where you can hear not only wolves and loons, but yourself.

6.

Not long after the Hwy. 65 bridge we were assaulted by a stiff northwest wind—some gusts up to forty miles per hour. Since the Little Fork's general direction of flow is to the northwest, the river banks and bends offered little protection. We'd come forty miles downstream, and the river had widened and flattened. It had dropped an average of 2.7 feet per mile up to Highway 65; from there to the mouth the average drop was only 1.3. There were still some violent rapids ahead—including a long Class II-III called, ominously, Deadman's—but they were separated by long stretches of flat water, and the naturally helpful current was noticeably slower. We battled the wind as if we were crossing a neutral, and, therefore, unforgiving lake.

We rearranged our packs, shoving them up to the bows, and I added a hefty rock for good measure. The weight up front kept our profiles low and our keels in the water. That made it possible—barely—to track through the waves into the wind. Here was the downside of solo canoeing. With two paddlers in a 17-foot canoe, that head wind would've been no more than a little extra resistance. Alone, it was a constant, energy-sapping struggle. We hugged the banks, stealing as much shelter as possible, and repeatedly cutting across the river to take advantage of the changing lee. Neil called out, "No stopping!" and it was true. You couldn't ease your paddling for a moment or the wind would blow you sideways and push you back upstream. The current was more than canceled out.

About seven miles beyond Hwy. 65 we got a little relief. Over the steady monotone of the wind we heard the roar of Nett Rapids. It was labeled Class I, but the map indicated it was nearly a mile long and included a major bend. Given the width of the river—over a hundred feet—that added up to an automatic Class II in my book. I tossed my ballast rock overboard and dragged my gear back toward the stern. I went through the usual primping of life jacket and eyeglasses, and steeled myself for a long run.

We entered the whitewater one after another, about thirty feet apart, with Neil in the lead. The rapids was a wide field of round boulders. The river didn't narrow much as it started to drop, and the main flow split up immediately. We were suddenly faced with three or four viable paths down through the white-caps, and we split up. Neil cut left and John dodged right, and I followed John until I heard his keel grind against rock. I dodged further to the right down another arm of the rapids and began to pick my own way through the choppy cascade.

It's beautiful to be in the midst of rapids and watch someone else running them at the same time. I kept one eye on my own business and tried to study Neil and John. There's a certain rough and tumble choreography to a burrowing paddle, a rolling hull, and a sparkling volley of spray. John knelt ramrod-straight in the stern, absorbed by his pitching bow. His arms and shoulders flexed and tightened—sharply, precisely—as he ruddered, stroked, or made a single thrust with a quick backpaddle.

The rapids was a series of shorter, steeper drops interspersed with longer, shallow, low-wave runs. There were a few big waves in the steep parts, and a lot of maneuvering required everywhere, but on the flatter stretches I had a little time to gawk, especially when I ran aground. I did it twice, and finally gave up on sight-seeing. But the first time I got hung up was on a bed of small rocks near the middle of the major bend. I was caught firmly, as stable as one of the boulders, so I relaxed for a minute.

All of the river was whitewater—rapids behind, rapids ahead, rapids all around. Neil and John fought their way out of sight around the bend, and I was alone with the thundering river. I enjoyed a rare frame of mind. That bright whitewater alertness was mingled with a peaceful, meditative reverence—for the river, for the trees, for the sky. The excitement of the rapids enhanced the state of contemplation. Here, I thought, was a new mystical discipline. The novices could work their perilous way to a high point in the middle of a rapids, and then, borrowing from the great mantra of the current, an ancient metaphor of time and renewal, they could seek rest and enlightenment. Hell, with the proper location, combining accessibility and danger, plus enough soulful hype, a dedicated entrepeneur could climb aboard the New Age-Aquarian Conspiracy bandwagon and cash in. I could see $300 for a two-day metaphysical orientation seminar, leading up to a journey into the rapids. That is, after the appropriate waivers and disclaimers had been duly signed by all concerned. And maybe some liability insurance would be a wise investment.

I could picture the classified ad in the New Age Journal: "Go with the eternal flow. Merge with the riverine consciousness. A weekend of holistic irrigation for true aquarians. Call Little Fork Cosmic Excursions." Even better, of course, would be to find a nice little stretch of whitewater on the Nile.

But here on the Little Fork you couldn't linger for long, at least not in June. We'd noticed that over every length of swift water there hovered a squadron of hungry deer flies. Two and three at a time would dive out of the sun in vicious sorties. The targets were the very tops of our heads, at the relatively open spot where the hair seems to whorl out of the center of your skull. And they hurt—like a jabbed needle. It was especially irritating to be concentrating on the water ahead, innocently charting a course through rapids, and then have your scalp drilled. If you put on a hat, they went for the face. It was blatant, bloodthirsty aggression, and we often became pre-occupied with self-defense.

But it's very poor form to be swatting at flies with your paddle as you enter whitewater. So Neil developed a more tasteful, and far more effective way to deal with the menace. He figured the flies were blitzing heads and faces because these were high points—they were like tall trees in a thunderstorm, attracting wrath—the proverbial high-profile targets. So before and after a rapids he'd lay back on the stern of his canoe and raise an upturned hand over his head. Sure enough, the deer flies would land on his palm to take a bite, and Neil'd make a quick fist and crush them. It was efficient and satisfying. There was even a certain aesthetic charm to temporarily triumphing over a race of insects without using some sort of chemical hazardous waste.

We theorized the deer flies were hanging around the swift water because that's what the deer were doing. Four times that day we snuck up on deer that were in or on the edge of a rapids. Deafened by whitewater, they never heard us coming. They were engrossed in drinking, wading, and shaking the flies off their ears. Besides, they had little reason to expect danger from the river. More often than not, rivers and lakes are a place of refuge for whitetails. They're fine swimmers, faster than wolves, and it's a good way to elude the pack.

But wolf packs don't come floating downriver (though maybe they should), and on the Little Fork not many canoes do either. We slipped to within a few yards of one deer. It was a strange, un-human feeling to be able to smoothly and easily creep up on a creature so wild and wary as a deep-woods doe. There was an inspiring sense of god-like jurisdiction in being able to see her eyes blink. For a little while it was as if we were incorporeal observers, drifting ghosts with the freedom to spy and pry without being detected. Now there's a myth worth living—to be some kind of disembodied forest spirit, flitting through the woods noiselessly, odorlessly, and finding out how things really are. Like how wide are the eyes of a cornered moose? What does the forest floor look like from just behind the left ear of a great gray owl? How is the underwater world in November—under thin ice, under a full moon? Do the northern pike shine as they dart and lunge after minnows?

7.

About nine miles down from the Hwy. 65 bridge we saw our first osprey. It drifted into view over the tops of some tall cedars and made a swooping pass over the river. It was low, maybe a hundred feet up, and *resplendent* is the only word. Saturated with the rich light of the afternoon sun, the body was a downy, linen-white. It was framed by huge, crooked wings, dappled and lined with black. The tail was a wide-open fan with alternating dark and light bands that rippled in the wind.

It was the first of ten osprey sightings—all sudden and dramatic. The birds seemed to just materialize overhead, waving their two-foot wings and zig-zagging across the river hunting for fish. Or sometimes they'd hover, floating almost perfectly still 50-100 feet above the water, waiting in high, sun-backed ambush. They looked like fancy oriental kites; pinnioned by air, suspended in the wind.

Ospreys are purists. They feed only on live fish—no carrion or helpless hairy rodents. Their name is derived from Latin and originally meant "bone-breaker." It's a fitting title for a beautiful, but tenacious predator that'll dive completely underwater if necessary. We would have loved to see that. Imagine the glory

of a hawk with a four or five-foot wingspan (and big red eyes) bursting *out* of the river. Such a vision was denied us, but we did see an osprey fly over with a glistening smallmouth bass clutched in its talons. It was a nice catch, perhaps one or two pounds. The osprey held the fish in a natural, lateral position. We saw the full profile of both bird and bass, as if the fish were flying along with the osprey, just underneath. The hawk spouted off with a series of loud, ringing whistles as it passed over—either bragging and taunting—and it was true, we wouldn't have minded owning a fish like that ourselves. We toyed briefly with the fantasy of having a trained osprey, like a hunting falcon. We could release it over a fecund lake or stream and watch it dive for our supper—the ultimate fishing gadget.

John brought along a rod and reel, and he did a little casting, but I know he envied the ospreys. That's how he'd really like to fish—diving after bass or pike and catching them with his bare hands. There's a delicate suspense to the manipulation of hook and line, but it's more like trapping than hunting. Angling is not so much a sport as it is a game of chance. Devotees talk of "playing" a fish. Various tools and toys are used as mediators between man and fish. The prey is not stalked or chased, but rather cajoled and deceived by bait and lures. Imitation talons are fashioned from metal and plastic. It's fun, but it's not primal, blood-rushing sport. If John had wings he'd be an osprey—a true, sky-patrolling fisher.

In contrast to the soaring ospreys we had the paddling alligators. From a distance we saw a long, low silhouette leaving a wide wake. It looked for all the world like a cruising gator. For a moment the illusion was perfect, and in spite of common sense and common knowledge I did a double-take. The mind is always ready for fantasy. You don't have to kick-start the imagination— it's strictly electronic (or electrochemical) ignition—the mere touch of a button. It's an endearing human characteristic much appreciated by politicians, preachers, and would-be lovers. But when it comes to the Little Fork, I'll stick with trained ospreys. Gators might savor plump northern muskrats, or careless canoeists, but come December they'd find ten inches of river ice to be a huge inconvenience. Gators are poor skaters.

The body of the "alligator" was soon resolved into a dozen tiny ducklings and a red-headed adult merganser. With the slightest ripples the twelve tiny feather balls were set to bobbing like comical rubber toys. They strained to keep up with mama, zeroed in on the point of her tail feathers. The impression was that their new webbed feet were churning furiously. They cut and turned as a unit, as if linked by one nervous system.

Everything was fine until mother decided we were too close. She rose partway out of the river, beating the surface with her wings. The brood erupted. They tore downriver in a frenzied, frothing stampede. You wouldn't think a batch of soft, tufted floaters could raise such a violent commotion. Half-running, half-flying, they whipped the water into bubbles and foam, and seemed to lift themselves on a cushion of air, hydroplaning for the bank. The sudden fuss died down only when they were all partially concealed by grass, reeds, and overhanging brush. Mother continued to lead them downstream, ducking (so to speak) in and out of cover.

All was calm and unruffled until we made up the distance, and then there was another burst of wings and water, and another panicky charge downstream. This dance went on for two or three miles. Since the mergansers were hugging the left bank, we pulled way over to the right, trying to be as innocuous and unthreatening as possible. We were afraid that these constant alarms were going to exhaust the little ones and make them easier prey for somebody who really did want to catch and eat them. But mother was unimpressed by our friendly gesture, and kept on fleeing before us until I guess *she* finally got tired. She certainly put a lot of effort into mothering. I suppose it was such behavior which first inspired the symbolic, mythological associations of ducks and geese with the Great Mother and the universal maternal bosom. I give you, for example, Mother Goose. Storks and the delivery of babies are in there somewhere too.

One of the most pleasing things about these middle reaches of the Little Fork are the homogenous stands of cedar. The aromatic evergreens are massed on both banks, dense and verdant. The forest lives right at the water's edge, flourishing in the wetness of the river flats. Many stout trunks lean out over the current, some growing nearly horizontal from the bank. They reach out from the sides of the stream as if trying to close it up. It's a jungle-like atmosphere of foliage meeting water without the influence of dry land. The river appears to be contained not by banks, but by natural dikes of prospering vegetation. And in the sunlight and wind they were stirring, waving walls; living palisades of greenery.

The trunks of the cedars are brown and stocky, and have stringy, primitive-looking bark. The general impression is of a Mesozoic Era cycad forest; or at least how that ancient locale was pictured in a dinosaur book I pored over as a kid. The illustrator had created a watery world that seemed to support only cypress-like, moisture-loving trees (not far-removed from cedars), and the giant "lizards." Whether accurate or not, it's the picture I still carry in my head. And if I could briefly see an "alligator" swimming in the Little Fork, I could also imagine a thirty-foot Tyranosaurus rex parting the tops of two cedar trees and striding into the river on legs as thick as the trees themselves.

It's jaws are agape, lined with ivory daggers, and the cold reptilian eyes focus on the three long, shiny objects floating on the surface of the river. They're moving, so they must be edible.

The towering carnivore lunges for Neil's canoe, flicking a snake-like tongue the size of a boa constrictor. Neil leaps up to face the descending maw. With an agile, forceful jab, he shoves his paddle into the dinosaur's mouth, jamming it vertically between the upper and lower jaws. For an instant the paddle holds, and the rex's mouth is locked open. Neil dives into the river and strokes for the bottom.

With an enraged, gurgling roar, the dinosaur snaps its jaws and the paddle splinters. The mighty tyranosaurus grabs Neil's 17-foot Alumacraft and crushes it at the center. There's a horrible screech—like fangs on a blackboard—as the sharp teeth stab into the metal.

But there is no satisfying gush of blood from raw meat, and the dinosaur realizes that the best part of the canoe has already gone over the side—this is only some kind of shell. It tries to spit out the Alumacraft, but it's stuck. The canoe is firmly impaled on the bottom row of six-inch teeth, and the jagged rips and tears in the hull have lacerated the rex's gums. It whips its head in pain and frustrated madness, trying to shake out the canoe. A shower of blood is flung from its mouth. As it struggles, the tyranosaurus slips into deeper water, and now only its head and upper torso are above the surface.

From just behind me comes a loud, ferocious whoop. In a moment John is past me, paddling furiously. He's aimed his prow directly at the dinosaur. "No stopping!" I yell. "No stopping!"

While thrashing around, the tyranosaurus has inadvertently shoved the canoe back into the river, and the bow and stern sections have filled with several hundred pounds of water. The creature is now having difficulty raising its head completely out of the river. The back of its neck is low and exposed. John pulls his canoe alongside and leaps onto the dinosaur's neck. It's slippery, and he almost loses his grip—sliding partway into the river. But he claws his way back onto the spine and then yanks a Swiss Army knife out of his pocket. He starts hacking away with the longest blade.

Just then Neil surfaces a few yards away. "No, no, John!" he shouts. "Use the corkscrew to drill into its brain!" John starts fumbling with the knife as Neil swims over.

I'm hovering in the near distance, watching closely and taking notes. Somebody's got to write all this down. Unfortunately, Neil's camera was on the bottom of his canoe. . . .

Actually, the most intriguing creatures we encountered that day were bugs. We saw them at sundown. At the end of a long day of thirty-two river miles and fifteen rapids, we found a wide sandbar nestled against the left bank. Compared to the previous evening's muddy clay and thick brush, this spot was an oasis. It was soft, dry, and open, with easy access to the water. In essence, we were camping on a clean beach. We could see a lot of sky.

After supper, Neil broke out the beer he'd packed in, and we laid in the warm sand, utterly content. We watched our neighborhood. It was a point where the Little Fork makes a short jog to the West Northwest, and the sun was setting directly downriver. As it reached the tops of the trees it backlit what appeared to be a blizzard of flying insects. From the surface of the river up to about fifty feet, the orange evening air was filled with darting, looping bugs. There were hundreds of thousands of them—a dense, swirling snowstorm of black "flakes." A few mosquitoes flitted around our campsite, along with some insects I didn't recognize, but it was nothing like the rolling mass downstream. If you'd paddled into that cloud, you'd be inhaling bugs.

And that's what the birds were doing. Dozens of swallows and night hawks were swooping in and out of the cloud. We saw them in silhouette—diving, banking, and zooming through the storm. It was a grand feast and air show. The birds would appear out of the shadows of the forest and darkening sky, shooting across the bright face of the sunset—dodging, cutting. And then one would peel off our way, swinging upriver and passing overhead. Their dark forms were then lit up, taking on the reddish glow of dusk. They'd dart in and out of the path of light—one moment a black profile, the next a red-orange reflection of sun on wings.

Soon there were so many birds engaged in complex aerobatic stunts that we expected to see a collision. It was as if the air was so saturated with insects that the birds couldn't decide which to pluck out of the sky. We saw dips, stalls, barrelrolls, twisting loops, and other maneuvers so quick and violent that they would've sheared the wings off the best, man-made stunt planes. Some of these natural dogfights unfolded only ten feet over our heads. We could hear the rush of air past wings, and the fast, low drumming of vibrating feather tips.

We sat there until dark; until the birds retired, and the center of the Milky Way galaxy was a bright band from horizon to horizon.

8.

The next morning we navigated through another phase of soothing mist. Slipping downstream enveloped by moist, tempered sunlight is like savoring good coffee—it introduces you gently to the new day. There's promise, but it's unassuming and tolerant. What will be, will be. It may indeed turn out to be "the first day of the rest of your life," that is, giddy and tinged with hope. Or it may be the final day. Whatever, It's enough to be gliding downriver, sipping mist with the prow of your canoe.

After four tranquil miles the canopy of fog burned off, and we faced Seller's Rapids. The map: ". . . a quarter-mile of Class II boulder bed . . . The rapids washes out and becomes easier in high water." Well, it was nowhere near washed out, but it was still easy. There was one interesting arrangement of three or four bow-kicking, water-shipping waves, but we'd been well seasoned by our thirty-one previous runs. I could paddle this rapids and be relaxed enough to study it. I was alert, but I didn't clutch my paddle in a frightened death-grip, prepared for some capricious *deus ex machina* or malevolent river god to wipe me out. I could take the time to feel what was happening to the canoe in various configurations of current and waves. I could determine just how a given force applied with a certain stroke would affect my degree of control.

Your first whitewater encounters are like your first time on a bicycle, or the first leap off a diving board. There's a tendency to just hang on for the ride and hope like hell you survive. It's why a novice's first rapids shouldn't be a Class III.

Seller's has a developed portage, and before we shot the rapids we took a break and walked it. We found a giant. Near the middle of the portage was an impromptu campsite that appeared to have been used by several parties over the decades. The old fire pit was choked with compacted ashes, and someone had left a small grill. We focused on that first, then looked around behind us, and collectively said something deep and reverent like "Holy cow!"

It was a gargantuan cedar—overwhelming. It was monumental in the literal sense of being a monument, a living tribute to the full potential of cedar-kind. I had no idea they could get that big. John and I embraced it, throwing our six-foot armspans around the trunk. Our fingers barely overlapped. That tree was nearly twelve feet in circumference. (Later research showed that the official record white cedar in Minnesota is 132 inches in circumference, and eight stories high. It's in Koochiching County, as is this one. Perhaps they're related.)

It was humbling to realize this was a living, respirating thing, possibly over two centuries old. This tree was a sapling long before our great-grandfathers were born, before white men had come to the Little Fork to fell timber. It was a seedling before there was a United States, back when canoes were made out of birch bark, pine gum, spruce roots, and strips of white cedar. They weren't recreational watercraft. They were harvested from the woods and formed. A birch bark canoe was as much a "tree-craft" as a watercraft.

And such canoes had passed by this magnificent cedar. If they'd run the rapids, perhaps they'd crossed its shadow. If portaged, they'd brushed its limbs. Men had seen this cedar who now had been in their graves for over 150 years. If we worshipped trees, this would be one of our sacred icons. As it was, previous travelers had felt compelled to inscribe the thick bark with some crude legend as evidence of their passing. It seemed important to get down the date—to have initials and the time of their carving grow imperceptibly skyward with the massive old cedar. The most ancient date we could find was 1957. I was hoping for something like: "Pierre Cadotte, 1801." We left nothing ourselves. It seemed better to just hug the colossus and move on.

About seven miles downriver we came to Deadman's Rapids. It's catalogued as a Class II-III, which means it's changeable and dangerous. The map said that it's "considerably less difficult than its name implies. . . ." That wasn't necessarily comforting. It wouldn't be difficult at all to be a dead man in a rapids.

It was stirring up an intimidating, channel-filling roar. It was one of those wild pitches that quickly drops out of sight, both vertically, and around a bend. We pulled over to the portage on the right bank and studied the hairiest run—a long slide narrowed to a chute. We looked, gestured, and exchanged opinions and judgements. These consultations are always uplifting. They're conducted analytically, with an air of veteran confidence; even if you're not completely sure you know what you're talking about. It's a boldness-building communion. If our expedition was being filmed (perhaps for a PBS—National Geographic Special), this would be a dramatic scene. On the edge of the "cataract" Neil points (with straight-arrow authority), I peer (with frowning concentration), and John nods (with a grim, bracing satisfaction). Over the din of the rapids, the audio track would record snatches of our technical discussion, peppered with terms like "chute," "backroller," "eddy," and "dead meat." In a voice-over, the narrator—I can hear Robert Redford—would remark on our expert weighing of risk against challenge, our courageous calculations of the odds, and our meticulous strategy to maximize them. He'd say nothing, of course, about our being too damn lazy to take the portage.

The analysis of Deadman's established that a precise entry would be absolutely definitive. There appeared to be only one feasible angle of approach to the gate of the chute. Deviation from that course would be defined as: sunk. The tricky part was that the real rough water was prefaced with a stretch of Class I-II through a maze of boulders. If you were deflected by any of those rocks and lost control, you might enter the chute sideways or backwards. You then had an opportunity to hit either solid rock walls, or two to three foot waves, followed by a long, cold swim

through an additional half mile of I-II whitewater.

We thought it was time Neil had relief from his role as test pilot, so John went first. We watched him advance toward the chute, and you could tell by his stiff posture that he was a little nervous. But he executed three or four nice zigs and zags, and hit the slide in fine form. He fired down through the chaos of lunging whitecaps and into the tamer rapids beyond.

I went next. I was at the top level of concentration, consumed by the machinations of the river and the feel of my canoe. I focused on each black rock, scraping one, barely missing another, trying to keep a heads-up-and-deal-with-it attitude toward the entry of that chute. The fear was in the background, energizing the run. But it was ready to leap up and take over if things fell apart.

John had taken an oblique route to the chute, arriving almost perpendicular to the main flow, and then making a sharp, last second cut to the right just before it truly was too late. But there appeared to be another viable course, one that swung up alongside the left bank. There were more rocks to dodge, but there was also room for error. I had at least twenty feet of straight, smooth (though fast) water before the top of the slide. It would probably allow enough seconds to correct any mistakes made among the boulders.

I made a last cut and ruddered into the chute. The current sucked at the canoe and things got blurry. A sheer stone wall flashed by on the left as I surged down the slide and braced my knees for the white rollers. The bow jounced and reeled, and the foaming lip of a fractured crest turned along the gunwale and slopped into the stern. But I'd hit it right, and I sliced and humped through four or five big waves and then was in the clear. I followed John the rest of the way, through a wide Class I with room to roam. I giggled in simple happiness. Neil came after, grinning. I didn't have to see it to know. It was the thing to do at a place called Deadman's.

9.

After two-and-a-half days on the river we were mutants. Seventy-two miles of paddling had drastically altered the organization of our thought processes. They'd been honed and streamlined. The usual life pattern of a late-20th century American is multi-faceted and intricate. Reality is a jigsaw of obligations, decisions, promises, needs, desires, hopes.

There's the work or career life, a whole set of demands and experiences entangled with a job, usually located outside the home. In many cases, the job environment is like being on another planet. There's the private or home life, a complex set of relationships pressurized from within and without by a rapidly changing culture. This life is often beset by a certain level of fragmentation and confusion. Then there's the outside world, or "media" life, the steady, heavy bombardment by the vanguards of the so-called Information Age: television, radio, newspapers, magazines, video casettes, telephones, (a personal computer and modem perhaps)—they make us crazy, but we're addicted, taking in the flow of images, sounds, and data as if it were an intravenous connection to the nectar of the gods.

Living in Side Lake has sheltered me from some of the more obtrusive aspects of the modern scene, but after seventy-two miles on the Little Fork the usual life patterns had been erased. The routine links to the manifestations of the zeitgeist had been severed. The only flow was that of the current. Reality was reduced to a single line of direction, a single goal. Life was defined by the river, bounded by the unambiguous banks. The only obligation, meshing with my greatest desire, was to follow the river. There was only one physical activity—paddling. Alone in my canoe, the Information Age was distilled to one input, tuned to the clear channel of personal mind. This was especially true in the afternoons. As we tired, the fresh banter of morning gradually subsided, and we eased comfortably into the listening posts of our own heads.

Because rapids—those spasmodic information gluts—were infrequent now, such listening came easily. As we neared its lower reaches, the Little Fork slowed and widened. According to the map, there wouldn't be another Class II for thirty-five miles. It was time to dig in for the long haul.

There was a natural, assuasive monotony to the river now—mile after mile, bend after bend, hour upon hour—all pretty. It was far from boring. The beautiful sameness was a liberation. The ceaseless paddling was a meditative device. The body was productively occupied, calibrated into a pattern of travel it could sustain without the aid of consciousness. The mind was alone and free; and for awhile that afternoon mine was soaring.

There is, of course, a biochemical aspect to what I felt. The pituitary gland manufactures groups of proteins called endorphins. These substances can have a powerful effect on mood, memory, and pain, and are chemically related to opium-derived narcotics such as morphine. It seems that prolonged physical activity is one of the ways to stimulate their secretion. Distance runners are familiar with, and probably hooked on, the feelings of euphoria and indestructibility that naturally come with their sport. But the dosage appears to vary, and on some days exertion will only reward you with pain and fatigue. I suppose a lot depends on the *kind* of physical activity, and how you feel in general. When I was spending a lot of time digging ditches, for instances, euphoria was rare. (Unless we were laying plastic pipe, and I was getting a whiff or two of PVC glue.)

On the Little Fork the environment was conducive to good chemicals. There was the inherent suspense of the wild river. The banks had a certain primitive, bionomic uniformity, but you never knew what was around the next bend. There would be an uncharted rapids, a fat deer, a swooping osprey, or a particularly splendid tree. There was always that justified sense of expectation. And the taste of adventure and exploration was spiced by the loyal, unflagging presence of beauty. Almost anything can be pretty—if the lighting is right, if your mindset is right. But a woodland river doesn't have to model, isn't subject to aesthetic accidents. Its beauty is immanent, perpetual, infused. The river has a symbiotic relationship with endorphins.

About an hour past Deadman's I felt a physiological surge. It was early afternoon and we'd already covered nearly twenty miles, but suddenly I was revitalized, awarded a second wind that was psychological as well as physical. All the positive aspects of the journey seemed to peak on some internal graph, and shift into a mode of geometric progression. I was high.

My pace picked up. I soon left Neil and John far behind. My shoulders had been a little sore, but all discomfort dropped away. There was absolutely nothing I wanted to do but paddle, to move downriver under blue sky and puffy cumulus clouds. The mood was ravenous and fed on itself. Strong strokes led to stronger, and stronger seemed easier. There was a sense of speed and compressed distance.

Born to paddle! We'd joked about it a few times. We were like the Blues Brothers: "on a mission from God." That's what the surge felt like—an express commission to revel in the wonder of the river, in the wonder of the mind. I started to sing. That too was self-generating. Songs invigorated the paddling, and paddling looped energy back into the songs. It's an old Voyageur trick. The French-Canadian paddlers were chosen not only for their strength and endurance, but also for the quality of their singing. Thomas L. McKenny, a contemporary, wrote: "A Canadian, if . . . gifted with a good voice, and lungs that never tire, he is considered as having been born under a most fortunate star." Another observer noted: "Of such use is singing, in ennabling the men to work eighteen and nineteen hours a day (at a pinch) through forests and across great bays, that a good singer has additional pay."

My voice isn't worthy of a raise, but there was no one to hear it, and cadence was the important thing. I sang and paddled for an hour and a half without breaking stride. Nearly six miles of river passed under my keel, including a short stretch of Class I rapids that I barely noticed. Motion, melodies, and sunshine on the water were the three basic elements of the world. I felt disembodied, as if operating a biological machine via remote control. No pain. I was suffused with deep satisfaction. For the moment, at least, life was complete; my purpose was fulfilled. The Voyageurs would have sung:

> Je prends mon canot, je le lance
> A travers les rapides, les bouillons,
> La a grands pas il s'avance
> Il ne laisse jamais le courant.

> I take my canoe, send it chasing
> All the rapids and billows across;
> There so swiftly see it go racing
> And it never the current has lost.

> Tu es mon compagnon de voyage!
> Je veux mourir dans mon canot.
> Sur le tombeau, près du rivage,
> Vous renverserez mon canot.

> You are my voyageur companion!
> I'll gladly die within my canoe.
> And on the grave beside the canyon
> You'll overturn my canoe.

There was a touch of that kind of giddiness—a great love for the present moment; not the last instant, nor the next instant, but the pure essence of now. That's what mattered. It's a great way to travel.

But you're not in control, and you can't sustain it forever. I finally pulled up onto a sandbar and waited for my companions. I was a little tired, but happy and satisfied.

In the midst of my outburst, I'd passed beneath the second Highway 65 bridge. After so many miles of organic banks and unbroken sky, it was startling and alien, like a UFO, or . . . or like a bridge on the Little Fork! It was a symbolic end to the wildest country. There was still a lot of dense forest left, but now there'd be an occasional sign of human (and Hereford) occupation; though nothing terribly oppressive. It was still thirty-seven miles to the *next* bridge.

We paddled another ten miles that day. I was no longer serenading and cruising along at the top end, but the afterglow of my natural high lingered, and the miles seemed like friends. John and I put our packs in the bows and then sat up on our sterns, feet on the back seats. This put our eyes about a foot higher than normal, and it changed our whole perspective of the river. The view was more expansive, superior. The extra foot provided an illusion of dominance, and the canoes seemed suddenly throne-like, a little royal. We were like pharoahs on our barges. Plus it was much easier to stretch out our legs.

Our sandbar camp of the previous night had convinced us that was the only way to go, so we paddled until we found a sandy bank. It was comfy, and a convivial place to swim, but it was also steep and narrow. There was no flat place big enough for a tent, so we had to do some "Boy Scout engineering." With bare hands we excavated the bank, forming the sand into a couple of ledges. We had two levels, each ditched for runoff, and each only precisely as large as necessary. It looked rather stylish. "Terrace tenting" we called it. I suppose by now it's all the rage on the Little Fork.

An hour before sundown a wind-torn wave of black clouds rolled in from the southwest. It was one of those leading edges of weather that seem to fly at the speed of sound. In less than five minutes the blue sky was consumed. A false dusk darkened the river, and thunder grumbled in the distance, trying to catch up with the wind. Each series of low reverberations was a little nearer—the heavy artillery being brought up from the rear. We lounged in the sand and listened, full of supper and camaraderie. John tried a little pre-storm casting. On up-turned faces we felt the benediction of the first fat drops of cool rain. It was a perfect evening.

Before we shoved off next morning, we returned most of the terraced sand back to its original slope, and buried the remains of our fire. From ten yards downriver the place looked pristine. Given the mutability of river banks, and the low camper density of the Little Fork, we may be the only people ever to sleep there. Especially since pitching a tent requires a mining operation.

10.

It was twenty-two miles and five rapids to the town of Little Fork and Neil's pickup truck. The storm had blown by as quickly as it had come, and the day was blue and blazing. Around noon we hit Flat Rock Rapids, a short, though violent Class II. I went first, a tribute to the basic simplicity of the run. But there was one massive standing wave, and Neil positioned himself below it, just out of the main flow. He dug out his camera and urged me to portage back up and run it again. Photo opportunity. I guess you've reached a dubious plateau when you start running rapids not for yourself, but for posterity.

On the first pass through Flat Rock, I'd skirted the big wave, knowing it was being generated by a huge submerged rock. There'd been enough water to dodge to the left and play it safe. It was a prudent, "professional" maneuver. But now that a lens was focused on me, realigning the natural path of the ambient photons, my brain waves became hopelessly distorted. (It's why many primitive peoples refuse to be photographed. A lens does suck things out of you—intelligence, for one.) To ensure a dramatic shot, I aimed for the middle of the big wave. No wisdom this time—I'd hit that sucker dead-on.

It came up fast. My bow leaped—aimed at the zenith, it seemed like to me—and blasted out a fan of spray. If I'd been able to stay atop the middle of the wave, I would have nose-dived from the crest and "tunneled" into a small backroller on the breaking side. I would've been swimming. But the current forced me to slide off the side of the whitecap. My stern hit the submerged rock, grinding as it sheared against the left edge. For the merest split second it seemed to hang up, threatening to grab and capsize; and then I was free. Part of the wave dumped into the canoe and shoved me forcefully away downriver. It was the closest I'd come to wiping out on the entire trip, and the resulting photo doesn't look nearly as exciting as it felt.

Most of the final leg into Little Fork was slow, flat water, but there's a quarter-mile length of Class I-II rapids at the town, just upstream from the Highway 217 bridge. It was wide, shallow, and very rocky. From the top it looked like a labyrinth of potential paths and dead ends. It wasn't dangerous, but it would take considerable skill or considerable luck to get all the way through without hitting a rock. We assembled briefly before we made the plunge, and Neil said, "This is the last one; we've got to do it perfectly." He grinned and added: "No stopping!"

We entered the rapids together, and for the first few yards we were right on each others' tails. Then John cut to the left down an alternate route and I lost sight of him. I stayed behind Neil for a ways, copying his moves. But then, on impulse, I cut to the right, into a channel that looked deeper. It was for a while. There didn't appear to be one best way through this stretch of whitewater, and it was a constant battle of steering, backpaddling, and directly fending off collisions with the blade of the paddle. If anyone was watching from the bridge it must've looked like a giant pinball game. We charged from side to side, darting to the left, then spinning, almost stopping, and cutting to the right. My paddle was flying from port to starboard—digging, ruddering, shoving.

With a lot of luck and a lot of frantic work, I was making it. Move after move, the canoe slipped downstream. I lightly scraped a few times, but nothing serious. The bridge loomed nearer, and I noticed that Neil was clear of the rapids and waving his paddle in triumph. I was back on his route, following his lead into calm water.

I was five yards from the end when I rammed the rock. It was flat and just under the surface, and I didn't see it until it was too late. I piled up onto it, my bow completely out of the water. I stuck there as if welded to the stone. Damn!

As I put out a foot to push myself off, Neil gave me a rueful, sympathetic smile. I saw him mouth our motto in mock reproach. I laughed.

Necessary Storms

Just before bed I strolled outside to patrol the summer constellations. It was midnight, and the sky was clear and still. The
silky July darkness was speckled with fireflies, and the warmth of
the previous afternoon still lingered. Lyra and Sagittarius were
impassive, offering no hint of the approaching tumult.

Six hours later there was a flash of sunrise. Upstairs, from
the eastern window, I glimpsed the full, unfiltered sun. It was
drenching the treetops with glossy radiation, but in five minutes
the sun was just a pale smear. A vanguard of clouds was advancing quickly out of the west.

I was planning to leave on a canoe trip that morning, so the
weather was a prime concern. I tuned in the early weather report,
and the meteorologists were unequivocal: we were going to get
pasted—soon.

Neil called. He was on board for this canoe venture, and had
also risen at dawn. "Get down to the lake!" he said. "You've got
to see what's coming in."

With our dog in the lead, Pam and I hurried down the path to
the lakeshore, and when we broke out of the woods we exchanged
an excited "look at that!"

It was an eldritch pile of cloud; beautiful, but terrifying.
Turbulent lumps burgeoned and tumbled—half-round and roil-

ing from the core of a distant maelstrom. It was as if a mass of protoplasmic storm matter was undergoing mitosis—doubling and redoubling in the form of gigantic, vaporous balls. They had the texture of dense smoke.

But they were also fringed and suffused with an ethereal pink, the final glow of the disappearing sun. The rosy accent was alien and scary. Not the pastel pink of young girls' dresses—but rather the shade of pale blood, the froth on the lips of a lung-shot deer. And it was hustling. The grim heap of cloud grew taller as we watched.

Just above the pinkish cluster—about halfway to the zenith—there was a sky-wide black arc. It was the leading edge of the storm slashing forward. Encompassed by this curve, and trapped by the expanding balls from below, were several white curls. They twisted and coiled in place, the seeds of a funnel cloud, spinning against a background of translucent gray. It was a hole in the sky, a cosmic lacuna that wouldn't come to focus. I stared and grew dizzy.

To the north, flashes of lightning were creeping around the rim of the front. There was no sound, but the clouds were ominously lit from within. To the south we could see the brunt of the storm. The iron-colored clouds soared to an incredible height, as if a titanic mountain was rising out of the earth and collapsing forward. The clouds were polished by wind and looked hard and solid. I could imagine a 10,000-foot granite precipice, or the carapace of a fantastic, apocalyptic monster unleashed by gods. I was reminded of a verse in the Book of Isaiah: "And all the host of heaven shall be dissolved, and the heavens shall be rolled together as a scroll . . ."

I felt diminished—shrunken to a mote of vulnerable flesh. We were at the mercy of a hostile, world-eating giant. If there were sirens out in the backwoods, they would've been wailing. If we were pantheists, it would've been time to fall prostrate, or open the jugular of a prized goat. Even in legal parlance the term is "an act of God."

Especially unsettling was the calmness of the lake. The sky was seething, but the lake was a mirror, reflecting the storm back on itself. It was too placid, far too composed. It contained the image of the tempest, and when I looked only at the lake, the storm appeared to be boiling out of the depths. Surely this glass was going to shatter.

Then we saw the wind. At the far side of the lake it thrummed the surface of the water. It plucked at the smoothness, breaking the tension with long swaths of ripples and wavelets. In a moment the gusts hit. There were a few sporadic blasts, and then the wind was steady—a seamless wall of driven air. The lake was churned to whitecaps.

Suddenly the dog was alert. He'd been nosing around the lakeshore, restless, and apparently impatient with our motionless gawking. As usual, he was oblivious of what was overhead. But when the wind hit, he froze. His ears perked, his tail went stiff, and he actually stared at the sky. I'd never seen a dog fixated on clouds. It was chilling.

The pink mass was racing towards us, bearing down at thirty-five to forty miles per hour. It was a juggernaut—charging, swelling, unstoppable. The gigantic balls were now fully over the horizon and rolling overhead. We were being enveloped. Below the bottom edge of the pink glow was a widening band of bluish-black clouds charged with rain.

It was a wild ferment of Olympian disorder, and we'd never seen anything like it. But we couldn't stand still; our feet started to move. We felt targeted for destruction, and we made an instinctual dash for safety. As the first raindrops struck, we half-walked, half-ran back up the hill through the woods. There was thunder now—not sharp claps, but a loud, continuous rumble. It was the symbolic voice of ultimate power—a few words from the Deity. The trees were waving. Mature birches bent and rebounded like saplings, and I was certain that some were going to snap and come crashing down.

There were no more pastels. The sun had been consumed, and all was black and gray. The rain fell in sheets, and for a few minutes the world had the temper of hollow dusk.

Then the wind stopped. It rained for only fifteen minutes, and the western sky began to lighten. There was no tornado. It was almost disappointing. The attack of the storm had been a grand display of aerial rodomontade. We'd been toyed with; the end was not yet.

But we'd been wise to be nervous. Other storms, though far less flamboyant, had imbued us with respect. Once, up on the Vermilion River, we'd suffered a taste of what it must be like to endure an artillery barrage. We'd spent an early-June day drifting downriver and fishing for smallmouth bass, and as evening approached we pulled our canoes onto the bank and made camp. There'd been intermittent showers throughout the afternoon, bracketed by sunlight and rainbows—some thunder and lightning, but nothing serious.

At first it seemed that sunset was heralding an end to the recurrent squalls. We cooked supper over a genial campfire and gazed up at Vega through a canopy of balsam fir and aspens. But before the rest of the stars appeared, the sky was obscured by more black clouds. Our smoke was rising straight up, but we could hear the wind coming. The sound of violent gusts among distant trees quickly grew louder, and the first splattering of rain sent us scurrying for our tents.

It rained for only a few minutes, but the wind hit us with a series of sudden, tree-lashing blasts, and powered up from there. We had a free-standing dome tent with a sturdy fiberglass frame, but the nylon panels were soon resonating like swinging drums. The gale howled and roared through the forest, ripping away leaves, twigs, small limbs, and small birds. Through the screened window of our tent I could see the tree trunks reeling. They creaked under the strain, like the timbers of a wallowing schooner. One of the mature poplars near our tent was seesawing and moaning, and I was afraid its roots were going to surface any minute, twisted, stripped, and torn.

In the distance we heard a tree crack and collapse. It sounded as if the top half of a large trunk had been sheared off and slammed into the frangible tangle of its neighbors. I started to recall every story I'd heard about tents and campers crushed by falling trees. Only a couple of years before a man had been killed on Agnes Lake in the Boundary Waters. A windstorm had dropped a large pine onto his tent and the sharp stub of a broken limb had been driven through his torso, spiking him to the ground. Or so the story was told. His companions had huddled on the shore of the lake, as far from the trees as they could get, outlasting what must have been a long and terrible night. Several years earlier, at a state park on Side Lake, two boys had been killed when a large tree dropped across their tent. Now, whenever a serious storm threatens, the campground is evacuated. Of course you can't always know what storm will be especially dangerous.

But there was no doubt about this wild night on the Vermillion River. I stared up at the dim outline of our crisscrossed tent poles. Light and flexible, they were surprisingly strong, but I had no illusions about them breaking the fall of the poplar next to us. And it was no good to seek shelter outside. The forest was very crowded clear down to the water's edge, and we would always be within the reach of several trees. There was a wide section of river a little way downstream, and we could possibly paddle there and ride out the storm in our canoes, but the river would be a turmoil of cold whitecaps, and it seemed no better to be out on the dark water.

Then there was a loud, splitting snap, like a thunderclap at ground level. It sounded close—only several feet away—and we flinched, expecting to get clobbered. A gruesome shredding noise was immediately followed by a crashing splash as a tree hit the river. We were relieved, but shaken.

Pam and I stared at each other for a moment, silently sharing fear. There was nothing we could do. Even if we had a shovel, we couldn't dig foxholes to hide in. The bank was bedrock covered by a thin stratum of dirt. That made me wonder—were the local tree roots holding as tightly as they would in deeper soil?

For a while my imagination revved up and ran unchecked. I could hear the old poplar ripping out of the ground. We would have a moment to decide—which way is it going? Then the bent fiberglass poles would shatter in our faces, and we'd have a split second of horrifying realization. The knobby log would slam into us, breaking bones. And if it didn't kill us outright, we would lay there, pinned and in agony—perhaps for several hours. The rent nylon of our tent would be a bloody shroud. My mind spun out a series of grisly scenarios, jumping like a startled squirrel each time I heard the slightest snap or creak.

It required a conscious, sweaty effort to focus my mind on a calm center of resignation. I forced myself to be fatalistic. Either a tree would hit us or it wouldn't. That simple axiom was comforting. It acknowledged that the situation was out of our hands. If there was an aspen with our names on it, well, c'est la vie.

This off-putting was a religious act. I temporarily relinquished any command over my life and fate. I had no control, therefore I had no responsibility; with no responsibility, I had no problem. I couldn't calm the wind or deflect a falling tree, so

I could do nothing. Since the matter was out of my hands, perhaps it was in someone else's. This mindset is the essence of supplicatory prayer. All that remained was to exercise the faith that we wouldn't get nailed, to be utterly convinced that it couldn't happen to us. ("Faith is the substance of things hoped for . . ." Hebrews 11:1)

The effectiveness of the tactic was erratic. For several minutes at a time I would be engulfed in my personal eye of the storm—at peace, with a potential for actual drowsiness. Then suddenly the fear would burst through, driven to the fore by a particularly vicious gust of wind, and I'd be staring at the tent frame, certain that I was about to eat it. In little pieces.

Thus passed the first several hours of the night. We were "under fire," and I vacillated between dread and morbid acceptance. Shortly before dawn the wind eased and I finally fell asleep.

We arose at midmorning and discovered that the nearby tree we'd heard die had been standing across the river, perhaps a hundred feet away. It was a large birch, and its remains clung to a shattered stump. Half of it was submerged in the river. If it had been on our side of the stream and had toppled in the same direction, it probably would have struck our tent.

I'm ambivalent about storms. They're at once splendid and terrible. They showcase the power of Nature, and they kill people. But their greatest attribute is their inevitability. In several regions of the world—including northeastern Minnesota—folks are fond of the cliche: "If you don't like the weather, just hang around for ten minutes and it'll change."

Storms are dramatic uprisings in this cycle of mutability, the sweeping revolutions that change everything—at least for the moment. If the sky is ever dull and unresponsive, it's not that way for long, not around here. Analogues to the human condition are often and easily built, but my favorite is found in a letter from Thomas Jefferson to James Madison in 1787: "I hold it, that a little rebellion, now and then, is a good thing, and as necessary in the political world as storms in the physical." Amen. I offer praise and thanksgiving for hell-raising thunder and lightning, for the cleansing insurrection of windblown rain and driven snow. But the best results are often subtle. Storms offer caresses as well as slaps.

One summer evening Pam and I were driving home from

town, heading north on a lonesome county highway. We had just crossed the Laurentian Divide, and ahead we could see the remnants of a huge thunderstorm. Overhead the sky was clear, and behind us a full moon was halfway to the zenith. The retreating storm looked like a range of mountains—a black cordillera that spanned the horizon. As we watched, the peaks were suddenly wreathed by a strange, glowing arc. At first I thought it was an aurora, but then I veered onto the shoulder of the road, and we hopped out of the car for a better look.

It was a rainbow—at night! The moist thunderheads were galvanized by moonlight, and had produced a near-perfect arc. But there were no colors. The bands of the rainbow were cast in shades of gray. It was a delicate blend of tones—a tapestry shimmering from vibrant black to white. It was like gazing at a life-size Ansel Adams print, reveling in the paradox of intensified vision through a fraction of the natural spectrum. Pam and I were amazed by the miracle of a sterling gray rainbow.

As are most wonders, it was a fleeting phenomenon. In a few minutes it was gone—a victim of the fluid celestial geometry. But this, we agreed, had been a marvelous storm. The distant thunderheads had been of that troubling, but necessary species—clouds with silver linings. To paraphrase Nietzsche: "That storm which does not kill you makes you happier."

We returned to the highway, pursuing the tempest. There was lightning at the base of the black mountains.

". . . let them dream life
just as the lake dreams the sky."
MIGUEL DE UNAMUNO

Crossings

I'm in a canoe on Big Sturgeon Lake, crossing two miles of calm, cold water. It's dusk, and the world is cast in shades of blue. The water, the treeline, the sheen on the blade of my paddle—all mimic the luster of the twilight sky. I'm paddling south, my prow aimed at a massive bank of receding thunderheads, their stratospheric pinnacles tinged with fading pink. To starboard the western horizon is still deep orange, suffused with rays of crepuscular light. A wide arc of translucent bands reaches up to the zenith, like a stylized symbol of sundown. Nimbus clouds, black as midnight, are slanting in from the northwest. They're new, just now closing in from beyond the curvature of the planet. Their tops are high, windblown and streaming, unaffected by the serenity far below. They're rimmed with a dull orange glow, and one has the shape of a horseman, a cumulus knight with a nebulous lance. He will conquer the sun. Venus is low in the west, a hard and radiant point of brightness amid a patch of mackerel clouds. She seems to wink, flirting in and out of shadow, teasing the approaching darkness.

This is an insistent sky. It raises hard questions. You're confronted by the feathering interface between yourself and the rest of space-time. It makes sense to consider them as separate. Though you're breathing the sky, and though the cells of your body are more like lake water than anything else, you are apart, detached from the firmament. And under this dome of trenchant dusk the independence means both comfort and insanity.

It's the crossing that makes it all so vivid. It's movement, the forsaking of the shore. From the beach the scene would be static, like a framed painting hung in safe stillness. But I'm paddling steadily, creasing the placid lake with my keel. I'm seated in the stern with my bow high, with a little roll to the hull as I knife along. A mist is rising, and the edges of the world are soft and ghostly. Tendrils ascend and pass. I have a sense of deep water—of distance to a cold, shadowy bottom. A loon calls—tremulous, phantasmal notes—loud but melodious. There's an answer from across the bay, and it could have come from a light year away. A lake expands as you cross it. When you're at the middle, the shore behind does not recede, the shore ahead does not approach. For a few moments you're trapped. You'll paddle forever and nothing will change. This is the madness—that your actions are meaningless, that the struggle has no resolution.

I recall a time on Knife Lake, up in the Border Country—six miles of open water and a head wind like a stone wall. We paddled against that stiff resistance—spray in our faces, our ears stoppered by roaring air and a metallic rapping as the canoe bottom slapped whitecaps. We made slow, infinitesimal headway toward a vague green shore, our muscles hardening, relaxing, tightening, releasing, but unable to rest for a second lest we be whipped sideways and swamped. Ten tough strokes—twenty, thirty, forty, a hundred, and still the distant shore had not changed in perspective. It was toil, wearying toil, a mechanical impulse of existence. No transcendent meaning. No spiritual goal. Simple physical work which we felt compelled to perform. Is that how a salmon feels when it struggles upstream to spawn? On and on and on?

After a time my strokes became rythmic and self-controlled. My mind wasn't present. The world was waves and a dullness in my back and arms. Exhaustion began to set in, and I lusted for the far shore and an end to motion. A salmon turns belly-up and dies.

But on Big Sturgeon the paddling is easy. The water ahead is a crystalline sheet—as flat, and dark as coffee in a cup. The ripples of my wake fan out behind, a wide purling triangle that eases away to invisibility, lost against the shoreline. I pass the halfway point,

and the pines on a wooded peninsula begin to grow. Their pointed, rayless silhouettes are gently backlit by the palest yellow—the last vestige of the sun's waning aura. This is the comfort—that my actions have effect, that enveloped in benign beauty my directed energy will carry me to a real goal. There is satisfaction in forward motion; in redeemed, rewarded effort.

I remember a late-August afternoon on Saganaga Lake. We were paddling "down" from Ontario, crossing the border on a westerly breeze. For three days hard winds had battered us. We rounded American Point and headed east, facing four miles of heaving water. The far shore was obscured by whitecaps—only the tiny treetops were visible, glimpsed between crests and troughs. Out in the open, the zephyr became a blast—a glorious tailwind, thirty miles an hour. The lake was like a vast set of rapids, a tossing, foam-flecked plain of waves. We whooped and entered the raging flow.

We rode the whitecaps for almost an hour. We dug in with our paddles, cutting the backs of breakers, seesawing through the chop. At times we were "surfing," shoved from behind by a three-foot ram of water, our prow bucking up and spray winging by over our heads. Even as we flew across Sag, pushed between islands and singing, I recall thinking that I would never forget it—that this was just about as high as you could get.

And now, on a tranquil evening on Big Sturgeon, I'm in-between. The joy of Saganaga and the despair of Knife are memories dimmed by the shadow of the present. I'm closing in on the south shore of the lake. I can see the warm lights of a friend's cabin—that's where I'm headed. The details of shoreline and clouds are fading. Deepening darkness and thickening mist are welding lake and sky, blurring the boundary between air and water. The reflections of the brightest stars are perfect mirror-images—I'm paddling across the Milky Way. My canoe is a starship.

Crossings. Journeys from shore to shore—at root they're all the same. But how you cross; that makes all the difference.

Portages

Every canoe trip has a first portage—usually a humble haul, from the car down to the water's edge. Every portage is a gate; this first one is a portal between worlds.

On the Little Indian Sioux River, off the Echo Trail in north-eastern Minnesota, you park your vehicle in a newly graveled lot complete with guard rails, garbage cans, privies, and most indicative of civilization, directional signs. It's forty rods down to the river, just 660 feet, but it could just as well be forty miles. The transition from the twentieth century to the seventeenth takes only a few minutes.

As you wend your way among venerable white pines, padding softly over the bare rock of the exposed Canadian Shield, you can hear the roar of rapids below. The violently aerated water, frothing against glacial debris, sends up a wild aroma. You can smell the wilderness. It's a cold green smell of fish and fur.

At the riverbank, where eddies of foam trace the outlines of jagged boulders, where thick black spruce lean over the stream, it could be three hundred years ago. If you're wearing a watch, this is your last chance to take it back up to the car and leave it where it belongs. Time will be measured by sunlight, starlight, and the phases of the moon.

The first portage sets the mood. Your canoe, resting on

shoulders meant for work, is as much a talisman as a boat, a symbol as much as an object. Though it may be fashioned out of aluminum, fiberglass or plastic, it is an archaeological artifact. The materials have changed from the days of birch bark and pine gum, but the idea and form are ancient. Outboard motors are allowed in some regions of the Boundary Waters wilderness, and they certainly have their uses. But a motorized boat is mere transportation, a purely utilitarian kind of locomotion. When you paddle a canoe, you not only cross water, you pass through history.

If you've ever fought your way across the wide expanse of Saganaga Lake against a stiff northwest wind, you've caught a bit of the spirit of the Ojibway and the voyageurs (and facefuls of spray in the bargain). But nothing evokes the aura of wilderness travel like portages. As you struggle over one of the more rugged portages, where moose have churned the trail into a quagmire, or deadfalls have claimed it as their own, you often get the feeling that few have passed that way before.

But it's humbling to realize that when George Washington was president, French fur traders had already been crossing many of these portages for more than a century—and the Indians, of course, for centuries prior to that. Hundreds of years before I-35 headed north from the Twin Cities, portages were highways of commerce. They were, literally, gates between worlds. They tied the North American continent together, and they linked the New World with Europe.

Among the most storied is the Grand Portage, a nine-mile trek from the Pigeon River to Lake Superior. It was created near what is now the Minnesota-Ontario border, to bypass a long stretch of almost continuous rapids. In the 1680s, the French became the first white men to explore the region, and the Grand Portage outpost on the shore of Lake Superior quickly became a hub for international trade in furs. It wasn't unusual for more than a thousand Indians and traders to rendezvous at Grand Portage at the peak of the season, delivering furs from as far away as Saskatchewan and the remote northwestern Athabasca country. Occasionally, during the great assemblies of the tribes, as many as 10,000 Indians would filter out of the wilderness, by canoe and on foot, to meet on the shores of Gitchie Gumi.

By the late 1700s, when the British had come to dominate the trade at Grand Portage, furs were arriving from as far west as Oregon and as far north as the Arctic Circle. Most of North America was accessible by water, and portages were the linchpins of a vast network of routes.

At the head of the Great Lakes, near where the city of Duluth, Minnesota, now stands, is the Grand Portage of the St. Louis River. The voyageurs would paddle out of Lake Superior through Spirit Lake, then for a short distance up the St. Louis River until they met ferocious whitewater. They were forced to endure a difficult, seven-mile portage around the treacherous stretch, but then the entire continent lay open before them—up the St. Louis to Savanna Portage into Big Sandy Lake, and from there to the Mississippi River, which, along with the Ohio and Missouri rivers and hundreds of other tributaries, went almost everywhere to the south, west, and east. From the St. Louis, you could also travel north to the Pike River, and into Lake Vermilion. From Vermilion, the entire north country was open to exploration. Hundreds of portages, short and long, were the indispensible shunts connecting this great circulatory system of lakes, rivers, streams, and, eventually, the Atlantic Ocean.

Today, as recreational trails, these portages are living museums. Rather than content ourselves with reading about our past, we have the opportunity to duplicate it—or, more likely, approximate it—for the voyageurs' route was a means of travel that few of us moderns could sustain for long. Many of us pride ourselves on the ruggedness of our canoe trips—and if you've experienced the 220-rod portage from Heritage Lake to Loon Lake or the 560-rod ordeal from Rose Lake to Daniels Lake, you've tasted the rigors of wilderness trekking. But only tasted.

Odds are that your pack weighed little more than fifty pounds, your canoe not much more than that. The voyageurs— who were shipping cargo, not mere camping supplies—were accustomed to carrying two or three packs (or "bales," as they were called) at a time, each of which weighed about ninety pounds. As with any commercial transportation, time was money and faster was better. A contemporary wrote:

> Sweating, panting, dark with mud and covered with mosquito and fly bites, the voyageurs dogtrotted, punctuating the carriage with many a "sacre!" . . . [T]wo or three bales or 180 to 270 pounds of goods were held on the bent back by a portage strap which passed around the voyageur's forehead and reached to the small of his back.

The voyageurs' portages were measured not in rods or meters, but in rest stops, or "poses." Depending on the difficulty of the trail, the distance between poses could be from one-third to one-half mile. A voyageur would carry his load to a pose, drop it, and head back to the canoe for more packs. In this manner the loads would be transferred from pose to pose until the portage was made.

A long, difficult haul—such as the Grand Portage of the St. Louis River, which required the voyageurs to pull their huge cargo canoes up and over a near-vertical bank about seventy feet high—would take three to five days in favorable weather. When the weather was bad, a voyageur might devote more than a week's labor to that one portage.

They performed their arduous feats on a quart of dried peas or corn and an ounce of grease per day—plus whatever else they could find, such as fish, game, or berries. Try to imagine that the next time you're in the woods zipping open your dehydrated dinner of spaghetti and meatballs or pigging out on granola bars and gorp.

And try this: Take off your treated-leather, Vibram-soled boots or your nylon running shoes; replace them with deerskin moccasins. Remove your Gore-Tex rain pants or your denim jeans; pull on deerskin leggings that reach to just past the knee. Shed your Thinsulite underwear and don a breechcloth—your thighs will remain bare. Chuck your goosedown jacket in favor of a short woolen shirt and hooded coat. Now try a long, wet-weather portage through swampy, rocky, mosquito-choked territory. (The one consolation of your voyageur imitation is that in place of your stylish Patagonia label—or, sacre!, Calvin Klein—you may wear a brightly colored sash.)

The horrors of our imaginings are, of course, a subjective product of our time. A voyageur transported to the twentieth century might consider it an unreasonable test of courage and endurance to drive a delivery truck in downtown Duluth. And he might gape, awestruck, at anyone bold enough to hang a roaring, smoking, meat grinder of an outboard motor on the stern of his eerie silver canoe. We moderns accept such curiosities as a matter of course, and paddling and portaging are for us a vacation, not a vocation. Pity.

Nonetheless, we still have the portages. We still have the

gates between worlds. We still can traverse large sections of North America by canoe if we so desire. And after we've done that—after we've picked our way among the myriad islands of Lac La Croix, have ridden the breakers on Basswood, have glided serenely across Ruby Lake—it's still the portages we remember best: Devil's Cascade, Elm Portage, Stairway Portage, Curtain Falls. A portage exists because some obstacle is there to be surmounted, and obstacles are inherently interesting. A gate is always its own invitation. Usually, in the case of a portage, an invitation to struggle and sweat—and therefore to sweetness.

A few years ago, toward the end of a long canoe trip, my friend Mick and I were heading south out of Iron Lake, bound for Stuart Lake and the source of the Dahlgren River. (We'd just left the portage around Curtain Falls. The force of that wild cataract sent vibrations through the rocky trail—we could feel the Falls on the soles of our boots before we actually saw it.) We would be crossing three small lakes between Iron and Stuart. Our map showed four portages in quick succession: Seventy-two rods, sixty-seven rods, sixty rods, and then a whopping 320 rods, or one mile. It promised to be a heavy morning's work. We joked about how rewarding that final portage would be.

At the end of the second portage, between Dark Lake and Rush Lake, we stopped to rest. I wandered off a good distance into the woods to relieve myself, and there I stumbled upon a relic, a representation and emblem of portages and portaging. On the forest floor, embedded in dead leaves and slowly sinking into humus, was an old wooden canoe. It was severely weathered and partially decayed. A young birch tree, about two inches in diameter, had grown up through the ribbed bottom.

I called Mick over to view this humbling artifact, and we could find no evidence that the canoe had been seriously damaged before its abandonment in the woods. Why had it been left there? Only imagination limits the possibilities—Mick posited a dramatic theory about smuggling and Mob violence along the Canadian border, but I had a hard time visualizing wild rice and blueberries as contraband. One thing we were sure of is that wooden canoes are very heavy. Perhaps someone tried to follow too closely on the heels of the voyageurs and was forced to give it up. Such canoes are not cheap—it was an expensive lesson.

But no matter what its history, the rotting canoe seemed an

appropriate object to find near a portage. It was like a work of art that precisely fits its surroundings. It was like a set of native pictographs on the face of a cliff. It was like a stone lion before a gate.

We resumed our journey, looking forward to that 320-rod portage. It was a good one.

Revival

The rain began sometime during the night. Wet pounding on the tent fly stirred me awake, and I faced the chilly blackness for a few moments before returning to fitful sleep. I hoped the weather would clear by morning.

But the dawn was gray and soggy—a watery world of low clouds and dripping pines. Heavy, damp air leaked in past the tent flap, and, though I hate the confinement of a sleeping bag, I was glad to linger for a while in that warm custody.

Our cold breakfast was eaten out in the drizzle, and as I gnawed on a piece of jerky I felt an icy rivulet course down my back. Socks and underwear were clammy. The day's paddling promised to be bleak, but traveling in the rain was better than sitting in it, so we bundled our wet packs into the canoes and pushed out into the lake.

In less than an hour we were stroking through a downpour that dumped nearly an inch of water into the canoes. It sloshed around our feet and seeped into our gear. My poncho was useless, and soon I was soaked to a uniform state of misery.

The portages were sticky quagmires of ankle-deep mud— black and slippery. My much-abused boots were talking to themselves. They uttered a squishing slurp going into the mud, and a loud sucking gasp on the way out. But while carrying the aluminum canoe, I could barely hear them. With the portage yoke resting on my shoulders, my head was in an echo chamber. The rain drummed violently on the upturned bottom of the canoe, trying to hammer us both into the ground.

As the flat and groveling sky went from dark to darker, signifying the approach of sunset, we found a campsite and tried to get "comfortable." With the grim diligence of the condemned, we spent an hour coaxing a sputtering fire out of saturated kindling. Our sleeping bags had been wrapped in plastic, but they were still damp. The tents, of course, were wringing wet, and the ambient moisture seemed to have permeated the very rocks. Accompanied by the incessant pattering of yet more rain, we struggled into a restless, chilly sleep.

The new morning offered no relief. Mist shrouded the forest, hanging in soppy stillness. Soon it condensed to intermittent drizzle. There was no hint of movement in the air, and we realized such weather could tarry for days. We grew increasingly depressed as we downed another cold breakfast, and our spare dry clothes gradually became drenched. Feeling like clumps of sodden moss, we shoved off for another day's journey.

Several hours later, as we pulled into our third melancholy portage, I felt the soft touch of a breeze on my cheek. Glancing up hopefully, I thought the overcast appeared a few shades lighter—perhaps. Hope can be deceiving and cruel. There was 160 rods of muddy, uphill trail ahead. I lifted the canoe and started picking my way over greasy roots and rocks. While weaving between the water-stained tree trunks, I felt a definite tug on the upturned prow of the canoe. There was a breeze—out of the northwest.

I reached the crest of the portage trail and could see part of the next lake below. It began to sparkle. A filtered shaft of sunlight suddenly burst through the sagging leaves overhead, and a gust of wind sent a final shower ricocheting off the canoe. I raised the prow so I could see a patch of sky, and there was a long jagged rip in the clouds to the west. It revealed a swath of sunlit, metallic blue. Ahead, one of my partners let out a whoop and ran slipping and sliding down to the water's edge. He let his pack flop onto the ground, and then did a joyful little jig in the mud.

In less than ten minutes the sky was torn and wild—filled with fleeing gray-white puffs scudding away against a broad blue dome. The dismal overcast was shredded by a dry and freshening wind. The lake was choppy and bright, awake and alive after long stillness. The afternoon sun was yellow and warm.

We hurried our canoes out into the lake—wanting to catch this miracle full in the face. We raised our paddles in happy salutes to the blazing sun we thought had forsaken us. I broke into the chorus of an old French canoeing song, and we all laughed in taintless delight, cleansed and high. I felt reborn. I felt as if we'd emerged from a long, black span of mourning—from the throes of unbearable grief into a new installment of life.

We were like dormant aspen buds, pullulating in the warmth of the April sun. We rejoiced as if it was the first real day of spring after a huge bitter winter. Suddenly I was convinced: our lives are not ended forever by death. The revelation came in a rush, unbidden. There amid the new waves, tossing under the new sky, I felt the confidence of hope. Leaping from depression to song at the touch of sunlight is not an accident of nature. The symbolism is too potent. We weren't happy just because our wet shirts would now be dried. We were happy because we could see the future. And like the beclouded sun, cut off by overcast or night, we will not sleep forever. Blue sky and aspen buds have told us so.

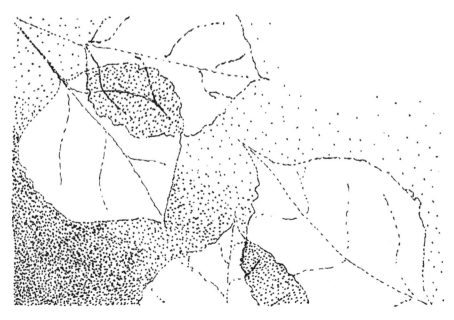

The Avenger

CAMPERS FLEE T

"I know it sounds crazy," says wife

EXCLUSIVE

In Search of
the Talking Bear

The Architectural Avenger picks me up at 5:00 a.m. We set out immediately for the Canadian border, bound for wilderness glory. Along the way he condemns several mobile homes and other offensive fabrications to well-deserved destruction, indulging in his fantasy of a militant crusade to banish vulgarity from the landscape.

"There's another job for the Architectural Avenger," he says, aiming the finger of judgement at a grotesque example of the "manufactured home," lewdly squatting in a pristine grove of aspen and birch.

The Avenger is a Harvard graduate who now teaches science to 1980s' "vidiot" children in Washington, D.C. He spent his internship as a cabbie in Boston. He still drives like one, cursing the universal ineptitude of other drivers. Since he is now piloting his own car, he refrains from ramming anyone.

"Those were the good old days," he says wistfully, recalling vindictive fender-benders, abusive lectures, and other demonstrations of authority.

At the Minnesota/Ontario border we pass through Canadian customs on Highway 61. A humorless customs official asks us the purpose of our visit. We bravely answer, "pleasure," hoping for the best.

In Thunder Bay we pause to feed diesel fuel into the Avenger's Volkswagen. The city sports a belching, aromatic paper mill, and on this foggy, mizzly morning, the local atmosphere resembles that of the planet Venus. We don't plan to linger, but being an inveterate browser, I can't resist a peek at the gas station newsstand. My curiosity is amply rewarded. The headline of one of the tabloids reads:

CAMPERS FLEE TALKING BEAR

Terrified Couple Says Bear Told Them To Leave Washington Park

"I know It Sounds Crazy," Says Wife, "But The Bear Did Speak To Us."

Joyfully, I show the paper to the Avenger. He instantly falls into a bear-like half crouch. "My park!" he growls. "Grrrr—get out of my park!" Suddenly we have a mission: we shall search for a talking bear. Fired with fresh purpose, we brazenly motor out of Thunder Bay, plunging deep into Canada "owut" along the northern shore of Lake Superior. On this rugged coast of an inland sea, rain, mist, and fog are *de rigueur*. The Avenger, who's ravaged this area before, once asked a native if they ever had clear weather. "Come back in February," was the reply.

On this soupy August morning we content ourselves with brief glimpses of magnificent wooded headlands, which lure us closer to Pukaskwa (puck-a-saw) National Park. The Ojibway word means "something evil," and the Avenger and I have been irresistibly drawn to this wild place. Surely, if an articulate bear exists, we shall converse with it here.

The Pukaskwa is a 1,127-square-mile wilderness area on the Northeastern shore of Lake Superior. It's roughly halfway between Thunder Bay and Sault Ste. Marie, and from either direction the drive itself is worth the trip. The chief attraction of the park is the Coastal Hiking Trail, a thirty-six mile jaunt along stupendous Superior shoreline. From bedrock ridges draped with boreal forest, to wide, sandy beaches hemmed in by palisades, the trail is always a scenic delight. In addition to a thriving black bear population, there are moose, wolves, and a small herd of woodland caribou. The half dozen rivers offer decent, uncrowded fishing—rainbow and speckled trout, northern and walleye pike, yellow pickerel. For anthropology buffs, there are the "Pukaskwa

Pits," the long-forsaken remains of an unidentified Indian culture. The park brochure notes: "Upon Pukaskwa boulder beaches are mysterious, shallow rock structures fashioned by man. We can only speculate about the purpose of these 'pits,' who arranged them, when, and why." However, a colorful display at the Hattie Cove visitor's reception center portrays the pits as ritualistic constructs—places of power where people could position themselves for meditation and/or worship. Modern sojourners are free to examine the pits and entertain their own speculations.

At tiny, weatherbeaten Heron Bay, the last ragged outpost of refinement before the Pukaskwa, we are stopped at the Canadian Pacific Railroad. Four locomotives and a long line of boxcars straddle the highway. We spend the next half hour speculating on the reason for the delay. Moose troubles, perhaps? Twice the locomotives move, jerking to within fifteen feet of clearing the intersection. Seven autos collect to enjoy the suspense. It's quite a snarl for this part of the world. We can clearly see the engineer. He's laughing, talking on a phone, lighting cigarettes, and waving to fellow employees out on the tracks. The Avenger is convinced that the man is taking bets on how soon he can strand an even dozen autos. It makes sense to me; a body could get lonely on the Canadian Pacific. But this never happened in Boston, and the Avenger begins to rumble ominously, his hack-driver's heart thoroughly unamused. But before we're transfigured into ugly Americans, the train finally chugs past the intersection. It's the smelly curtain of civilization being drawn aside. We courageously shoot the tracks, and in a few minutes enter the soggy Pukaskwa.

After the empty formality of registration (they'll never rescue us alive!), we heft our backpacks and hike into the rainy forest. We're bemused by Canadian hospitality. We find that the "primitive" campsites are complete with roofed outhouses, displaying men/women symbols on the doors. Worse, over the best mudholes and across otherwise attractive swamps, the park people have constructed footbridges. Stinking bridges! We're sorely disappointed until we realize these effete conveniences are intended for the lowly "day-trippers"—folks who drag in coolers and kids. Soon, a few miles into the bush, the maternalistic structures peter out and leave us with a terribly honest path. We gratefully ease into ankle-deep mud, right next to the moose tracks.

We follow moose prints for two-and-a-half hours, and I'm deeply mystified. Over the course of five miles or so, despite hundreds of hoof impressions, we see no droppings. Piles of "moose berries" should have been abundant. Strangely, we would end up covering twenty-two miles replete with moose tracks, and we would see no scat. What's the deal? I wondered. The Avenger, drawing on his background in biology, suggests that the park rangers create the tracks with moose feet attached to sticks, in order to impress the urbanites. I argue that anyone who invested so much care into constructing wilderness privies would surely know enough to scatter some fake moose droppings. I theorize that there's one real moose, and this individual is severely constipated. The Avenger concedes this single moose, but maintains it's been potty trained by overzealous environmentalists.

In any case, we reach the White River. The frothing cataract—they don't call it "white" for nothing—cuts through a spectacular gorge, about 150 feet deep and seventy feet wide. The chasm is spanned by a narrow, swinging suspension bridge. The Avenger is delighted, giving it his architectural seal of approval. The flimsy looking structure, squeaking and yawing under our weight, is right out of a Tarzan movie. As we gingerly traverse the wet boards, surrounded by misty forest and dripping cliffs, I can imagine the Ape Man screaming through the Pukaskwa. Leaping from spruce to spruce in his loincloth, he's fair game for billions of lustful mosquitoes. The winters are also rough. His northern companion, Cheater, a rabid red squirrel, provides little comfort. In desperation, a distraught Tarzan dives into the raging White River after a man-eating walleye pike, and vanishes forever. Good riddance.

The White River is a relatively notorious canoe route. Experienced paddlers—emphasis upon experienced—can make a 115-mile trip from Negwazu Lake just north of Obatanga Provincial Park, all the way to Lake Superior. The river drops 765 feet and encompasses sixty-eight rapids and waterfalls. Its lower reaches are roadless and remote, and the whitewater is treacherous. People have died on the White. "Respect" is the key word, but it's a beautiful, challenging run. Paddlers must finish the trip by canoeing about four miles up the Lake Superior coast to Hattie Cove, and that is probably the most dangerous segment of the trek. There are portages around the whitewater, but Superior has to be negotiated on its own terms. The Ontario Ministry of Natural Resources' map/guide for the White stresses that paddlers must allow time to be "degradé" on Superior. That is, windbound—like the Voyageurs of old, you may have to camp for a day or two (or three) and wait for calm waters.

As for the Avenger and I, we make camp on the edge of a foamy pool at the base of a stretch of rapids. While fishing and gawking beside the stream, we see a boat materialize out of the fog. A thumping/buzzing/cranking indicates an outboard motor. There are four humans in expensive raingear.

"Motorheads!" I hiss.

"Motorheads?" queries the Avenger. My grimace of disgust says it all. The Avenger has a new cause. As an adjunct to his architectural purification, motorboats must be expunged from the wilderness.

"Motorheads!" he spits, his voice reeking with practiced cabbie scorn.

Even so, they're sharing the woods, so we wave, a deceptively congenial gesture. But since they don't see an eighteen-foot Lund with a sixty-horse Mercury, they take us for an optical illusion. Any motorhead knows that humans don't *walk* that far.

In the morning we strike our tent, pack up our self-righteousness, and head out into the fog. We follow the sanitary moose onto a high ridge which is blanketed with a mind-boggling blueberry patch. The little suckers are ripe; the sensation is orgasmic. We drop our packs and wallow in the patch like snorting hogs. This is black bear nirvana, a free buffet, but we see no droppings or tracks. The Talking Bear has not yet arrived.

Our tongues blue, we push on to a campsite at the mouth of the Willow River, on the shore of Lake Superior. Late in the day some motorheads cruise in. The Avenger engages them in a friendly conversation about poor fishing, and they promptly leave. His strategy is devilishly subtle.

Shortly thereafter, three kayaks ride the breakers onto the beach. One of the paddlers is a little pale. We amble over to chat and find out that his two "friends" have just taken him for his first kayak ride—several hazardous, heaving miles on Lake Superior. He is not happy; impressed, but not happy. He talks only half-jokingly about portaging his kayak the ten trail-miles back to Hattie Cove. Though definitely not for rookies, the

Pukaskwa coastline is a popular stretch of water with paddlers—using both kayaks and canoes.

The sun, or what we surmise to be such, pokes out briefly toward evening, but it's soon overwhelmed by more clouds and mist. Nevertheless, we catch a glimpse of some nice scenery that is at least three hundred yards distant. The next morning visibility is back to a comfortable one hundred feet, and we set off into the fog. About a mile down the trail, on the crest of another rocky ridge graced with blueberries, we meet the Talking Bear. We're just humping along, our brains on autopilot, when there he is, a large male with shiny black fur and decorative little ears. He's standing a mere thirty feet away munching berries, and we startle him. He startles us. For a moment we all freeze, staring. Then I slowly backpedal toward the Avenger, contemplating an evasive jump off the nearest ledge. The bear, making definite eye-contact, emits a loud, snuffling snort. He then turns and gallops off into the trees and is gone.

"Did you hear it?" I shout. "The bear spoke to us!"

"Absolutely," replies the Avenger. He's obviously awestricken.

In the next day-and-a-half we encounter nine more bears, mostly face-to-face, but they are mute. Enough has been said. We respect their unencumbered wisdom. The sun emerges full blast, clear sky and all, and the blueberries sweeten on the bushes. Bears fill the patches and we no longer loiter there. It seems slightly tacky, and somehow stupid.

Presently we leave the Pukaskwa and venture back into the wilds of highway and truck stop. Somewhere near Nipigon we pass a KOA Kampground. The parking lot is choked with ungainly RV units, Winnebagoes as big as sperm whales. Motorheads! The familiar A-frame building is one of their shrines. The Avenger and I begin to chant: "Koa! Koa! Koa!" In the midst of the infidel we offer sarcastic, heretical homage.

But we are secure, fulfilled; we've left our testament. The solicitous park people had installed a guest register at the White River campsite. On a blank page the Avenger had scrawled in dark illegibility: Death To The Motorheads! Below that, in a benign and elegant script, I entered our revelation: *I know it sounds crazy, but the bear did speak to us.*

Autumn Books

By mid-August anticipation is building. Not with pounding heart and sweating palms, but with keen expectations in the mind. Autumn is coming. The land will be transformed, vibrant with colors, odors, and textures alien to the rest of the year. When you walk through the autumn woods you sense an undercurrent of restlessness in the world. It's easy to imagine being on an exploration of terra incognito, on a glorious quest in the company of strange and wonderful wayfarers. It's no accident that the famous trek of Frodo Baggins began in September. It's time for changes and adventures. One grows tired of summer; it's much too benign.

I had a secret when I was younger: I looked forward to returning to school in the fall. It wasn't because of football or the girls, or because I didn't appreciate the carefree days of summer vacation. It was because of the books. A new textbook was such a grand mystery, like a green leaf turning brilliant orange. Where would it lead? What new paths would be uncovered in those first fresh days of September? Who could say where I would be by Halloween? Autumn was a season of quests, of journeys into hollow trees where secrets lay in wait for eager eyes.

The crisp blue winds and whirling leaves kindle a rebirth of those youthful days of wonder—days when each sunrise described a new horizon, when just looking at the stars could rede-fine the earth. There's a unity to existence, and layer by layer, as our perceptions dissect the world, each event is significant. Is it easier to hear a peal of thunder, or an autumn leaf hitting the ground? They speak with equal voice. If one is too loud, or the other too soft, we have our own ears to blame.

But even the books of autumn, wise as they were, could only tell so much. Soon the final page was turned and fell like the last brown leaf of November. A soft sound, but as momentous as thunder. For one day I too will have told all I have to tell. I'll be brittle and shaky in the October wind, and the journeys of autumn will end. The restlessness will sleep. One grows impatient with autumn; it's much too lucid.

Like spring. Once, in April, we ran our canoes down the East Branch of the Sturgeon River. It's a narrow stream, only runnable in springtime, but then it's fast and deep, dropping sixty feet in five miles. The rapids come one after another, short but brisk. We whipped along, riding waves around bends, dodging over-hanging boughs, shooting down small slides. The river was rarely more than twenty or thirty feet wide, the banks thickly wooded, and we had the feeling of paddling through tunnels. At one spot, a violent rapids, that was all tumbling waves and foam, filled the constricted channel, pounding the banks. It made a sharp bend at the start, and as I fired around the corner, paddling hard to avoid a large boulder, a whitecap broke over the gunwale. For an instant I wallowed, but the momentum of the stream and my digging paddle launched me out of danger. It seemed as if the canoe was weightless. The close quarters produced a magnificent sensation of blinding speed. I hit a straight stretch and flew down the rapids, laughing. Neil and John were waiting in the pool below. They were both grinning. We were as high as the bald eagle we could see soaring overhead.

Then, unexpectedly, we came to a small footbridge spanning the stream. Whitewater boiled under it, reaching almost to the deck; there appeared to be enough clearance for the prow of a canoe. We followed Neil in, fighting the rapids until the last mo-ment, and then ducking to the bottoms of our canoes as we were swept under the bridge into the waves beyond. There had been about two inches to spare.

For two hours we rode the river down through the forest,

reveling in illusions of speed and freedom, sharing the satisfaction. The river compelled us—a pouring and gushing of icy snow-melt at the peak of its power. On the last stretch of rapids I nailed a rock dead-on. I was hung up for a moment, struggling to pry free with the paddle. But the relentless current spun the canoe on its keel and tipped it back into the river. I fought for balance, but the river surged in, swamped the canoe, and flipped me into the water. We flowed downstream together, clutched by the current, flotsam in the roiling stream.

But autumn comes. You can take a trail down to the banks of the East Branch, and follow the now tamed and quiet brook. The commanding torrents are gone, reduced to ripples. Where we blithely cruised over submerged logs, they're now exposed as barriers, dried by summer sun. There's plenty of room under the footbridge. The once-swollen pools are rimmed by cracked mud. Here is a book, an autumn revelation.

Still, you remember the springtime river, the exaltation in the midst of whitewater, the thrill of rounding choppy bends. I was here in April, you say—when we flew down this river like gods. I remember the cold, fresh foam, and the waves as bold as new life. You can always remember—especially in autumn. You can allow the restlessness a free hand. Bring on the long winter, you'll be back in the spring.

A Species of Exercise

It's mid-September, and I think I'll take "the grand tour." That sounds a bit showy for a mile-and-a-half stroll through a nondescript patch of woods. But it's a jungle out there, a wild cosmos to be sensed and examined. I usually take a leisurely hour to cover the distance, cradling a .410 shotgun, ostensibly hunting for grouse. It's been years since I actually bagged one. Last season I had a single clean shot, and missed. This armed stalking is more of a congenial autumn ritual than a serious dragnet.

I guess the practice is in tune with the walks of Thomas Jefferson. In 1785, in a letter to a nephew he wrote: "A strong body makes the mind strong. As to the species of exercise, I advise the gun. While this gives a moderate exercise to the body, it gives boldness, enterprise, and independence to the mind. Games played with the ball, and others of that nature, are too violent for the body, and stamp no character on the mind. Let your gun, therefore, be the constant companion of your walks."

A gun is appropriate company in the backwoods. It's not that you need it for self-defense, it just helps you to fit in. Everybody else is armed. They have fangs, claws, quills, stingers, talons, beaks, pincers, venom, and thorns. Our grizzled old shotgun, nicked, scratched, and taped, is as unobtrusive as a sheathed talon. It's naturally camouflaged by the dullness of age and hard use.

133

If I laid it on the leaf-strewn ground and walked off ten paces, it would be hard to spot. It's a good forest companion, quiet (unless called upon), and impervious to distance. It fits the land.

We consider the government land east and south of the cabin as "our backyard." Though we officially share it with the rest of the citizenry, not many others know it. Deer season is usually the only time I encounter another human out there. I give it up then, conceding superior firepower. Besides, I would feel like a jester (and a high-profile target) rambling around in a blaze orange ensemble.

In late afternoon I leave the cabin and walk past the woodpile. It's a mongrel stash, a little mixed up and inelegant. A lot of folks like to precisely construct a neat and homogenous woodpile—a compact cube of all birch or all ash. Our pile isn't messy, it's just asymmetrical. It's inherent imbalance, both in style and content, is unpleasing to the critical eye. It's higher on one end than the other, and contains a wide sampling of species—aspen, birch, jack pine, white spruce, maple, white ash, balsam—whatever's handy. I think there's even a chunk or three of dense (and smelly) balm of Gilead, or "bombagilly," as I've heard a local logger call it.

But the red squirrels love it. The pile is parked right at the edge of the woods, and for the squirrels it's an accessible and sheltering labyrinth. The irregular chunks of wood, not too tightly packed, provide them a veritable castle of passageways, dens, and caches. One January, I broke apart a frozen row of wood (a mid-November rain had "cooled" before it dried) and uncovered a plush rodent suite. Some enterprising squirrel had found a roll of fiber-glass insulation we had stored in the garage, and had smuggled out enough to line its entire den with Owens-Corning's best. The pink contraband must have made for a particularly cozy nest, but I can't imagine how the squirrel could stand to sleep in the midst of that scratchy, itchy, irritating stuff. I had to wear a long-sleeve shirt (disposable), gloves, and a face mask when I was installing it, and after fifteen minutes I still felt like I'd been staked out on an ant hill. I suppose if I had a skin-tight fur coat it wouldn't have bothered me either. On the other hand, the squirrel would have had to transport the fiberglass in its mouth. They're a strange breed. When I hear someone referred to as "squirrely," I picture a distracted, chattering individual, their shorts stuffed with fiberglass insulation.

The woodpile looks massive now, nine cords of solid, no-nonsense matter, about 120,000,000 latent BTUs. But in a few months it will have vanished, transformed into heat, light, smoke, and a surprisingly small pile of ashes. Nothing we do around here is at once so substantial and so ephemeral. Putting up nine cords of firewood, from stump to woodbox, is the essence of reality—tangible, authentic work. It's a sweat-stained exercise of life and will. And then, in one season, it literally goes up in smoke. If someone were innocent enough to ask, "Where did your woodpile go?", I would have to point at myself and say, "Here. I absorbed the BTUs, and despite winter's best, I'm still alive." On one level, I am the woodpile. Because of its mass and energy, I can now go out and cut some more. It's a curious little epicycle, entangled with the larger, but no more profound, cycles of the cosmos. (Or so it's helpful to theorize at the start of the work.)

Just beyond the woodpile is a scrub oak. This region doesn't produce the giant, gnarled oaks of fantasy and paganism. Only along the river flats will a northwoods oak grow much beyond an eight-inch trunk. But in the fall the leaves turn a deep russet-maroon, a touch of somber refinement amidst the flamboyant maples and aspen. The leaves eventually turn dead brown, contemplative and unfashionable, and hang onto the tree long after the snows have arrived. It's a tenacious gesture, a symbol of resistance that's appreciated by those who intend to survive another winter.

A Canadian jay flits about the branches of the oaks, its feathers a pleasing blend of white, gray, and black. It whistles at me, a loud "wheeoo," a big sound for a big bird. A jay can be up to ten inches long, and is almost always friendly—to a fault. This one wings off behind me, headed, no doubt, for the dog's dish. They prefer dry dog food to the sunflower seeds we provide for the rest of the birds. It's rare to see them at the feeder, even in darkest January. Their cousins, the blue jays, loiter at the feeder all winter, but the gray jays would rather peck at Purina Puppy Chow. Or better yet, anything that humans peck at. It's nothing to get them to perch on your fingers and pluck peanuts out of your palm. I once saw a jay swoop down and grab a wiener off a hot grill. It took off like a torpedo plane, the frankfurter held parallel to its direction of flight. It was a heavier load than anticipated, and the weight of the wiener almost dragged the jay to earth before its pounding wings managed to lift it to the nearest tree. We loudly cheered its impudence.

I pass beneath a natural archway of thick balsam limbs, and purposely brush against them. A rich coniferous aroma is released and drifts along behind me. The green, piney smell lays a fresh edge on the autumn air. It's evocative of deep woods, Christmas trees, and log cabins. I rub some needles on my wrist and keep it to my nose for a while. I pluck one and chew; it tastes like amber and gin.

There's a faint trail twisting off into the forest, a path I've made myself by simply walking through. Here it's fringed by ferns and purple asters. The ferns are brown, crisp as corn flakes; the early frosts have finished them. But the asters are at their peak, healthy and tall. The little yellow centers of the flowers dip and wink in the breeze. The path leads to a small open area where I've done some logging. I felled a few dead aspen and balsams, and now their stumps have almost rotted away. I see a black bear has ripped one out of the ground, searching for tasty black ants. I stacked all the limbs in one huge brush pile, and its been there for about five years now. If I were to climb on top and jump a bit, I wouldn't be surprised to see a rabbit come scurrying out. Anyway, I left it there for them.

The open area is rimmed by orange, red, and yellow maples, afire with sunny color even though the sky is steel gray. The maples are backed and topped by aspen and birch, their leaves still green, the last hurrah of summer. This bright, chromatic clearing is in strong contrast to the neighboring bog. The mixed forest drops off a short, steep bank to the muskeg. Several acres of spongy sphagnum moss support a scattering of black spruce and tamaracks. The tamaracks lose their needles in late fall, but before they drop, they turn a fine pastel yellow, trimming the muskeg with swaths of color. The muskeg surrounds a large fifteen-acre pond (or small fifteen-acre lake, depending upon your point of view), and you can just see the open water from the edge of the woods.

At a quick glance all is damp and dull green, but the bog is an intricate, surprising world. The moss is thick and hardy, and is also remarkably clean. During the Russo-Japanese War of 1904-05, sphagnum was used as a sterile battle dressing. The oxygen deficiency and natural acidity of bog water prevents the growth of microorganisms. Dried moss was also the traditional chinking material for log cabins.

Beneath the lumpy layer of moss is a stratum of coal-black peat, a sealed reservoir, a huge organic sponge. It's a fossil fuel in the making, but not a very good one (if there is such a thing). Politicians around here have been excited about it off and on for over fifty years, but I believe an Ojibway spokesman was right when he said that the peat is fulfilling its most important duty right where it is—as an inherent part of the watershed, and a source of life for all.

And sometimes a preserver of death. If you shove a body down under the moss into the heart of the bog, it won't decay— at least not for a very long time. It's that lack of microscopic decomposers. A few years ago in Scandinavia, a corpse that appeared to be newly dead, perhaps a few days gone, was uncovered in a peat bog. In fact, the man had died (apparently murdered and hidden) a thousand years before. About 2,000 so-called "bog bodies" have been found in Europe. Many were probably sacrificial victims. Bogs were uninhabited, deserted places, so they were deemed the abode of gods and spirits. The sacrifices were rendered (and sometimes partially eaten), and left for the gods, and us, to find. So if you wish to dispose of the evidence, stay away from the bog.

But not if you appreciate subtle beauty; like pitcher plants. The green and reddish fluted spouts grow in the folds of the moss, opening to the sky. These strange leaves collect rainwater and partially fill. Flies and other insects easily crawl inside, but treacherous, downward-pointing hairs prevent an easy escape. Many victims drown inside the plant and are dissolved and digested by enzymes and bacteria. In summer this insectivore produces a dark red flower at the end of a graceful, nodding stem. It's an altogether alluring and devious killer. But it's not without its nemesis. One mid-November day, when the pond ice was just thick enough to walk on, I noticed a flock of wheeling ravens on the far side of the bog. I counted thirty of the large black scavengers, and I had never seen more than a dozen together before. What would draw so many carrion-eaters? As I approached, the ravens squawked (irritably, it seemed) and flew off, leaving their banquet. I was prepared for some gorey corpse, but all I found were dozens of shredded pitcher plants. Apparently the ravens were tearing them apart to get at the "meat" dissolving within. Were these ravens desperate, or are pre-digested insects an exotic delicacy? I was unable to tell.

Cotton flowers also proliferate in "our" bog, and at their height in late June the muskeg sports a low canopy of white fluff. There are thousands of them—long, spindly stems, each capped by a pure white cotton ball. On windy days it's like a tossing sea of foam. To butterflies it must be stupendous—like a layer of clouds, another dimension in which to dodge and glide.

Twining through the moss and blending into the enveloping greenness are the tiny leaves and "vines" of the low bush cranberries. Sometimes you must bend over and stare to see them. Even when the plump berries, as big as grapes, turn from white to cherry red in the fall, they can be hard to see in the moss. We pick them in early November, from our canoe if the lake is still open and the bog unfrozen, or on foot if all has hardened. One year we wore skates, gliding along the edge of the ice and reaching back into the moss on hands and knees. In a good year we'll get enough for two or three pints of cranberry sauce to tide us over the Holidays. It's especially satisfying to provide your own cranberries for Thanksgiving—very Pilgrim-like.

Other plants in the bog include Labrador tea, the leaves of which the Indians used for making just that; bog rosemary and leatherleaf; and false Solomon's seal, whose roots are a folk remedy for arthritis. (Haven't tried that yet.)

The muskeg and the lake/pond are a magnet for wildlife. Anything interested in water, food, or shelter usually finds its way to the bog at one time or another. We've seen beavers, otters, muskrats, and mallards swimming around, and a pair of loons has recently begun to nest there. They mold the nest out of sedges and reeds on a soft, semi-floating mat at the edge of open water. The egg or eggs—we've never seen more than two—hatch in early to mid-June, and it's a big event when a little loon makes it. Unfortunately, the track record is poor.

The first year I kept a daily watch on the loon nest with binoculars, and on the night of June 9th I heard the loons break into a wild and ecstatic song that swept along for several minutes. The next morning I saw the parents, and one tiny black feather-ball swimming in the middle of the lake. We have a canoe stationed at the water's edge, but while the nesting was in progress we kept off the lake. It seemed crass to intrude upon mother and eggs. But with the nest empty and maternity achieved, we thought it appropriate to paddle out and greet the little one.

First we glided up to the empty nest and discovered it wasn't exactly empty. One egg was all in pieces, its recent occupant now out in the wide wet world with mom and dad. But the other was only partially opened, a dead chick folded up inside. Its feathers were still moist, flat against its body. It looked fully developed. I later read that sometimes the adult loons become so preoccupied with getting the first hatchling out of the shell and into the water, that they neglect the second, and it may not complete the critical transition on its own.

Still, we were happy about the one that was free, and for the next few days we watched and took photos as the new loon cruised the lake, sometimes riding on the back of one of the adults, often closely sandwiched between them. It was pleasing to know that by fall we could expect to hear three loon voices melded in ethereal melody. But one day they were all gone. It was only two weeks after the birth, and by all accounts a loon can't fly until it's ten or eleven weeks old. The unpleasant conclusion was that some predator had nabbed the youngster, and the adults had left. The chief eaters of baby loons are northern pike and birds of prey. It could have been a snapping turtle, but we've never seen one around. It was sad; we can use all the loons we can get. The avian guidebooks call them the "common loon," but there's nothing common about them. Only the timberwolf can make night music that's more spine-tingling. But no creatures cry out with such melodious, wide-ranging harmony. As we lay in bed (or next to some remote campfire) and listen to the sometimes melancholy, sometimes rapturous notes drift in through the screens and pass by in the darkness, all is right with the universe.

So we were excited the following spring when the pair of loons (we assumed it was the same family) arrived to construct a new nest on the opposite side of the lake. The old one was still there, bits of the brown eggshell littering the bottom, but it appeared a fresh start was in order. Sadly, it ultimately came to even less than the previous season's effort. The loon remained on the nest until the third week of June, and when she finally swam off it for good, there was nothing there—no trace of an egg. Either something had stolen them intact (or eaten them whole), or she had never laid one in the first place. It seems that creating a full-grown loon is no mean feat. Perhaps that's why their songs are often so mournful.

But the lake/bog is not often an unhappy locale. It's a place where timid whitetail deer sip water at dusk, where squadrons of Canada geese briefly pause on their October trek to the south, and where zooming woodcocks will buzz by like strafing F-14s, making the dog jump and bark. Once I looked up from the moss just in time to glimpse the hindquarters of a moose slipping into a thicket of black spruce. The irony was that I was preparing to drive a hundred miles north that afternoon to go moose hunting. And so now, whenever I approach the bog, I keep an eye out, hoping for a more intimate encounter.

But the moose isn't out in the muskeg today, and my path veers away from the moss and past two old landmarks. One is a dead jack pine, the other a dead birch. They're side-by-side amidst dense alderbrush, and they've both been dead for years. The jack pine is defiantly erect. It's hard trunk and branches are almost bare of bark, tempered by sun and weather to a smooth gray finish. It's rotting at the base, where lifeless roots still cling to the damp, fecund soil. One day it'll topple, broken by a southwest wind, but it'll be a tree to the end.

Birch, however, don't pass away with dignity. Their lovely white bark is drum-tight and unyielding. It's not readily decayed, and so locks degenerative moisture inside the dead trunk. Mushroom-like fungi called polypores burst through the bark like alien parasites, sucking the hardness out of the heartwood. In a year the insides of a dying birch are turned to mush, and it collapses at the slightest pressure. The bark may remain intact for years, a cylindrical case for soft, rotten wood. A dead-fallen birch trunk is a fragile thing; I could rip it to shreds with my bare hands. But the soggy tube will be there for a long time, lying in the shadow of the naked jackpine. It's like walking past the graves of two old friends. One died well; the other took it hard. They'll all go one day.

I'm about two hundred yards from the cabin, and the trail leads up a ridge past a couple of granite boulders—the detritus of the last ice age's receding glaciers. The rocks are fragments of an expansive formation of rock that stretches north to the Arctic Circle, and is never very far beneath the surface.

At the crest of the ridge I'm in a grove of young aspen. The area was logged off a dozen years ago, and the aspen immediately took over. For the next quarter mile the straight, greenish-white saplings form a dense natural monoculture. When all their leaves turn butter-yellow and are backlit by a westering sun, the color is like a mist hanging in front of your eyes. The yellow is so vivid, so concentrated and overwhelming, that if your retinas were on circuit breakers they would certainly trip out. You must occasionally glance at open sky to cool them.

But this is a wicked stretch of woods. Amidst the aspen, the regenerating forest has produced a mass of raspberry and blackberry bushes. The berries are sweet and succulent in their seasons, but are vigorously defended by prickers and thorns. The raspberry stems aren't too bad, their coating of stingers is fine and pliable and you can ease through a raspberry stronghold with only mild discomfort. But the blackberry stalks are liberally armed with hard, sharp thorns, like tiny fangs or splinters of bone. They catch, rip, and stab—and never one at a time. They work in platoons and battalions, one puncturing spike leading inexorably to the next as the stalk bends into the body of its adversary. Barging into a "stand" of blackberries is like having a pair of fighting cats dropped into your lap. Those plants are angry. There are some ancient traditions that have Christ's Crown of Thorns being made of blackberry brambles. True or not, those thorns could easily be employed for torture of some kind. I've pushed back or broken all the stalks that have assaulted me, and I now have a narrow, but safe passage through the tangle.

But for the birds it's a haven and buffet. The little wood warblers and black-capped chickadees trill and chirp as they hop around in the thicket, unstuck and unflustered, with berries to boot. I've seen grouse in there too, but one flap and they're gone, swallowed up by the foliage. I have time to cock the hammer and get excited, and that's it.

The trail of thorns gradually widens into an old logging road. The right-of-way has almost melted away, reclaimed by woods, but a few bare, sandy patches remain, and they're perfect spots to check for tracks. I almost always see the hoof prints of deer, and today is no exception. It looks like two of them—a large adult and a juvenile, probably born last spring. We are traveling in the same direction, but the prints have caved in at the edges and aren't fresh—perhaps this morning or even yesterday. I'm no expert, but I'd say this pair is long gone.

There are also some canine tracks, possibly wolf or coyote. Occasionally we hear timber wolves howling, and packs of coyotes yipping and yapping, and once Pam looked out an upstairs window and saw a huge gray wolf standing nonchalantly in our driveway. By the time she hustled outside it had evaporated into the brush, but it taught us never to take our windows for granted. (I keep telling her that some moonlight winter night we'll look out and see Sasquatch.) According to the Department of Natural Resources, this land is within the territory of the Sherry Lake wolf pack. The last I heard, it had twelve members and appeared to be thriving.

Of course these canine tracks could also have been made by somebody's dog. They're not amazingly large, and we're not far away enough from what passes for civilization to preclude it. But for now I'll go with the wolf interpretation. There's no evidence to contradict me, and I feel wilder and more free in their presence.

One February, out on skis not far from this spot, I picked up a fresh blood trail. Interspersed with the bright red drops were the tracks of a deer and a wolf. I fell in behind and took up the chase. Soon I noticed more tracks—wolf prints on either side, gradually closing in on the original track. I felt like part of the pack, hungry to see what was ahead. I assumed the blood was leaking from venison, and that somewhere over the next ridge I could witness the climax to this feral drama. In the deer versus wolf pack contest, the odds are in favor of a healthy deer, but since this one appeared to be bleeding, the advantage could have swung over to the pack. I might catch them feeding. But it was late and overcast, and darkness descended before I reached the end of the track. I turned back, hoping to resume the search in the morning, but it snowed heavily overnight and the story was lost; at least to me.

Near the canine prints I find the three-toed scratchings of a grouse. I'm reassured that my quarry has at least been in the neighborhood lately. This one crossed the old road and headed east. I'll be alert for it when the trail banks that way. There are a couple of oaks over there, and the grouse might be after some acorns.

I'm almost half a mile from the cabin now, and I wade into a ten-by-thirty-yard patch of sweet fern. It loves the sandy soil and grows to my knees in an homogenous, pungent plot. Despite frost, it's still green, and the weedy smell rises off the leaves in an invisible cloud. It dominates the surrounding air, spicy in a rough sort of way. I've often thought I should roll around in it sometime; surely this scraggy perfume would mask my human scent and render me a little less detectable to the local residents. I'll try it one day.

Just beyond the ferns is a long stretch of grass, clover, and small "bombagilly," and I've often seen whitetails leaping across this exposed swath for the security of the balsams beyond. When they're gone I rush up to look at the prints they've made in flight. Their hooves dig deeply and launch together, and just looking at the tight pattern of tracks can impart a sense of the power and agility at work. One of my visions of paradise is to be endowed with the speed, grace, and savvy of a large buck, and turned loose in a beautiful autumn forest. Bring on the wolf pack and let me leap and run and run and leap—for days and nights and never tire. I can understand how notions of reincarnation as various animals arose—it was out of envy for their prowess.

The fading right-of-way soon merges with a two-track logging road that was still usable (with a truck) up until a few weeks ago. The road was deteriorating, and the county sealed it off at the main road. There wasn't much traffic, but now there's none, and that's fine with me. The old road borders a plantation of Norway and jack pine, and the young greenness is always refreshing. The seedlings have done well, and are now bona fide trees, secure from those who are looking for Christmas decorations, or a free transplant for the front yard back in suburbia. In fifty years they'll be magnificent, and I hope I'm still around to see it. It'll be worth a few more winters.

The two-track road turns to the east and rises. It's a short, steep hill, and in the winter, when all the leaves are gone, I can catch a glimpse of our cabin snuggled in the woods. The isolation is visible then—a solitary roof in an ocean of trees, a whiff of smoke from the chimney—a secluded warm spot that would've been a natural for Currier and Ives.

At the base of the hill there's a sudden flurry off to my left, a flapping and a rustle of ferns. I raise the shotgun, but it's no grouse. A yellow-shafted flicker scoots off into the trees, winging and dipping in its curious, jerky flight. It's a big, colorful bird, with a golden, mottled breast and a conspicuous red patch on the back of the head. From the rear it sports a white "flag," like an airborne deer. There are a lot of flickers around this year. I aim at it just for drill, imagining how I would lead my shot to catch it on an upward swing. It's not a lot smaller than a grouse. I'd probably miss.

About halfway up the hill I stop to inspect the old stuffed chair. I first walked this way a decade ago, and the chair was there then. Someone was too lazy to trek to the garbage dump, and just rolled it off their tailgate and pushed it into the woods. I was irritated the first time I saw this rotting human artifact, and pushed it a little further into the brush. I jumped on the arms and back to break up the frame and make the chair more compact and less obtrusive. I made a note to drive in and pick it up, but I never got around to it, and now there's no point. This furniture carcass is familiar now, an old acquaintance. It's camouflaged and ambient, the fabric and stuffing decayed almost to the level of humus, the wooden frame black and punky. The steel spring skeleton is exposed and rusty, and one day I'll bury it in a shallow grave. A clump of asters has pushed up through the seat, and a bumble bee is molesting the blossoms. The forest resigned itself to the old stuffed chair a long time ago, and soon it'll be assimilated.

From the chair out to the main road is about one third of a mile. I take the road and turn south for about one-hundred yards. The main road is gravel and closely bordered by the woods. It sees some traffic in the summer, but it's never what you'd call busy. Nevertheless, there's always at least one aluminum can or other piece of litter for me to pick up before I angle off back into the trees.

A relatively new trail shoots off the main road and heads due west. It was formed in the last three years (a blink of the eye in forest time) by one of technology's more unfavorable mutations: "three-wheelers," those all-terrain tricycles for motorheads. Someone has made this path as a part of a regular route for his or her gasoline-fired predations. As if dirt bikes and snowmobiles weren't enough, we have at least one more way to make noise, burn fossil fuel, trample plants, and let our muscles and minds grow soft. If it wasn't for the toxic fumes, it would be a satisfying diversion, or rather an exciting sacramental ritual, to gather all the ATVs ever made into one huge pyre and fry them in their own petroleum juices. We could joyously cavort in the light of the flames, celebrating the at least partial return of peace and security to the planet. Those who refused to sacrifice their noxious machines would be banished to the bowels of some metropolis, where their penchant for producing racket, fumes, and wheeled vandalism would go unnoticed. There's no place for them in the woods. I wish.

But apparently the path is here to stay, an example of multiple *mis*use, and I follow it downhill to a low, wet area that supports a grove of small willows. In the spring this hollow is often under water, alive with the croaking of frogs. It's not exactly high and dry now, but I can walk through without sinking. There are some puff balls growing in this soil—succulent little mushroom tabs that seem to erupt from the ground overnight. I pick one and eat it, savoring the fungal aroma.

I climb out the other side of the hollow, scanning for grouse in another stand of fresh aspen growth. High over the trees a couple hundred yards ahead, I catch intermittent glimpses of a soaring red-tailed hawk. It banks in a tight orbit, cruising the drafts and hunting. All raptors seem to me bold and audacious—a lofty, majestic race that has little in common with the rest of the living. They look down on us from graceful blue arcs, with eyes like telescopes. In ancient Egypt the hawk was a symbol of the soul, the rising, ephemeral core of being.

Unlike robins, wrens, jays, or other of their perching cousins, images of birds of prey do not generally decorate greeting cards, dishes, or children's clothing. Raptors are taken seriously. They appear on coins, military uniforms, official documents. They've been conscripted by sober, no-nonsense government. It was inevitable, I suppose, that so many of these necessary, but inherently dismal organizations, should choose to be represented by a creature that is the antithesis of ponderous restriction. Hawks and eagles are free and soaring; they can see for miles. It would be more appropriate if government seals were festooned with images of pythons and rattlesnakes.

We once boarded a red-tailed hawk for a couple of months. We were driving along a local highway when we spied a strange, feathery flapping in the roadside ditch. We stopped to investigate and found a wounded hawk. One of its wings was shattered, and it was trying in vain to take to the air. It fixed us with a menacing eye and squawked a warning, but it seemed doomed if we didn't help. Using my sweatshirt as a net/shield, I caught the bird and we carefully wrapped it in the shirt to the point of immobility. We ran it into a veterinarian in town with a reputation for taking on wild animal emergencies free of charge.

He took our hawk, and his assistant gave us another crippled red-tail. Some idiot had shot it and permanently ruined one of its wings. The vet had patched it up, but the hawk would never fly again. The assistant had been caring for it at home, but was now moving and would have no place for the invalid. Since we seemed to care about hawks, she asked if we would take on the responsibility. We agreed, and "Big Bird" took up residence in our basement. Alice, our cat, was not amused.

We fed Big Bird chicken parts (necks, gizzards, etc.) and an occasional mouse, and the hawk dined with alacrity; but it never grew to trust us. It never learned—getting anthropomorphic here—to *relax*. There was always a wary cast to the eye, an alert, *aiming* kind of stare. The sharp, hooked beak was always ready to grab and tear. To be shot from the sky and transported to a basement was perhaps the human equivalent of a star athlete being paralyzed in some senseless accident. Big Bird seemed always on the verge of attack. Given the opportunity, my finger would have served as well as a chicken gizzard. Like the man says, "parts is parts." But we weren't bitter. A red-tailed hawk belongs in the sky; what a blow to give up flight! We were just careful of the hands that fed it. After all, they were the same kind of parts that pull triggers.

We finally gave Big Bird to a family that took care of all kinds of wild animals, and he lived out his life in a barn, hopping after mice like a common earthling.

The motorhead trail takes me back to the old logging road, headed toward the cabin. I retrace my steps past the stuffed chair, and then, on impulse, cut into thick woods, following an indistinct deer trail. It's a barely visible scar in the forest, marked only by bent stalks, pressed grass, and an occasional deer track. I come across a huge one, a massive hoof print gouged deeply into an ant hill. The hill is soft, so the track is exaggerated, but I'd like to see the whitetail that made it; there's got to be a few three-hundred-pound bucks patrolling this area.

There's another burst of wings in the woods. I whip the shotgun to my shoulder again, but this time it's a pileated woodpecker. They're large birds, and always startling. Up to a foot-and-a-half long, with wide, expansive wings, they seem to be too substantial to be dodging through the trees at low level. The black wings and body are crowned by a magnificent banded head—it's striped black and white with a slash of red at the base of the long beak, and topped by a rakish red plume. It's a luminous red, almost irridescent. A white band tapers down the neck and flares out on the underside of the wings, which are bordered in black. At a glance, the impression is of some misplaced tropical bird, perhaps a seriously wayward parrot. I catch sight of a pileated only a dozen or so times a year, so it's a lift to encounter one, especially up close.

But it's also sad, because I'm reminded that it's a cousin to the ivory billed woodpecker, a bird of the same size and configuration, but with its red, white, and black colors arranged in a different pattern. Or at least they used to be, because no one has seen an ivory billed since the 1930s. It was in the southern U.S., and enough unsuccessful searches have been mounted in that region to convince many in the bird-watching fraternity that the big woodpecker is gone forever. Still, it's comforting to speculate that somewhere deep in the southern woods, perhaps in a remote corner of the Okefenokee, a few members of the species hang on, pounding out picidean rhythms on the trunks of ancient trees. I'll hold that thought.

I slowly follow the deer trail for about three-hundred yards, always on the verge of losing it. But it's well-defined by the time I rejoin the old logging road. Compared to what impact the deer have had, my passage resembles that of a Sherman tank. But the deer don't seem to resent it. That dim path is always there, apparently used year-round. If I was a deer hunter, I'd know where to lie in ambush. (And I'm not telling.)

I walk along the overgrown road all the way back through the aspens and blackberries. At the top of the hill where it narrows into my personal path to the cabin, I strike off cross-country to do a little exploring. I'm right at the boundary of our forty acres, and I like to occasionally scout around in the portion of our woods that we don't see very often. This is the best time of year for it.

In the spring, and for a good part of the summer, the wood ticks are as thick as the brush.

The ticks used to be of scant concern to me, just another species of "insect" out to take over the world. The dog was so obviously appreciative when I picked a half dozen a day off him, that it was almost enjoyable. But now a tick-borne malady, Lyme's disease, is spreading into our area. It can cause severe arthritis, coronary problems, and neurological disorders. There's even been one reported death (out in New England). So now I'm more cautious. It's not that it keeps me from burrowing into the bushes, but the post-burrowing debriefing takes more time. The particular tick that carries the disease is much smaller than the variety we're used to plucking, so we've got to closely inspect our clothes and skin. Before, it was convenient to just wait until we felt one of the little pests crawling around in our pants. I'm not a blood-thirsty person, but I admit there are three creatures whose destruction I relish: mosquitoes, horse flies, and woodticks. And it's not a prejudice against "creepy-crawlers," because I adore spiders. I guess those three are the only things that personally assault me, unprovoked, on a regular basis. Constant self-defense has rendered me callous and a touch depraved.

I'm no more than three steps off the path when I see a rabbit crouched on a fallen birch. Six or seven years ago the rabbits were almost as numerous as the ticks. During the winter, the snow in our yard was literally packed down with their tracks, and the dog got to the point of ignoring them. They were like mobile lawn ornaments. Everywhere the forest was carpeted with "bunny berries." But now the population seems to have cycled to a nadir, and rabbits are not at all common—though I've seen more this year than last. I take practice aim at the rabbit and slowly approach until it bolts. I get to within fifteen feet. That's one reason they're compelled to be such prolific breeders.

A half-dozen steps further, next to the copse of birch, I find a deer bed. A ten-square-foot patch of ferns, grass, and strawberry plants has been flattened. Some whitetail spent the night curled up here, and it does look cozy in an open, under-the-stars kind of way.

Our forty is a mixture of old and new growth. Aspen saplings shoot up between stately balsams and birches—survivors of both fire and logging. As I slip through the woods I can see scattered, charred stumps, now mossy and decayed. In a few more years there'll be no obvious trace of a fire. The logged stumps are not as far gone, but they too are fading fast. In a decade, tall, straight aspens will dominate this land. That's fine with me. They're good habitat, good fuel, and good looking.

I make a wide sweep through the old/new forest and pick up my path just before it emerges back at the woodpile. I pause next to our winter stash and unlock the .410. The shell pops out of the chamber, and I drop it into my pocket. As I walk toward the back door of the cabin, I hear a low-pitched booming/thumping/batting far back in the woods. The murmurous drumming seems barely audible, at the edge of normal frequencies, and I *feel* it as much as hear it. It's a male grouse, perched on some log and beating its wings in a precise pattern and rhythm. It sounds like it's up among the blackberry bushes, just off the old logging road. I may have walked right past it. But it's hard to tell; grouse drumming fills your ears from all directions at once—like it's part of the air.

Well, I'm glad I heard one. It's been another good hunt.

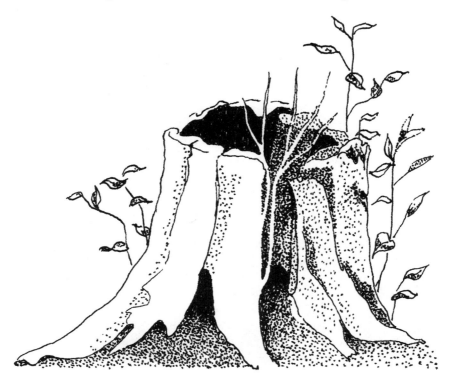

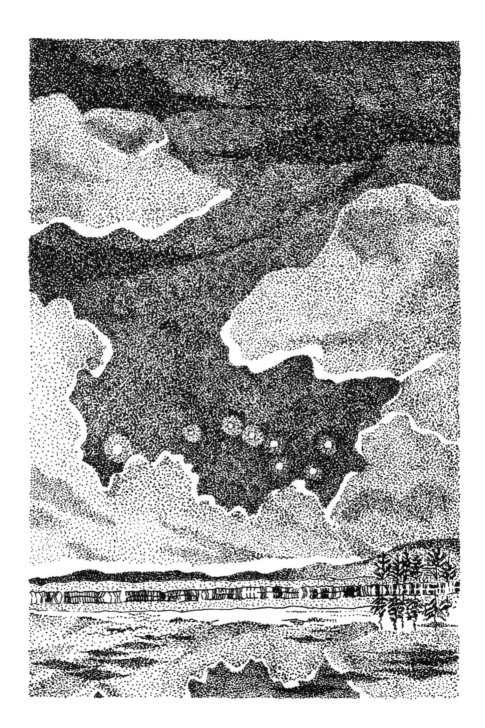

The Bear Guardian

1.

Mick reached across the campfire and passed me the pint of Yukon Jack.

"Whoo!" he wheezed. "I can feel that down to my ankles."

I took a sip of the Canadian whiskey and felt the rush of bitter, artificial warmth. The rest of the hunting party grinned at my 100-proof grimace.

"What's that label say again?" Mick asked.

I lifted the bottle into the firelight and read: "Yukon Jack is a taste born of hoary nights, when lonely men struggled to keep their fires lit and cabins warm."

It sounded like just our stuff. A cold September rain was beating on the tarp we'd strung between some jack pines. Southeasterly gusts whipped the rain into our campfire, hissing and sputtering among our blackened cooking pots. We kept feeding pitch-laden sticks, hoping to beat the wetness. That fire had been tough to start in the rain—an embarrassing three-match effort—and we labored to keep it alive. We were on the shore of Lake Agnes, four portages and seven miles into the Boundary Waters Canoe Area Wilderness, a short paddle from the Ontario border. We were hoping to shoot a black bear.

It's not something you just waltz in and do on an itchy autumn whim. Mike and I (Mick was along to haul meat, converse, and pass the Yukon Jack) had entered a state lottery for bear licenses. We hoped to get at least one permit between us, but we both ended up winners. Theoretically, we could kill two bears. As a precaution against such fortune, we followed the official Minnesota Department of Natural Resources (DNR) advice, and packed in two large coolers with thirty pounds of dry ice in each. Actually, the government recommended one hundred pounds, but they obviously hadn't been quoted a price of three dollars a pound! You'd think we were trying to cut a deal for cannabis, chocolate truffles, or some other overpriced narcotic. We finally found some ice for ninety cents a pound, and then debated about buying it at all.

It's true, as the DNR reasoned, that it can get warm in September, and the proper handling of bear meat is critical to its palatability. You need to strip off the pungent, viscous fat and then cool the meat as rapidly as possible. If the wilderness happens to be graced with an Indian summer day, the dry ice might make all the difference.

Nevertheless, we were skeptical. Three years before, we'd packed out six-hundred plus pounds of moose meat in cheesecloth bags, and it was delicious. It had been the first week in October, but it was also mild, and we had farther to go. Besides, once we shot a bear we didn't plan to loiter around watching flies congregate. We'd hustle our cargo out of the woods and into somebody's reefer. Even so, we caved in to government pressure and bought some dry ice. We called it insurance.

Mick, Mike, his wife Barb, and I planned to stay in the bush for five days or a bear, whichever came first. Barb was the only member of the party who hadn't been on the moose hunt, and she had to pay for her wisdom by enduring yet another retelling of the moose story, a tale inevitably conjured up by the company and the fire. We had bagged a thousand-pound cow on the first day, but that business-like schedule probably wouldn't hold for the bear hunt. The success rate for Minnesota moose hunters hangs consistently around ninety percent; for bear hunters it's closer to forty percent.

As we sipped our whiskey and hot chocolate in the deepening gloom, two otters surfaced just offshore, gliding back and forth a few feet from the rocky bank. Occasionally they'd rise up like furry periscopes, getting a better look at us. They snorted.

The otters appeared confident and comfortable in that cold, rainy lake—perfectly at home. That's how our bear would be, I mused; secure in his niche, knowing the wilderness as well as he knew the scent of cedar-stashed honey. We human hunters were outsiders, prowlers; and slightly bumbling at that. Here was a little icy precipitation and we needed raingear, a tarp, tents, a fire, and of course the Yukon Jack. The bears had their birthday suits. No wonder the otters snorted.

But we also had large caliber rifles, and that great backfiring human foible, strategy. Rifles: .35 cal. Remington, .300 Savage; 200-grain bullets. Strategy: baiting and ambush.

At dawn, with the sky still gray and the woods still dripping—Mike, Barb, and I broke out compasses and struck off into the forest. (Mick would patrol the portages, hunting for grouse.) We picked our way through dense brush for a couple hundred yards until we found a high spot that was relatively open, affording a field of fire. Mike and Barb decided to set up a bait station there. I pushed on to the north, constantly checking the compass, keeping the rifle barrel away so as not to deflect the needle.

About a quarter-mile from camp, where a hillside rose gently out of a swamp, I found my ambuscade. The ground was rocky and mossy with little underbrush, and I had a clear view for fifty to sixty yards all around. That was about right. While running a few practice rounds through my borrowed rifle the week before, I'd decided I wouldn't take a shot longer than fifty yards. Beyond that, my chances for a clean kill dropped dramatically, and a wounded bear was very low on my wish list.

Of course an unwounded bear is also a dangerous beast, even a black bear. A popular misconception is that while grizzlies and polar bears are certified man-killers, black bears are skittish cowards. It's often said that banging a couple of pots together will run them off, and some campers have been known to pelt them with rocks. Ninety-nine times out of a hundred they may indeed turn tail, but black bears are killers as well. Their behavior is unpredictable, and that one time when a black bear doesn't retreat can lead to mayhem.

In the United States, from 1929 to 1986, grizzlies in the wild attacked 125 people and killed sixteen. Black bears attacked 102 and finished off seventeen. While there are a lot more black bears around (they live in all but a dozen states), and therefore more encounters with humans, they also seem more likely to carry an assault to its climax. And though they're generally much smaller than grizzlies, black bears can be terrible assailants. Jim Zumbo wrote: "The animal can be a bundle of fury, a ferocious beast that has no equal among the strongest men. With a quick slap of its paw, even a medium-sized black bear can break a man's neck. Its bite will shred a human leg or arm."

My friend Greg briefly pondered the aggressive nature of black bears a couple of summers ago. He was hurrying along a wilderness trail when he came around a bend and saw a large bear a short distance away. He was startled, and he reasoned he should warn the bear of his presence. Experts stress that bears are unappreciative of surprises.

There are a lot of things Greg could've shouted. A simple "Hey!" might've been effective. But the first thing that came to his mind was a game he often played with his young daughter—he would imitate a bear and growl at her. So he growled at the black bear. Wrong, wrong. The bear immediately whirled and charged. Greg leaped away at full speed, threw his arms around a large aspen and prepared to shinny up—like a rocket—when he took a quick glance behind and saw that the bear had stopped, and was now ambling away. A false charge. Well, it'd done the trick. Greg, the growling intruder, had been routed, and he'd probably never growl at a bear again. Impersonation apparently ranks right up there with surprise on the bears' index of irritations.

But on this hunt I intended not only to surprise, but to seduce. I dug into my kit and pulled out a backpacker's propane stove. I put a small pot on the burner and dumped in some honey and a dose of Liquid Smoke. I stirred well and let simmer. It did smell enticing—sweet, tangy, and a touch juicy—like some kind of care-less-camper Oriental dessert. If a bear wasn't attracted to that, he was already a rug. (Though I did consider simply toting in a basket full of peanut butter and jelly sandwiches.)

I crawled off behind a rock and waited. In less than three minutes two Canadian jays arrived. The scroungers swooped into the lower branches of a jack pine and gave me the once-over. They cocked their black and white heads, each inspecting me with a dark, shiny eye. Despite my hardware I was deemed harmless. In a moment one of the jays was perched on the rifle barrel. I lifted a hand, extending the index finger, and the other jay landed on my knuckle. It made a few tentative pecks at the skin of my palm, but found no peanuts or dried fruit. The head cocked again, and I was favored with a "Hey, what's this?" stare, and then the jay indignantly flew off. I felt like St. Francis of Assisi, but the jays had no time for sentimental communing with humans. They're practiced panhandlers, after goodies, and they'd flatter the gentler aspects of my nature for only so long. I sighed and rooted around in my pack for some nuts and fruit. I scattered a few bits on a nearby rock and the jays immediately returned to pounce on them. That was more like it.

A red squirrel approached next, cautiously skittering in little jumps. But when I tossed a slice of apple in its direction, it squealed and darted off. Squirrels lack the audacity and shamelessness of jays, and free food merely scares them.

I laid in ambush for six hours, now and then adding materials to the bait pot and giving it a stir. My nose grew accustomed to the odor of honey and steak sauce that was permeating the neighborhood. I broke a nodule of pine pitch off a nearby trunk and deeply inhaled its coniferous vapors for some relief. I also watched my neighbors—a half dozen wood warblers, a couple of downy woodpeckers, a raven, and two piles of picturesque, but uncommunicative moose droppings.

We had come to this area because it was known bear country, a happy hunting ground for Ursus Americanus and its appetite for just about everything. Eighteen campsites on Agnes serve as inadvertent bait stations all summer. Unarmed paddlers tantalize the bears for months with the alluring effluvium of American supermarkets. We weren't naive enough to think we'd have bears rushing to us immediately, but six hours was enough for the first shift, and I scraped the contents of my bait pot onto the ground and headed back to camp.

On the way I spotted a ruffed grouse. The bird ran out of my path from beneath some ferns, and ducked behind a fallen tree. It lowered its head almost to the ground and froze, assuming it was concealed. The grouse wasn't accustomed to tall predators. I raised the .35 caliber and debated. This was not a bird gun. If I hit the grouse in the body, I might as well have thrown a grenade. There'd be precious little left for roasting. Besides, after half a day of solitude and tranquility, I was reluctant to fire that cannon in the first place. On the other hand, I had the itchy trigger finger of the hunter who has seen no sign of his quarry, and the ruffed grouse is a decidedly tasty upland fowl. I took lengthy aim, and fired. The grouse jerked twice and died. My bullet, as big as a bomb, had gazed its back at the base of the head. It was quick, neat, and probably lucky.

I dressed out the bird on the spot and carried the entrails back to my bait station. Here was more odor for the bears. Back in camp, I wrapped the grouse in aluminum foil and cooked it over the open fire. All we lacked was wild rice and a maitre d'.

It rained again that evening, and the next day was also overcast and intermittently wet. There was a sick joke about hunting for a "drizzly bear." It was the autumnal equinox, and on the way to my bait station I thought it fitting that a flight of about sixty Canada geese ("honk if you love Florida") winged over heading south. Whenever I watch such a formation fade away into low, gray skies, I have a sense of a vast army poised just beyond the northwest horizon. Great white blizzards, barely restrained, are waiting impatiently for the last goose to lift off the Canadian tundra. In a few weeks the first waves of blowing snow will swoop down across the border—no mercy. But it's not an unpleasant thought.

I approached my baiting area slowly and quietly—no telling what might be there after all the enticements of the day before. And sure enough, there'd been a few guests. Except for a small length of intestine, the grouse organs were gone, and in their place were two kinds of droppings. One looked like field mouse or squirrel, and the other like weasel or fisher. There was no bear sign.

Barb had hooked a small northern pike the previous afternoon, and I had a chunk of it for bait. I flopped it next to my honey pot, and a jay descended almost instantly to drag it off. In a stingy mood, I staked the fish to the ground with a stick. The jays were welcome to peck at it, but they couldn't take it all. I figured that having a couple of birds loitering around, nonchalantly feeding, would help create an illusion of normalcy around my hiding place.

I baited and waited for seven more hours and then launched an extended scouting mission around the area. On a narrow strip of beach not far from our camp, I found a set of wolf tracks, and followed them until they vanished into the woods. They were spaced in the pattern of an easy stroll—appropriate for a beach.

Maybe the wolf had been hunting for the sun, an elusive entity that no one in these parts had seen for three days. Later in the afternoon Mike and Barb saw a pine marten running along in that same sand, and there were moose tracks there as well. Everybody loves a beach.

On my way back to camp I finally saw some bear sign. There were five piles of seed-laced droppings on a faint game trail that ran along the lakeshore. One pile was within a hundred feet of our tents, but the dark stools were all old and dry. Perhaps we were in the right area at the wrong time. We discussed moving our operation.

But just before dark we were encouraged. Two more bear hunters paddled into Agnes from the Moose River, and set up camp on a rocky point within sight of our fire. Mick wanted to see if he could bum a couple of cigarettes (he only smokes when he's out in the bush, and never brings enough), so we eased on over to chat. One of the new arrivals was a weather-beaten old-timer, who, Mick joyously noted, seemed to have two cigarettes burning at all times. Between puffs the man mentioned that he and his partner had bagged two bears at this spot four years before. They were delighted to hear we'd been baiting for two days already, and were confident of success. The last weather forecast they'd heard before coming in had promised sunny skies for the next day, and the oldtimer was sure that would put the bears on the move.

It was raining again when we crawled into our tents, but we resolved to rise even earlier than usual, and slip back to our same bait stations. I had this image of a huge bear, miles away, that got wind of our honey pots on the first day. It smells fine, so he starts working in our direction. Perhaps he's familiar with the eighteen campsites on Agnes—has had occasion to rip granola bars out of Duluth packs. He is constantly distracted along the way. In one spot he pauses to tear apart an old cedar to get at a beehive; a half-mile later he finds some venison carrion and scatters the feasting ravens. But each time he pokes his questing snout into the air, that same tempting odor wafts through his nostrils and lures him on. Ah, Liquid Smoke and honey—garnished with rotting fish. No doubt he'll be upset when he discovers it's a trap.

The next morning I simmered bait for another six hours or

so, and around noon the clouds scudded off, herded by a cool northwest wind. Even under the overcast the red, orange, and yellow sugar maples had been luminous, tongues of leafy flame amidst the gray-green wetness. Now they exploded in full sunlit radiance, almost too bright. I left the bait station to stroll in the warmth, to revel in the dry, colorful air. I ambled down to the beach, enjoying the sight of blue water. A nap in the sand? Sounded good, but were the bears sleeping in the sunshine? No way. No doubt they were up and feeding, and as a predator, I'd better do the same. After a snack, I returned to my bait pot and watched until dusk. Nothing.

The first stars were appearing as we ate our evening meal and planned for our last day. We'd bait until 11:00 a.m. and then head out. It would be perfect if we could get a bear in the morning. We could have it dressed and packed out by sundown. We were hopeful, buoyed by the good weather.

The sky darkened into crisp autumn clarity, presenting us with our first transparent night of the trip. I pushed off in my canoe to look at the stars. Jupiter and Mars were low in the south, so bright that they cast long sinuous reflections in the lake. I paddled out to the middle of a bay and gently spun around, watching the glittering skyscape rotate overhead. I grinned at the Big Dipper—Ursa Major—The Great Bear. It was the only bear, great or otherwise, that we had seen. Just to the west of the Dipper's handle, or the Bear's tail, was the brilliant star Arcturus. It means "bear guardian." Well, something's guarding the bears, I thought. We certainly hadn't been allowed to endanger any.

And then an omen. A slashing, flaming fireball—a huge meteor—streaked across the dome of the sky from the southeast. It was a bluish-white flash, as bright as a quarter moon, and it rocketed directly toward Arcturus. Just as it seemed to reach the Bear Guardian, it exploded, breaking into three pieces. For an instant the star was bracketed by celestial shrapnel, and then the fireworks winked out. Man! I sucked in a breath. Here was a portent. The Bear Guardian had been pointed out and then "circled," underscored by heavenly fire. Any ancient hunter would have instantly taken the meaning: we weren't going to get a bear.

I paddled back to camp and asked if anyone had seen the meteor. No, they had been watching the campfire. I didn't offer my observations concerning Arcturus, but needless to say we had no luck the next day either. We went home to regroup.

2.

Three days later Mike and I returned to the wilderness alone; we planned to hunt for another four days. This time we paddled down the Little Indian Sioux River and portaged into Shell Lake, about seven miles west of Agnes. We started baiting that evening, setting up stations about a quarter-mile apart on either side of a portage trail. We were encouraged. The trail had been littered with fresh bear scat—shocking heaps of glistening dung. It seemed that a bear was near. One pile was full of broken acorns, and being in the midst of a minor hemorrhoid flare-up, I felt a twinge of sympathetic discomfort. Here was a bear that was quite possibly irritable.

But the excrement was a valuable clue. If the bears were munching acorns, then they were hanging around the scrub oaks. The oaks flourished on the higher ground, growing out of cracks in the ledgerock. We hid ourselves up on the thinly-wooded, thickly-lichened ridges and waited—our bait pots shadowed by oaks.

It turned out that the oak groves were hot spots. I bagged two grouse that afternoon (I had a .410 shotgun along this time), and both had gullets full of acorns. Fresh deer and moose droppings also littered the rock. It appeared we had discovered a four-star wilderness dining area.

I baited until nearly sundown and then hiked back to camp. On the trail I met two late-season backpackers, and I guess I struck them as odd—perhaps dangerously so. I had the shotgun in one hand, the .35 caliber in the other, and a wicked-looking knife on my belt. I had an Army-surplus pack on my back that smelled faintly of steak sauce and grouse blood. We stopped to chat, and once they saw that my eyes weren't glazed over, and I wasn't foaming at the mouth, their expressions eased into bemusement. I was slightly embarrassed. I must've looked like a displaced Dirty Harry, or an over-earnest imitation of Rambo. All I needed was an imposing sidearm and an appropriate script. They impishly grinned and wished me luck, then headed off for a nearby campsite. Good, I thought; maybe they'd attract a bear.

I returned to camp at sunset, and Shell Lake was a fairyland.

The oblique rays of autumn sun resolved the water and trees into sharp focus. It seemed we could count leaves and needles a half-mile away. The surrounding forest, a tangled mix of pine and aspen, was melded into a green and yellow tapestry, shimmering in the breeze. The lake was an irridescent blue, gently ruffled and rhythmically lapping. To the north and east, mountainous, gray-black thunderheads were creeping away. They were laced with lightning, but too far away for us to hear thunder. As the orange sun slipped behind the treetops, a beaver appeared on top of its lodge across the bay and slid into the water. It swam into some reeds at the shore, and then dived. Here and there a fish jumped, and two mallards winged over and banked to the south. The peaks of the distant clouds were stained a dull orange, and soon after the sun disappeared and the clouds went black, an owl began to cry out from the west. Wup-wup-wup-wahooo—over and over in a mournful, dusky chant, until the sky was dense with stars. Then the northern lights, mingling with the lingering clouds and lightning on the northeast horizon, flared toward the zenith and danced—pallid green and silent.

Mike and I sat on the shore and took it all in—or tried to. As our campfire smoke wafted through the balsams and out over the water, I felt in tune, at home. Here was a niche worth filling, and it made me a little giddy. On impulse, I pointed toward Arcturus and told Mike about the Bear Guardian. He studied the star for a while and then looked at the horizon beneath it.

"Gee," he said, "it's right over our bait stations." And he laughed. It was true. Another portent? Was our quarry still being protected?

The next morning it was overcast, and by early afternoon it was pouring rain. That oldtimer back on Agnes had considered rain to be a poor bear-hunting ambience. But not long before the precipitation hit, Mike got a shot at a bear. He'd left his bait station, pack on his back, and was patrolling near the crest of a ridge. From the shelter of a small clump of oaks, the bear rose on its hind legs and sniffed the air. It looked tall and mighty. It was only fifty yards away. Mike was taken by surprise, and as he threw his rifle butt to his shoulder it slipped off the padded strap of his backpack. He hadn't practiced shooting while lashed into a pack. He re-shouldered the rifle, pushing it snugly into the strap. He was off balance now, and fumbled with the safety catch—another split second lost. The bear was still erect, but had seen him, its eyes were looking into his. Mike finally peered through his scope, the crosshairs centered on the bear's chest.

Then two things happened—or seemed to happen—precisely at once. Mike squeezed the trigger, and the bear fell to all fours and dashed off as quick as a rabbit, as agile as a doe. It was gone in a heartbeat. Damn! Had he missed? That pack strap had screwed him up.

Mike dropped his pack and hurried (cautiously) to the spot where the bear had been. He was fully alert, rifle at the ready with the safety off. He might have wounded it. But there was mostly bare rock all around, and he could see no blood. He circled and searched for over an hour, gradually working further out from the oaks. Nothing. No blood, no hair, no bits of bone. The bear charged off at top speed—it must've been a clean miss.

Back in camp, Mike described the scene and I agreed—the bear had no doubt escaped and was now much wiser. He'd probably leave the area altogether. We crouched under our tarp and listened to the incessant rain—watched it stream off the edge of the tarp and form muddy puddles around our feet. Arcturus wasn't visible, but we knew about the Bear Guardian.

That night I had a terrible dream. Transported back twenty years, I was working my old paper route, delivering the Hibbing *Daily Tribune*. It was winter and I was trudging through deep snow. Suddenly, from behind a parked car, a huge polar bear rose up on its hind legs. It was eight feet tall and it growled at me. I flung away my papers and began to run. The white monster leaped to all fours and chased me. I knew it was an experienced, appreciative man-eater. I slipped and fell, and the nightmare dissolved. I awoke shivering, and snuggled deeper into my sleeping bag. There was a real bear out there who'd been shot at. Was he frightened? Or merely enraged?

It was still drizzling in the morning, but stopped by the time we reached our bait stations. Against the leaden sky I saw a solitary goose. It was heading north. That was odd. Another omen? It was fun to think about, to extrapolate meaning from random events. The goose, I imagined, was lost and disoriented. It was alone and afraid, and some quirk of the wind had altered its course into a mistaken, fatal trajectory. The natural balance was upset—there would be changes.

Three hours later Mike found the bear. It was lying two hundred yards from where he'd shot at it. His aim had been true. The bullet had entered the chest, broken two ribs, pierced a lung, and exited the back. Perhaps the blood from the exit wound had soaked into the hair on the back and never reached the ground. Perhaps there'd been a faint blood trail and Mike missed it. In any case, the bear had collapsed on a stretch of flat, exposed rock, high on a ridge and open to the sky. It was an adult, but not huge— 150 to 200 pounds.

Mike gutted the bear at once, and then hurried back to camp to enlist my aid. I was off on a canoe ride, so he left a note near our fire pit, telling me where the carcass was. I found the note an hour later. By the time I arrived at the site, Mike had most of the hide off. We quickly finished that and started on the fat. In some spots, around the hindquarters, for instance, it was nearly two inches thick. Using fillet knives, we stripped off the wet, white layer, and then cut the carcass into chunks. In spite of the twenty-four-hour delay, the meat smelled and looked fine. The weather had been in our favor—cool and sunless. And the ravens hadn't spotted the body; either that, or they gave bears a little more time. We sprinkled black pepper on the meat to keep the flies off, and then Mike boned it and I dropped the red slabs into a cloth bag. (We'd decided against the dry ice this time.) It felt like about sixty pounds.

Before we rolled up the hide and slipped it into another bag, I lifted the head and looked into the bear's eyes. They were open and still moist, but as dead as brown leaves. The snout, from lips to eyelids, was a golden cinnamon, feathering delicately into black. The ears were round and stubby. It was a teddy-like face, even in death. As usual, with every successful hunt, there was a bitter wave of regret. Though Mike was going to preserve the hide, and we would process the meat, there was still sadness. A relationship had ended. We had talked about this bear, thought about it, dreamed about it. We had hunted it for eight days—prowling through wilderness forest and lying in ambush in the rain. I had enjoyed the hunt because it made me feel primitive; not barbaric, just more closely knit to the natural order of predator and prey. One way to understand something about animals is to be like one for a while—living in the woods and the weather, hunting for your food. We would eat this bear, and its blood would mingle with our own. You are what you hunt; and we were now part bear.

The killing and skinning wasn't pretty, but it was genuine, uninterpreted biology. We touched not just the sinews of a bear, but the sinews of the wilderness itself. This carcass was ours; we had created it. In an ecological sense, we hadn't destroyed the bear; we were just diassembling and redistributing it. Some would be used by us, some by the ravens, some by the ants and flies, some by the microbes in the soil where it lay.

Nevertheless, an individual life was gone, and there was mourning. The bear's death was our responsibility. We did it; we'll live with it. I laid the head down gently, respectfully.

As we carried the meat and hide down off the ridge, the westering sun slanted through the overcast. The rain had ended, the clouds were breaking up. We fixed a quick dinner in camp and packed our gear. We wanted to get the meat out as soon as possible. It was dark when we pushed our loaded canoes away from the shore, but we knew this country well. We would be out by midnight.

As we paddled for the first portage, I looked at the sky. To the south, Mars was shining—bright and bloody red. To the west, another bank of dark clouds was advancing. They had swallowed Arcturus.

Dogging It

The dog trained me well. I was too anxious at first, over-eager to advance. This was ignorance, of course. You can't rush a pheasant hunt, and only rarely can you flush a ring-neck by yourself. They're wily birds, hard to spook. A stalking human, even a large and loud one, won't make them stupid. You can literally step over one, and though its little gallinaceous brain must be wretched with anxiety, the pheasant will not budge.

I wouldn't have believed that if I hadn't seen it myself. I was out hunting alone one day (before the dog completed my education) when, in mid-stride, I accidentally kicked a fat male pheasant. It exploded like a land mine—a sudden burst of hammering wings that took a year off my life. I was so flustered that I never did locate the safety catch on my shotgun. What amazed me the most was that a male is an uproar of color—red, blue, green, white, purple—and the bird had been effectively concealed in six inches of dry brown grass. If I hadn't tripped over him, I would never have seen him. From then on I paid attention to the dog.

He was a Weimaraner, or at least most of him was. He had the distinctive gray coat and the bright, intelligent (slightly manic) yellow eyes. But he was bushier than he should've been, and we suspected his family line had been polluted by the blood of some other breed of retriever. It would've been a horrifying speculation for some. A guidebook published by "The Pet Library Ltd." noted that the Weimaraner had been "carefully guarded, for the promoters of the Weimaraner in this country are following the precedent of the Weimaraner Club of Germany, which was extremely careful concerning ownership of surplus stock, breeding practices, and prohibitions of the infusion of new blood!"

Well, our dog slipped through some crack in that system. He was a foundling, a stray that showed up on our doorstep. He had a collar and a vaccination tag, but when we phoned the vet who'd given him his shots, we were told that the owner would be pleased if we kept his erstwhile dog. A big orange September moon was just rising when we learned this, so our new companion had a new name: Moon.

He was a wild one, easily excitable, and as "hyper" as a kindergarten sugar freak. You couldn't keep him still, he loved to bark all night, and he was gun-shy—except when he had the scent of pheasant in his nostrils. Then he was a cool hunting machine, as silent as death, with ears and nose like radar.

So Moon learned his new name and I learned about bird hunting. The main thing was: follow the dog. Naturally I learned the hard way. I assumed that this playful, boisterous, run-after-the-hot-bitches kind of canine didn't know how to track and point. He was barely out of puppyhood, and we hadn't taught him anything but "come," "sit," and "shut-up!" (And he never did grasp the full meaning of that last command.) The first time we went out I figured it would be just a frivolous romp. Moon liked to pounce on field mice, and that's what he started to do. Since the mere sight of a gun was enough to drive him under the porch, I kept the 20-gauge in its case and held it behind my back until he got to chasing mice—then he forgot about it.

It was an innocent sylvan scene: man, dog, and gun; and no game. And then Moon's demeanor changed. His head bolted up and froze. His entire body tensed—ears perked, leg muscles taut to the point of trembling, nose twitching. He tested the air for a moment and then took a few furtive steps. He sniffed, and then suddenly composed himself into a beautiful point. His tail (undocked and therefore contrary to Weimaraner Club standards) was pointing straight up, as stiff as a rod. His right foot was curled up into his foreleg. His torso was slanted forward, hind legs braced and parted; and his nose, eyes, and ears were locked in—

focused like telescopic sights on a spot a few feet in front of his snout.

I laughed. It seemed a bit melodramatic for a mouse hunt. And then a pheasant burst out of the grass. It was exactly where Moon had pointed. Though surprised again, I managed to get off a shot. I missed, but now I was with the program: watch the dog; he was a natural. And now that he understood it was pheasants and not rodents we were after, the hunt began in earnest.

He'd catch the scent of a bird from a distance, sometimes up to a hundred yards. He'd follow—nose to the ground, nose in the breeze. I'd watch his tail. As he got closer to the quarry, it started to rise. It jacked up step by step, as if there was some sort of sensor or rheostat that linked his nose to his rump. And when that silver plume of a tail reached the vertical position, Moon would freeze and point. I could be certain that there was a pheasant six feet from the end of his flaring nostrils. And he wouldn't stir until the bird did. He was immobile, paralyzed by instinct into this elegant, deadly pose. He looked like a statue, a weathered basswood carving of a magnificent hunter.

And when the pheasant jumped I was ready—safety off and muzzle zeroed in. Roasted ring-neck became a routine entree at our table. Soon it wasn't the shooting that was exciting. It was too easy. Now the thrill of the hunt was watching Moon, following his nearly inerrant lead. In a couple of weeks we were a crackerjack team. I had the modern firepower, he had the vulpine cunning. I studied his moves and tried to anticipate. Through his mannerisms I could tell when he first got wind of a bird. I could tell if the quarry was stationary or moving. I could make an accurate estimate of how far away it was and if there was more than one pheasant in the vicinity. And I never saw a bird until Moon flushed it out—even if it was only a half dozen paces away.

Except once. I was on a small rise and Moon was below, nose to the earth. I just happened to catch sight of a moving male pheasant about forty yards in front of him. It was running in circles, making ever-widening rings in the tall grass. After a half dozen circuits it shot off in a straight line—still running low to the ground—for about fifty yards. There it started to make another set of concentric circles. In the meantime, Moon had hit the first set and was tracing every one, going round and round. Just about the time he'd finished, the bird ran off to begin a third set. Moon reached the second batch of diversionary tracks and paused for only a moment. He ran around the outside of the rings and picked up the freshest trail. He'd decoded that ploy. The pheasant was on only its second orbit when Moon arrived at the third set and forced the devious cock into open air. As far as I could tell, Moon never missed a bird. Once he had the scent the outcome was inevitable.

The only bad part was, when I shot a pheasant I had to beat him to the carcass. Though he was retriever, fetching was a foreign concept. He'd done most of the work, so why shouldn't he share in (or hog all of) the spoils? With a lot of travail I finally convinced him that he at least shouldn't rip the pheasants apart. We negotiated a compromise. If I didn't get to the fallen bird first, he could pick it up and hold it in his mouth for a while. With enough cajoling, cursing, and threatening, he'd even bring it over to me. But he'd never drop it at the "master's" feet. I had to gently work it loose from his jaws, putting in my fair share of effort.

Moon and I bagged over twenty-five pheasants that autumn. Our landlord had a game farm, and we helped him raise and take care of the birds. The various hunting parties he invited to the farm rarely got all the pheasants we put out, so Moon and I were the mop-up crew. We nailed the ones that got away, and I liked to think that these were the smartest, most challenging birds. We saw a lot of other hunting dogs, some rigorously trained, but none was better than Moon. (Except when it came to obsequious fetching, of course.)

Seasons and years pass quickly, and Moon is gone now. It's been over a decade since we shared the joy of the chase, and generations of pheasants may well rejoice. But I have a fantasy that one glorious day we'll be reunited. In some heaven, paradise, or happy hunting ground, we roam golden September fields—cool forest meadows concealing the wiliest pheasants that ever lived. Moon's yellow eyes blaze like sparks—vivified, renewed. We hunt as a skilled, artistic pair; Orion and his Sirius. And when he retrieves the fallen pheasants he still won't drop them at my feet. But I kneel to stroke his silvery head and say, "Good dog. Good dog."

"When Daniel Boone goes by at night
The phantom deer arise
And all lost, wild America
Is burning in their eyes."

STEPHEN VINCENT BENET

The Deerstand Slayer

It's a free fire zone. For two weeks every November the forest around our cabin fills with armed men. During deer season we feel under siege, surrounded.

One year I climbed onto the roof to clean the chimney, and I could pick out nine blaze-orange hunters from up there. Twice we've looked out our living room window and seen would-be deerslayers making an inadvertent drive through our front yard. Most of them look embarrassed to have stumbled upon a slice of civilization in the midst of their primitive quest.

Part of the problem is that our land was long considered to be in the public domain. Before we built our cabin and moved in, nearly everyone assumed our forty acres was kin to the government land that borders it on three sides. The first year we posted it, someone vindictively tore down all our "No Hunting" signs. We had purposely left the land unposted until a week before Opening Day, and then we didn't display "No Trespassing" warnings. We hoped this gesture would demonstrate that our aim was not to erect a legal force field around our property, but merely to shield ourselves and our dog from stray bullets. We weren't against hunters, we were just opposed to being hunted. Maybe I should have written all that on the signs.

As I labored in the snow to replace several dollars worth of placards, I figured this meant war. I fantasized about establishing a radio link with the Air Guard base down in Duluth. They had a squadron of F-4 Phantoms. When hunters encroached upon our territory I'd call in an air strike. Self-defense. Napalm. I'd probably have to do it only once. But in reality, my confrontations with intruders were much more pacific. I opted for psychological warfare.

One day, a week into the season, I was out cutting wood. In lieu of a flak jacket, I wore an orange vest and cap. Being a Stihl, my chain saw was also orange (and loud), and I didn't figure we'd draw any fire. Of course it's always sobering to recall that about seven percent of all males and one percent of all females are color blind, and significantly more than that are just itching to shoot—something. (And being over 200 pounds, I'd make a nice trophy.)

In the midst of felling a dead aspen, I saw a hunter emerging from the heart of our forty. He was dragging a buck. The temperature was at freezing, but the guy was sweating—toiling at the end of a rope he'd secured to the antlers. A bloody trail snaked off behind him. He punched out of the woods onto our driveway, and saw one of the "No Hunting" signs. Then he saw me. He looked abashed. Apparently he'd missed the posted announcements on the other side of our land, or was feeling guilty because he'd ignored them. In any case, he lugged the deer over to me. I killed the saw.

The damage was done, and we both knew he'd seen the signs, so there was no point to harangue about that. Instead, I decided to intimidate him for future hunts. I gave him a hostile, stone-faced, jackpine-savage stare. I narrowed my eyes and tried to make them smolder—broadcasting meanness like X-rays. I made them say: I am an anti-social, unbalanced backwoods crazy who probably eats raw entrails. I kept my finger on the trigger of the chain saw.

The hunter offered a tentative smile, but I ignored it, and he stumbled over his words as he asked me which way it was to South Sturgeon Lake. I hesitated just long enough to make him even more nervous, and then I merely pointed with the bar of the chain saw—a wicked little jab to the south. He thanked me, and then looked longingly at my pickup (also orange) which was parked nearby. He had to haul that carcass a long way, and I could see he was trying to work up the nerve to ask me if I'd give him and his buck a lift. I glanced at the truck, snorted, and fired up the Stihl, yanking on the starter rope more violently than necessary, and went back to my cutting. The hunter turned away, and started trudging down the road for South Sturgeon. I've never seen him since, and I hope he's told all his buddies about the malicious bastard with the chain saw.

If all hunters were savvy, dead-eyed reincarnations of Daniel Boone, it might not be so bad. But for many, deer season is an annual fling, a freaky few days of unaccustomed exercise and alertness. In Minnesota there are usually about 400,000 hunters in the woods—thirty-five divisions of infantry—and most of them probably fire less than a dozen rounds per year. Since bagging a deer is often literally a one-shot deal, and since many hunters are not sharpshooters, there is a high level of anxious anticipation and excitement out there in the brush. Tension is ambient, the idea of competition is pervasive. According to the Department of Natural Resources (DNR), the success rate for firearms hunters is rarely higher than thirty percent. A lot of people don't get a deer because they never see one, or have only fleeting glimpses of twitching ears and flashing tails. So it's not unusual for a once-a-year Hawkeye to see things that aren't really there. Common are the stories of gunshot cars, dogs, cows, and even fellow hunters, all of which showed up on somebody's retinas as honest-to-God ten-point bucks.

For example, during this past season a friend of ours stopped by her neighbor's house and asked if he had gotten "his deer." Oh yes, he replied, he had it in the living room. In the living room? She followed him into the house, and there, propped against a wall, was a life-sized cardboard cutout of a magnificent buck. There were three bullet holes in it. Her neighbor explained how he and his companion had spied this buck deep in the woods. They both took aim. While peering through his scope he had wondered why the deer was so still, not even blinking, but they had fired anyway. "So," he laughed, "we both shot somebody's idea of a practical joke."

"But," said our friend, "there are *three* holes in the 'deer.'"

Her neighbor looked sheepish. "Well," he replied, "I shot it once more when it tried to run away."

The DNR estimated that in 1986 there were an average of 19.4 deer per square mile in the Side Lake area—before hunting season. That means our forty acres contained 1.2, and I saw at least that many. But within a half mile of our cabin I know of at least four deerstands, and there are probably some I haven't seen. On Opening Day I'm sure the deer are outnumbered.

Shooting from deerstands is legal of course, but it's always seemed like cheating to me. You establish yourself up in the air—in a quarter from which deer have no reason to expect danger. Wolves and other natural predators don't hang around in the trees. When you're nine feet off the ground and waiting in ambush with a telescopic sight, you're a sniper, not a hunter. Other than staying warm, what's the challenge? Now if you were to drop out of the stand onto a deer's back, with only a rock, or with a knife clenched in your teeth, *that* would be hunting. That would be more fair.

With this bias against stands, I'm always a little irritated when I see one. No doubt a lot of hunters would say, "So what? That's your problem." True enough. Except one fine October day I made it somebody else's.

I was out grouse hunting and exploring—more of the latter than the former—and my expedition began poorly. As I was leaving our land I saw that someone on an ATV had run over some spruce seedlings we'd planted the previous spring. A couple of the trees were broken and would surely die. That put me in a foul mood. Planting trees is hard work. It's a vote of confidence for the future, and what could be more callous and ignorant than squashing them with a three-wheeler? We'd even had a sign there that said, "Trees Planted," to warn passersby that it was a sensitive area.

I pushed on through the woods, patrolling an old logging trail, and a few minutes later I came upon a brand new deerstand. Someone had hauled in two-by-four scraps and built a little platform between three closely spaced balsams. It was relatively low and fairly innocuous, but already there was an empty beer can and a candy wrapper lying on the ground beneath it. A set of three-wheeler tracks led away to the west—perhaps the same machine that'd trampled our young spruce. I picked up the litter and stuffed it in my game bag. My dark mood darkened.

A half hour later, when I found the next desecration, I lost control. It was another new deerstand, and even from a distance I could see it was illegal—at least three or four feet higher than the limit. But that wasn't what put me on the rampage.

The stand was constructed within the natural framework of a copse of four birch trees. It had a deck made of two-by-fours, sturdy and neatly done, and railings fashioned out of aspen saplings. Four stout and symmetrical ladder rungs, also made from aspen, were secured to two of the birches with 40d spikes. Someone had spent a lot of time—the stand almost looked nice.

But after he'd finished his little redoubt, the sniper had climbed onto the platform, looked around, and realized there was a serious tactical deficiency. He didn't have a perfect field of fire. His view to the southwest was partially obstructed by a balsam tree. It was six inches in diameter at the butt, a healthy adolescent tree, attractively formed and well on its way to maturity. The sheltering fir had been rooted there for thirty years, a haven for chickadees. One day it would be prime timber—a cabin log or several board feet of lumber. Its extensive root system was an integral part of the forest floor. It anchored the soil and protected its own small section of the watershed. It respirated in the sunlit air, manufacturing precious oxygen. And against a dappled white background of young birches, it was very pleasing to the eye.

But damn it, it was in the way—a full thirty degrees of horizon was obscured. Why build such a Cadillac stand and then reduce the zone of death? So the sniper had cut down the balsam. Apparently 330 degrees had not been enough.

I came upon the freshly felled balsam as if upon a corpse. The stump was a hacked ruin, as grotesque as a pile of guts. The tree was lying amid broken boughs, still green, but drying rapidly. In a couple of weeks the needles would be dead-brown tinder; the trunk would be starting to rot. It was a sickening waste—all for a little better shot. From an illegal stand.

I put down my shotgun and picked up a stick, a length of green aspen about the size of a baseball bat. It was a piece left over from the construction of the stand. I was maddened, consumed with fury. I was angry about our broken spruce seedlings, infuriated by the careless apathy that discarded beer cans in the forest, and incensed by the profligate killing of the balsam tree. Whoever had built this deerstand was going to pay for it all.

With a dozen vicious blows I broke all the rungs of the ladder. In a flurry of hammering I then beat the ends to splinters, leaving only the heads of the spikes protruding from the birch trunks. I exalted in the violence, swinging my club with energetic ferocity. I hit and cracked and ripped until the ladder was utterly destroyed. I picked up several of the fragments and cast them off into the woods. It was a three-minute orgy of demolition, a short reign of complete havoc. And then I slumped against one of the birches, my anger spent. I dropped the stick and picked up my shotgun. I felt guilty and a little embarrassed. I hadn't vandalized anything since I was an ignorant kid. On the opening morning of deer season, probably before sun-up, some eager sniper was going to come to his stand (and it was nice work; he could be proud), and be enraged to discover that he couldn't get up into it. His blood pressure would rise to a heart-stressing high, and that near-sacred Opening Day would be ruined.

For a moment I felt bad. And then I looked again at the slaughtered, wasted balsam—the wantonly violated tree. Okay, I thought, I'm a fanatic. So be it. That tree was worth it.

Night Ski

This is as close as I'll come to being a hawk, a nighthawk. I'm riding the snow, but it doesn't feel like it. My skis are as light as sound waves; as buoyant as tail feathers, and almost as quiet. An owl could hear me from a long way off, but only because the night is so still.

Here at the start the trail is wide, and I have room to skate—pushing from edge to edge in long, flowing sweeps of skis and poles—as if side-slipping in wind. There's a slight crunch to the snow, but it's smooth noise, like rough air on raven wings.

The forest is awash with moonlight. The bright, full orb is arcing high, nearing the zenith. The shadows of trees are starkly projected onto the snow. The light is hard, and the images are perfect. Each branch and twig is reproduced in fine detail, and the intricate tracery of the forest canopy is there beneath my ski tips. Here is the real sensation of flight—that I'm swooping and soaring over the treetops, that these sharp-edged shadows of aspens are the trees themselves. They whip by, below and all around, and the closed-in black-and-white world fosters an illusion of breathtaking speed.

Above, the constellations have been polished by moonglow; only the brightest stars are visible. In Orion, Betelgeuse is a firey red; Rigel a coruscating blue. The trail turns north and I can see the cup of the Big Dipper rising beyond the woods ahead. Off to the right, blinking between pine boughs, is brilliant Capella. The tree silhouettes are utterly black, and, by contrast, the moonlit sky is a translucent shade of blue. It's the color of infinity.

Though the sun has been down for three hours, it's twenty-nine plus degrees—in January! (Twenty-nine below would have been closer to the norm.) I revel in this "subtropical" anomaly. The air is breathable and smells of cold crystal and pine needles. As it rushes past my face it feels cleansing and fresh—vernal air without that brittle Arctic edge.

I hit the crest of the first hill and snowplow just a little. In daylight, I would pole halfway down, digging for velocity. But at night it looks different; the bottom is indistinct, the bordering trees seem to hem it in. There's a wide curve at the base, and I sail into it—knees bent, poles tucked—like the nadir of a raptor's dive.

I ease into a rhythmic, floating glide, cruising the flats and whisking down slopes. Soon there's a stand of mature aspen, huge trees whose branches are concentrated in distant, lofty clumps. Here are only the shadows of arrow-straight trunks, a whole corridor of thick black striations on the snow—like a gigantic spectra of some mysterious star. As I race over them it's as if I'm flying past a picket fence, eyes winking in and out of bands of light.

And then I plunge into a dense bower of Norway pines. The track is invisible, absorbed into the murky umbra of deep, tangled woods. I feel my way along the track, tunneling through the blackness and focused on the bright snowfield beyond. It's a galaxy of crystalline sparkles—multi-colored pinpoints of moonlight. I burst into their midst, bedazzled by the sky come to earth. The snow is like a thick carpet of rhinestones.

At the halfway point there's a small clearing at the top of a hill, and I pause for a few moments next to a coppice of birches. Their paper bark is as white as the snow, and my eye follows the ghostly trunks upward. A bank of thin cirrus clouds is drifting past, a swath of milky fleece. In the dimness of the night the birches seem to form a frosty, two-dimensional link between land and sky—between pure snow and pure cloud—different manifestations of water and ice.

The clouds graze the moon, then briefly envelop it. A reddish halo forms and spreads through the vapor—like concentric waves in a quiet pool. This January cycle of phases is the Wolf Moon, and yesterday we heard a pack singing just after sunset; as the moon was climbing out of bluish eastern haze. I would love to hear the wolf pack now.

My rising breath forms a second halo, a pale aura wreathing my head. The sky is framed by the naked limbs of a maple, and my exhalations seem to curl among the branches before dissipating into the molecular ambience and rejoining the atmosphere of the planet. For a moment the cosmos is compressed, and I blow a breath at the moon. It doesn't appear to be that far beyond the top of the maple. A nighthawk could circle it. But the illusion is fleeting. This moon is far and high; it'll trek with the stars until past dawn, perched between Auriga and Orion.

I shove off down the rise, gliding into a winding flat stretch that leads to the crest of the Roller Coaster. It's two hills in one. The first slope is a steep curve. You must bank sharply to the right, and just as you straighten out, shoot up the flank of a ridge. There's another curve at the top, and you slide into it at speed, pivoting a little to aim your skis down the second drop. You make one quick stab with the poles and then tuck in and plummet— flashing through a grove of young aspens. When the trails are icy, it's a harrowing, ski (and bone) threatening run.

Tonight the snow is soft, but the Roller Coaster is dappled with blackness, deceptively lit. The moonbeams have modified its configuration. I'm going too fast when I hit the first curve—or that's what it feels like. I overcompensate, confused by the lunar radiation and how it's blended the darkness and light. I skid up the ridge off balance, fighting for equilibrium as I break over the top. Before I hit the trees, I sink into a crouch while making a little jump to the left. The skis slap the snow and grip, and as I start to hurtle down the second slope I feel stable and plumb. I just hang on until the aspens stop streaking past.

If someone was behind me I would turn to them and laugh, sharing the joy of evasion and escape. But I've chosen solitude this evening, and the sound of only one pair of skis. I must smile just to myself, but I don't regret the privacy. Often it's satisfying to feel remote, to be deliciously alone with the moon. You may listen, uninterrupted, to the shadows on the snow, or to the space between the stars.

In a minute I'm back into the tempo of the trail, weaving

through the forest—an apparition flitting between trees. Suddenly I feel watched. I perceive being the object of attention. Though if there is a pair of eyes upon me, they don't see much— a brief glimpse of swinging arms; a wavering trail of vapor. I have a sense of being airy, transitory. And yes, there *are* eyes out there; I know it. But I don't feel menaced; I feel escorted. Some nocturnal sentinel is noting my swift passing through these winter woods. A wolf? A fox? An owl? But the eyes feel neither wary nor alarmed. Perhaps it's only God. Surely God's near on a night like this.

A Good
Blizzard

In northeastern Minnesota, March is the traditional (and statistical) month of the heaviest snows. It's not unusual for a March storm to dump twelve to twenty inches of snow in a few hours, and then back it up with a short, but wicked sub-zero cold snap—all accompanied by vigorous winds. In the past thirteen winters, a span which encompassed a couple of the nastiest of the century, we had been truly snowbound twice—both in March.

It's a snug feeling. To be trapped inside a warm cabin by freezing drifts is timelessly romantic. As the radio narrates the event—announcing cancellations, closings, accumulations, and wind-chill factors—you stoke the woodstove with another chunk of seasoned maple and sip hot cider. With luck, it's a Tuesday or a Wednesday, and you may skip the twenty-mile drive into town for work, school, or a dental appointment. Outside, the car is interred, a mere bump in the deep snowfield of the yard. Good riddance. The windows offer a view of nearly blank whiteness. The spruce and balsams at the edge of the forest are dimly visible through a rushing curtain of snow.

Over a hundred years ago, John Greenleaf Whittier wrote of a winter storm in New England:

Shut in from all the world without,
We sat the clean-winged hearth about,
Content to let the north-wind roar
In baffled rage at pane and door . . .

Though Whittier's storm was in December, I've often been tempted to present a reading of *Snowbound* on some blustery March evening. But instead, I usually place a Bob Dylan record on the turntable. The Minnesota native rasps: ". . . get your mind off wintertime, you ain't goin' nowhere."

Well, maybe. No matter how cozy the living room, or how soothing the cider, I always feel compelled to venture outside. Storms are to be savored too, and the raw edge of winter has its peculiar attractions. Though it's invigorating to just stand outside and watch the wild union of forest and sky, it's better to have a specific mission—a legitimate reason to travel. A "matter of life and death" is good, but such diversions are rare. Usually an appropriate mission must be distilled from everyday needs.

A couple of years ago an early-March blizzard laid down eighteen inches of snow. In the middle of the twenty-four-hour storm, when only ten inches or so had fallen, I left our cabin on skis. Nancy had telephoned, and in the course of chit-chat had told Pam that she needed a pack of cigarettes and couldn't get to the store. It was mission enough.

I poled down our private road, breaking a trail through the clean snow. Now and then my ski tips would break the surface, but were otherwise invisible. The going was slow, and aside from an occasional creak of the bindings, I moved in a monotone landscape of profound silence. Visibility was cut to twenty yards, and my privacy was complete. I was sequestered in a soft cocoon of falling and fallen snow. The flakes piled up on my head and shoulders.

When I hit the main road and drew abreast of an old clearcut, I began to feel the force of the wind. Out of the defilade of the mature forest, I was now exposed to the direct pressure of the blizzard. It wasn't loud, but it was pushy.

As I looked across the clearing and saw the young aspens fade away to opaqueness, I had a sense of the weight of this storm—the breadth of its influence. Four states and half of Ontario were being layered with blowing snow. I was in the midst of an atmospheric convulsion that blanketed hundreds of thousands of square miles and was "local" in the sense that North America was the neighborhood. It was better to focus on those peeking ski tips and not on the vastness of the storm.

It was about two miles to the store, and then a half-mile to Nancy's. At both places I was greeted with the bemused deference reserved for a familiar village idiot. That's not to say I wasn't appreciated, but it *is* unsettling to see a frosted apparition emerge suddenly from the depths of a blizzard and pound on your drift-blockaded door.

Most of the two-and-a-half miles had been uneventful poling, gliding and trudging, and, as careless as the storm itself, I'd skiied down the middle of the road. That is, until I was nearly run down by a four-wheel-drive pickup. I just managed to hear the engine through the drone of the wind, and cut to the shoulder as the headlights rushed past. I'm sure the driver never saw me.

Though more traffic seemed unlikely, I couldn't be sure that there wouldn't be other kindred spirits on missions of mercy (or on desperate crusades to justify their four-wheel-drive), so on my return trek I decided to cut across Little Sturgeon Lake and avoid the main road.

As I skied onto the desert plain of the 325-acre lake, I was aware of the potential problems. The featureless expanse was under "white-out" conditions. Aside from what I could see of myself, there was absolutely nothing to look at. A few yards from shore I was effectively blind; I would have to "feel" my way across the lake. I knew the wind was pushing from the east northeast, but for purposes of rough navigation, I called it due east. If I kept the wind directly at my back, I should come off the lake near a bridge on the western shore. From there it was a short hop back to our cabin. I had to cover only about a half-mile of ice.

I jockeyed myself into position, adjusting my course until the wind seemed to be precisely astern. Then I set a fast pace and started cruising.

It was eerie. After two or three minutes (or was it longer? or shorter?) I was lost. Not in space, but in time. I had a very good idea of where I was on Little Sturgeon, or thought I did. At least I could visualize a map and project myself onto it. I had a specific journey in mind, but how long was it taking? Timekeeping is essential for navigation. Since I'd skied it before (in clear weather), I knew it should only be a ten or fifteen-minute jaunt. Because the snow was loose and deep, I could give myself twenty minutes.

I didn't have a watch, but I could've counted to myself—perhaps assigned an integer to every dig of my left ski pole and called that two seconds. When I reached six hundred, I should have been at or near my goal. But I didn't count, and in a "little while"—more than a minute but less than an hour—I was disoriented in time.

It was sensory deprivation. The contrast with the sound and fury of an ambitious July thunderstorm was striking. But this colorless, soft-edged blizzard seemed a lot more dangerous. Without a handle on the passage of time, I was confused. In spite of my conviction about spatial location and the support of the wind, I started to doubt my course.

It reminded me of the sensation of skydiving. Before I made my first jump I assumed that when I exited the aircraft I was going to experience a vivid sensation of falling, and that would be the great thrill. But, no. It turns out that with nothing rushing past, your brain isn't convinced that you're dropping. The sky is empty, and you're too high up for the earth to be rising to meet you. (That distressing perspective isn't achieved until you're about four hundred feet from the ground. If you haven't deployed your canopy by then, it's your last observation.) Hence, there is no feeling of falling. As far as your brain is concerned, the available data proves that you're merely suspended in midair. Gravitation is certainly operating, but you can't see it or feel it. And it's more than academic. Some skydivers, distracted by the glory of the experience, never open their parachutes. At one level, the brain senses no immediate danger—almost all the way to final impact.

Similarly, time is events. It's the methodical ticking of a clock, the surefire phases of the moon, the beating of your heart. You can mark time inside yourself, but you have to concentrate. In short, I should've counted.

Being lost in time, and therefore doubting myself, caused me to unconsciously alter my course. I suppose I was continuously correcting to assuage my confusion. But I didn't know that until I came upon a windblown, half-obliterated ski trail somewhere out on the lake.

My first thought was, "Hey! There's somebody else out here." But in a moment the embarrassing truth hit me. This was my own track. I'd navigated in a complete, right-handed circle. I was mortified; and a little scared. For I was convinced that I'd kept the wind directly at my back. How would this happen? I didn't know. This was a small lake, but I realized that if the blizzard lasted several more hours, I could stay lost long enough to freeze to death.

After an agitated moment of self-recrimination, I refocused on the wind direction, intensely concentrating on how and where I felt it. Since the temperature and the snowfall remained constant, I could safely assume that the wind hadn't changed. And as I resumed skiing I started counting. Every fifty beats I paused to reaffirm wind direction. In a "little while"—less than five hundred beats—a shoreline loomed out of the blankness. I was further north than I expected, but not too bad, considering.

Just before he died, Daniel Boone was asked if he'd ever been lost. "No," Boone replied, "I can't say as ever I was lost, but I was *bewildered* once for three days." That was precisely my feeling—though a northern Minnesota blizzard may not have allowed me three days of perplexity.

I once heard a man emphatically state that he "could never get lost in northern Minnesota." He knew the land too well, he said; not every acre, of course, but the general aspect of woods and water—the *feel* of the place. It bequeathed him an unerring sense of direction.

Perhaps. I'm not so confident myself. But in one way I'm never lost when I'm in the forest. I may get turned around physically—bewildered—but spiritually I know I'm at the center of where I belong. I reach out from wildness, making long forays into other habitats, but I always return. A forest wilderness is certainly not the only "way into the Universe," but it is a clear route.

Pam Leschak

Peter Leschak has worked as a freelance writer since 1984. His work has appeared in such national periodicals as *Harper's*, *The New York Times Book Review*, *The New York Times Magazine*, *New Age Journal*, *Outside*, *Outdoor Life*, *Country Journal*, *Fine Gardening*, *Writer's Digest*, *Astronomy*, *Backpacker*, *The Photo District News*, *Children's Magic Window*, and *TWA Ambassador Magazine* (He was a columnist and contributing editor there 1985-86.). A Minnesota author, Leschak has been represented in such regional periodicals as *Minnesota Monthly*, *Twin Cities* magazine, *Mpls/St. Paul* magazine, Minneapolis *Star & Tribune Sunday Magazine*, St. Paul *Pioneer Press/Dispatch*, *The Boundary Waters Journal*, *The New North Times*, *Lake Superior Magazine*, *Minnesota Fire Chief* magazine, *The Minnesota Volunteer*, *The Twin Cities Reader*, and the Hibbing *Daily Tribune*. His first book, *Letters from Side Lake*, was published by Harper & Row in 1987, with a trade paperback edition released in 1988.